ADMINISTRATIVE LAW AND PROCESS

IN A NUTSHELL

Fifth Edition

By

ERNEST GELLHORN
Late Foundation Professor of Law
George Mason University

RONALD M. LEVIN
Henry Hitchcock Professor of Law
Washington University in St. Louis

THOMSON

™

WEST

Mat #40111872

COPYRIGHT © 1972, 1981, 1990 WEST PUBLISHING CO.
COPYRIGHT © 1997 By WEST GROUP
© 2006 Thomson/West
     610 Opperman Drive
     P.O. Box 64526
     St. Paul, MN 55164–0526
     1–800–328–9352
Printed in the United States of America

ISBN–13: 978–0–314–14436–2
ISBN–10: 0–314–14436–6

*TEXT IS PRINTED ON 10% POST
CONSUMER RECYCLED PAPER*

PREFACE

Ernest Gellhorn, the author of the first edition of *Administrative Law and Process in a Nutshell* and co-author of all subsequent editions, passed away in May 2005. At that time, half of the chapters in the book had been revised for this edition, and Ernie had approved their contents after contributing his suggestions. All of the chapters, however, contain ideas, explanations, and turns of phrase that originated with him. His insights into administrative law, his worldly perspective, and his habitual clarity of expression will, therefore, animate these pages for years to come.

Ernie commanded broad respect as a professor, law school dean three times over, managing partner of a major law office, and leader in the administrative law bar. His familiarity with the worlds of both scholarship and practice enriched his writing and caused his views to be widely sought out. And his independence of mind, generosity, and good humor made him a delightful co-author. It was a privilege to work with him, and this edition is respectfully dedicated to his memory.

R.M.L.

*

OUTLINE

CHAPTER VI. PROCEDURAL DUE PROCESS

CHAPTER VII. FORMAL ADJUDICATIONS

CHAPTER VIII. PROCEDURAL SHORTCUTS

CHAPTER IX. RULES AND RULEMAKING

CHAPTER X. OBTAINING JUDICIAL REVIEW

APPENDICES

*

TABLE OF CASES

References are to Pages

XI

TABLE OF CASES

XV

TABLE OF CASES

TABLE OF CASES

TABLE OF CASES

TABLE OF STATUTES

UNITED STATES

UNITED STATES CONSTITUTION

UNITED STATES CODE ANNOTATED
2 U.S.C.A.—The Congress

TABLE OF STATUTES

3 U.S.C.A.—The President

5 U.S.C.A.—Government Organization and Employees

TABLE OF STATUTES

UNITED STATES CODE ANNOTATED
5 U.S.C.A.—Government Organization and Employees

TABLE OF STATUTES

XLII

TABLE OF STATUTES

TABLE OF STATUTES

POPULAR NAME ACTS

———

CIVIL RIGHTS ACT OF 1964

OCCUPATIONAL SAFETY AND HEALTH ACT

———

CODE OF FEDERAL REGULATIONS

EXECUTIVE ORDERS

FEDERAL REGISTER

TABLE OF STATUTES

FEDERAL REGISTER

FEDERAL RULES OF CIVIL PROCEDURE

FEDERAL RULES OF EVIDENCE

TABLE OF AGENCIES

References are to Pages

TABLE OF AGENCIES

L

ADMINISTRATIVE LAW AND PROCESS

IN A NUTSHELL

Fifth Edition

*

INTRODUCTION

Administrative agencies usually are created to deal with current crises or to redress serious social problems. Throughout the modern era of administrative regulation, which began in the late nineteenth century, the government's response to a public demand for action has often been to establish a new agency, or to grant new powers to an existing bureaucracy. Near the turn of the century, agencies like the Interstate Commerce Commission and the Federal Trade Commission were created in an attempt to control the anticompetitive conduct of monopolies and powerful corporations. The economic depression of the 1930s was followed by a proliferation of agencies during the New Deal which were designed to stabilize the economy, temper the excesses of unregulated markets, and provide some financial security for individuals. Agencies were also established or enlarged in wartime to mobilize manpower and production, and to administer price controls and rationing. The development of new technologies, ranging from radio broadcasting to air transportation to nuclear energy, often led to creation of new government bureaus to promote and supervise these emerging industries. In the 1960s, when the injustices of poverty and racial discrimination became an urgent national concern, the development of programs designed to redress these

1

grievances expanded the scope of government administration. More recently, increased public concern about risks to human health and safety and threats to the natural environment have resulted in new agencies and new regulatory programs.

The primary reason why administrative agencies have so frequently been called upon to deal with such diverse social problems is the great flexibility of the regulatory process. In comparison to courts or legislatures or elected executive officials, administrative agencies have several institutional strengths that equip them to deal with complex problems. Perhaps the most important of these strengths is specialized staffing: an agency is authorized to hire people with whatever mix of talents, skills and experience it needs to get the job done. Moreover, because the agency has responsibility for a limited area of public policy, it can develop the expertise that comes from continued exposure to a problem area. An agency's regulatory techniques and decisionmaking procedures can also be tailored to meet the problem at hand. Agencies can control entry into a field by requiring a license to undertake specified activities; they can set standards, adjudicate violations, and impose penalties; they can dispense grants, subsidies or other incentives; they can set maximum or minimum rates; and they can influence conduct through a wide variety of informal methods.

However, these potential strengths of the administrative process can also be viewed as a threat to other important values. Administrative "flexibility" may simply be a mask for unchecked power, and in our society unrestrained government power has traditionally been viewed with great and justifiable suspicion. Thus, the fundamental policy problem of the administrative process is how to design a system of checks which will minimize the risks of bureaucratic arbitrariness and overreaching, while preserving for the agencies the flexibility they need to act effectively. Administrative law concerns the legal checks that are used to control and limit the powers of government agencies.

Moreover, continued exposure to the same issues may lead not only to agency expertise but also to rigidity and ineffectiveness. Indeed, scholars and other critics have identified a wide variety of causes for regulatory failure: the basic theory of the regulatory program may be wrong, or the state of knowledge not adequate to support wise decisions; there may be a mismatch between the regulatory objective and the technique chosen to achieve it; the agency may be unduly influenced or "captured" by a powerful constituency group; agency officials may be incompetent or corrupt or lack incentives to produce quality work; and regulatory programs may simply be politically unacceptable in a particular time and place.

These substantive problems of administrative regulation are important and interesting, but they are largely beyond the scope of this text. This explanation of the administrative process will concentrate on how it operates, on "the rules of the game." There is admittedly artificiality and oversimplification in this approach. Administrative law as applied by the agencies and the courts cannot be separated from the particular mix of factors that make each agency unique—factors such as the nature of the agency's legislative mandate, its structure and traditions, the values and personalities of the people who work in the agency or deal with it regularly, and, most importantly, its substantive law. Even the procedural uniformity imposed on the federal agencies by the Administrative Procedure Act, 5 U.S.C.A. §§ 551–706 (see statutory appendix), seems to have weakened, as the Congress has at times been willing to prescribe detailed codes of procedure in enabling legislation. Thus, it is an open question whether the differences among agencies are more important than the similarities.

Still, there is something useful to be gained from the effort to view the administrative process as a whole. The student, the lawyer, or the citizen who is trying to penetrate the workings of an unfamiliar bureaucracy needs a general framework of principles and doctrines in order to understand—let alone to criticize or try to change—a given agency decisionmaking process. It is also important to remember that, despite their many differences, agencies also share several broad challenges. One is to design procedures that will strike a workable compromise among important and potentially conflicting public values. These values can be grouped into four categories.

(1) *Fairness*. Concern with the fairness of government decisionmaking procedures is a primary fea-

ture of Anglo–American legal systems. The basic elements of fairness, embodied in the concept of due process, are assurances that the individual will receive adequate notice and a meaningful opportunity to be heard before an official tribunal makes a decision that may substantially affect her interests.

(2) *Accuracy*. The administrative decisionmaking process should also attempt to minimize the risk of wrong decisions. The real difficulty, however, is in defining and measuring accuracy. Since the goals of many regulatory programs are not simple or clearly stated, and the consequences of agency decisions may be difficult to identify, there will often be differences of opinion as to whether a particular decision was accurate or wise—and how the procedures may have influenced the result. Nevertheless, there is widespread agreement that different procedures are more suitable for some kinds of decisions than for others. For example, trial procedures are generally considered most useful for resolving disputes over specific facts concerning past events, and least useful for making general predictions or policy judgments about the future.

(3) *Efficiency*. Efforts to increase the fairness of an administrative decision by expanding opportunities to participate, or to improve accuracy by gathering and evaluating additional information, can be very costly in time, money and missed opportunities. Since agency resources are always limited and usually insufficient to accomplish the full range of duties imposed by statute, it becomes necessary to consider the efficiency of decision-making proce-

dures. Typically, this takes the form of an inquiry into whether additional procedural safeguards are likely to increase the fairness or accuracy of decisions enough to warrant the costs and delays they will create.

(4) *Acceptability.* Because the legitimate exercise of official power ultimately depends upon the consent of the governed, it is necessary to consider the attitudes of constituency groups and the general public toward the regulatory process. That is, administrative procedures should be judged not only on their actual effects, but also on the ways they will be perceived by affected interest groups. There are probably few situations in which public attitudes toward agency procedures play a determinative role in shaping beliefs about the basic legitimacy of the regulatory decision or program. Still, it seems clear that a widespread feeling that a government bureaucracy makes decisions arbitrarily or unfairly can undermine the public's confidence in the agency and the regulated industry's willingness to comply with its decisions.

The administrative law system does not rely solely on procedural controls to ensure that officials will perform their functions satisfactorily. It also expects the legislative, executive, and judicial branches to supervise the substance of what agencies do. For example, the President appoints officeholders and chooses the overall goals of his Administration; Congress conducts oversight hearings and, when necessary, rewrites enabling statutes; courts enforce legal requirements and place outer limits on agencies' use of discretion.

The primary focus of this text is on federal administrative agencies, although some discussions of state administrative practice are included. As a practical matter, the numerous variations in state law make it impossible to cover the subject adequately in a brief survey. In any case, the basic objective of this book is to help the student of the administrative process develop a framework of general principles, policy considerations and methods of analysis that will be useful in understanding a wide variety of administrative agency procedures, regardless of whether they are found at the federal, state or local level.

CHAPTER I

THE DELEGATION OF AUTHORITY TO AGENCIES

The study of administrative law can be viewed as an analysis of the limits placed on the powers and actions of administrative agencies. These limits are imposed in many ways, and it is important to remember that legal controls may be supplemented or replaced by political checks on agency decisions. One set of legal controls that we will examine at length is the procedures that reviewing courts have required the agencies to use. Another is the rules specified by Congress in the Administrative Procedure Act (APA). Conceptually, however, the first question that should be examined is the amount of legislative or judicial power that can be entrusted initially to the agency by the legislature—the governmental body creating it.

A. THE DELEGATION ISSUE

Throughout the modern era of administrative regulation, agencies have been vested with sweeping powers. Some of these powers are assigned on an industry-wide basis, as with the Federal Communications Commission, the Nuclear Regulatory Commission, and the Maritime Administration. Other agencies are charged with enforcing certain norms of conduct throughout the economy. These range from the Federal Trade Commission, which since 1914 has enforced a ban on "unfair methods of competition," to newer health and safety regulators, such as the Environmental Protection Agency and the Occupational Safety and Health Administration. These grants of authority are commonly described as *delegations* from the legislative branch.

What makes the delegations particularly dramatic is that these agencies typically wield powers that are characteristic of each of the three principal branches of government. The statutes under which many agencies operate can be described as giving them *legislative power* to issue rules that control private behavior, and that often carry heavy civil or criminal penalties for violations; *executive power* to investigate potential violations of rules or statutes and to prosecute offenders; and *judicial power* to adjudicate particular disputes over whether an individual or a company has failed to comply with the governing standards.

For example, the Securities Exchange Commission (SEC) formulates law by writing rules that spell out what disclosures must be made in a stock prospectus; these rules may have the same effect as a law passed by the legislature. The SEC then enforces these rules by prosecuting those who violate its regulations through disciplinary actions against broker-dealers or through stop order proceedings against corporate issuers. Finally, the SEC also acts as judge and jury in deciding whether its rules have been violated; it conducts adjudicatory hearings to determine guilt and mete out punishment. In addition, administrative agencies are often unattached to any of the three branches of government (executive, legislative, or judicial).

Such delegations raise fundamental questions concerning the constitutional distribution of authority in our system of government. The federal Constitution, and most state constitutions as well, are based on the principle of separation of powers. Generally, law-making power is assigned to the legislature, law-enforcing power to the executive, and law-deciding power to the judiciary. With responsibility divided in this fashion, each branch theoretically provides checks and balances on the exercise of power by the other two branches. The combined powers of administrative agencies seem, at least formally, at odds with the three-part paradigm of government.

Practical justifications for these broad delegations of combined powers can be found in the institutional advantages of the administrative agency. Particularly in novel or rapidly changing fields of activity, the legislature may be unable to specify detailed rules of conduct. An agency, armed with flexible decision-making procedures and charged with continuing responsibility for a limited subject matter, may be better equipped to develop sound and coherent policies. Moreover, effective development and implementation of regulatory policy may require the exercise of all three kinds of power. A rule or a policy decision can be quickly nullified in practice if investigations and prosecutions are not vigorously pursued, or if adjudications are decided by tribunals that do not understand or support the regulatory goals. When the subject matter of a regulatory program is technical or complex, or when detailed knowledge of the regulated industry is essential to the formulation of sound policy, administrative agencies can bring to bear their superior experience and expertise. Uniformity and predictability are also important in many areas of economic regulation. Businesses need to plan their operations and make their investment decisions with some assurance that the ground rules will not be changed abruptly or applied inconsistently—problems that might well arise if decisionmaking power were dispersed among the three branches of government.

It should also be noted, however, that a substantial number of legislators, judges, and commentators are unpersuaded by these arguments. They argue that little real justification exists for continued sweeping delegations or for the combination of prosecutorial, rulemaking and adjudicative powers within one agency. See pp. 18–22 infra. Thus there is pressure to separate such functions, to establish an administrative court, or otherwise to limit the delegation of broad authority to the agencies.

B. DEVELOPMENT OF DOCTRINE

The so-called *nondelegation doctrine* asserts that the Constitution limits Congress's ability to confer

power on administrative agencies. Proponents of
the doctrine typically rely either on general separation of powers notions or on the language of Article
I, § 1 of the Constitution, which provides: "All
legislative Powers herein granted shall be vested in
a Congress of the United States." To be sure, that
constitutional language does not necessarily support
their position. One can think of an agency's role in
implementing a regulatory statute as nothing more
than an exercise of *executive* power, even if the
agency plays something of a lawmaking role along
the way. Nevertheless, ever since the earliest days
of administrative law, courts have encountered—
and occasionally endorsed—suggestions that at least
some delegations constitute attempts to transfer
"legislative powers" that Congress alone may wield.

The earliest judicial decisions discussing the nondelegation doctrine contained broad, uncompromis-
ing statements. A classic example is the Supreme
Court's statement in Field v. Clark, 143 U.S. 649,
692 (1892): "That Congress cannot delegate legislative power . . . is a principle universally recognized
as vital to the integrity and maintenance of the
system of government ordained by the Constitution." Nevertheless, the Court in its early decisions
consistently upheld delegations by minimizing their
significance. Typically the Court would claim that,
in the cases presented to it, the executive branch
had been granted nothing more than a power to
"ascertain and declare the event upon which . . .
[the legislative] will was to take effect" *(Field),* or a
power to "fill up the details," United States v.

Grimaud, 220 U.S. 506 (1911). In truth, the executive branch was not merely finding facts or supplying details in these cases; it was exercising a substantial measure of policy judgment. The *Field* case involved a congressional authorization for the President to impose retaliatory tariffs when foreign nations raised their duties on agricultural products; *Grimaud* upheld the power of the Secretary of Agriculture to issue regulations, backed by criminal penalties, governing the use and preservation of the national forests. The holdings of the cases, therefore, belied the Court's absolutist language.

However, as the modern industrial economy developed and demands for regulation grew, it became apparent that these narrow formulas were too restrictive, even when moderated by a liberal interpretation. Gradually the focus of judicial inquiry shifted to whether the legislature had provided *sufficient standards* to limit the scope of agency discretion. The Supreme Court's decision in Buttfield v. Stranahan, 192 U.S. 470 (1904), was the first case to articulate this modern version of the nondelegation doctrine. Later cases adopted this line of analysis, and in J.W. Hampton, Jr., & Co. v. United States, 276 U.S. 394, 409 (1928), the Court refined it in the often-quoted statement that, to be permissible, a delegation must contain an "intelligible principle to which the [agency must] ... conform."

Throughout this early evolution of the doctrine, the Supreme Court had never invalidated a congressional grant of authority to an administrative agency on delegation grounds. However, the Great

intelligible principle: did Congress provide sufficient standards?

Depression of the 1930s brought a wave of new regulatory agencies, armed with broad statutory delegations of authority, to control the economy. In the rush to find solutions for this overwhelming economic crisis, some regulatory statutes were poorly designed, poorly drafted, and poorly implemented as well. One of the most visible and controversial of these New Deal regulatory agencies, the National Recovery Administration, provided the Supreme Court with an opportunity to demonstrate that the nondelegation doctrine could become a very real constraint on the powers of administrative agencies.

The first major test came in the "Hot Oil" case, Panama Refining Co. v. Ryan, 293 U.S. 388 (1935). The National Industrial Recovery Act (NIRA) had authorized the President to prohibit interstate shipments of "contraband" oil. The purpose of this provision was to reduce economic disruptions in the oil industry, which was faced with falling demand and an increasing supply from newly discovered oil fields. The Court found that the statute gave the President absolutely no guidance as to the circumstances under which he should impose the prohibition. Accordingly, for the first time in its history, the Supreme Court struck down an Act of Congress as an overly broad delegation of legislative power.

The regulation that was challenged in *Panama Refining* also had a serious procedural defect. The "code" in question had never been officially published. Just before the case was argued in the Supreme Court, it was discovered that the code had accidentally been amended out of existence. One beneficial side effect of the *Panama Refining* decision was the passage of legislation requiring federal agencies to publish official texts of their regulations in the Federal Register. See Louis L. Jaffe, *Judicial Control of Administrative Action* 62 (1965); 5 U.S.C.A. § 552(a)(1). However, the opinion did not resolve the central questions about the constitutionality of the system of regulation created by the National Industrial Recovery Act.

Further questions about the constitutionality of the NIRA arose a few months later in the decision that is usually referred to as the "Sick Chicken" case. It involved a criminal prosecution for violations of the Live Poultry Code issued under another section of the NIRA. A.L.A. Schechter Poultry Corp. v. United States, 295 U.S. 495 (1935). As in the Hot Oil case, the Court was concerned by the lack of both substantive and procedural standards. The statute had empowered the agency (acting on behalf of the President) to issue "codes of fair competition" for particular industries if the code "tend[ed] to effectuate the policy of this title." However, the Court could not find a clear policy directive in the legislation; indeed, the congressional statements of policy seemed to pull in several different directions. The Act adopted the policies of preventing monopolies while promoting cooperative actions among trade groups, and of encouraging increased production while improving the wages and conditions of labor; it gave no indication of how these potentially conflicting values should be weighed or reconciled.

The Court also gave considerable emphasis to the procedural deficiencies in the Act. In contrast to prior delegations of authority to the Interstate Commerce Commission or the Federal Trade Commission, the NIRA did not require the agency to hold trial-type hearings, or even to provide interested persons with notice and a right to participate in the challenged decision. Nor did it provide an opportunity for judicial review to those who might be adversely affected. Thus, the Court concluded that the delegation was unconstitutionally broad.

A third Supreme Court decision invalidating a delegation on constitutional grounds was also decided in the 1930s. Carter v. Carter Coal Co., 298 U.S. 238 (1936), involved a system of industry "codes" for the coal industry, roughly similar to the "codes of fair competition" that were at issue in the *Schechter* case. In *Carter Coal,* however, the Court noted an additional factor that made the delegation suspect: decisionmaking power effectively had been granted to committees of industry representatives rather than to government officials. Because these private parties had "interests [which] may be and often are adverse to the interests of others in the same business," the statute was "legislative delegation in its most obnoxious form."

In retrospect, these three decisions were the high-water mark for the nondelegation doctrine. Although Congress has continued to grant sweeping, vaguely defined powers to administrative agencies in the ensuing decades, the Supreme Court has not invalidated any other statutes on nondelegation

grounds. Repeatedly, the Court has held that even
the vaguest of regulatory provisions satisfied the
"intelligible principle" test of *J.W. Hampton*. This
leniency is exemplified by Yakus v. United States,
321 U.S. 414 (1944). There the system of wartime
price controls was challenged on delegation
grounds. The statute empowered an Administrator
to promulgate standards that would be "generally
fair and equitable and ... effectuate the [enumerat-
ed] purposes of this Act." The Court upheld the
statute, noting that constitutional problems would
arise only if the legislation were so lacking in standards that "it would be impossible in a proper
proceeding to ascertain whether the will of Congress has been obeyed." This tolerance has continued right up until the present day. See, e.g., Loving
v. United States, 517 U.S. 748 (1996) (upholding
statute authorizing President to prescribe list of
aggravating factors that would support capital punishment in court-martial prosecution); Skinner v.
Mid–America Pipeline Co., 490 U.S. 212 (1989) (upholding statute authorizing agency to set "user
fees" for pipeline companies); Mistretta v. United
States, 488 U.S. 361 (1989) (upholding statute authorizing commission to write criminal sentencing
guidelines). The Court's unwillingness for over sev-
enty years to require precise standards in legislative
delegations has led some commentators to conclude
that this branch of the nondelegation doctrine is
simply unworkable, and ought to be abandoned
altogether. Yet, as discussed in the next section,

proposals for a reinvigoration of the doctrine have continued to surface.

C. MODERN NONDELEGATION CONTROVERSIES

A decision involving the Occupational Safety and Health Act of 1970 spurred broad discussion of whether the Court should begin anew to hold broad delegations unconstitutional. Section 6(b)(5) of that Act directed the Secretary of Labor to issue rules requiring employers to protect their workers, "to the extent feasible," from harm due to toxic substances in the workplace. The Secretary subsequently promulgated a regulation that called for expensive measures to minimize workers' exposure to benzene, a cancer-causing chemical. The Supreme Court struck down the rule in Industrial Union Dep't, AFL–CIO v. American Petroleum Inst., 448 U.S. 607 (1980), commonly known as the *Benzene* case. Four Justices, led by Justice Stevens, believed that the Secretary had not made all of the findings required by the statute. The fifth vote against the Secretary was that of Justice (later Chief Justice) Rehnquist, who would have held that the statute contained an unconstitutional delegation to the Secretary. He regarded the statutory phrase "to the extent feasible" as a "legislative mirage" by which Congress had simply avoided resolving the hard questions about the circumstances in which employers could be allowed to take some risks of injury to workers because of the high costs of protective measures. Resolving fundamental, politically divisive policy issues, he insisted, is the very essence of legislative authority and could not "unnecessarily" be left to a politically unresponsive administrator. See also American Textile Mfrs. Inst. v. Donovan, 452 U.S. 490 (1981), in which Justice Rehnquist repeated his position and was joined by Chief Justice Burger. In ensuing years, however, neither Rehnquist nor other Justices have tried to extend this argument to other situations.

The Clean Air Act provided the backdrop for a more recent effort to revitalize the nondelegation doctrine. The Environmental Protection Agency promulgated a rule that set limits on emissions of particulates (such as soot particles) and ozone. The relevant section of the Act directed the agency to set air quality standards at a level that is "requisite to protect the public health with an adequate margin of safety." A lower court set aside the rule, asserting that the agency had articulated no "intelligible principle" to channel its exercise of discretion. Any exposure limit above zero would entail some health risk, and EPA had "failed to state intelligibly how much is too much." American Trucking Ass'ns, Inc. v. EPA, 175 F.3d 1027 (D.C.Cir.1999), rehearing denied, 195 F.3d 4 (D.C.Cir.1999). Here the court applied the nondelegation doctrine in an unusual fashion, by claiming that the agency itself, rather than Congress, must supply the needed clear principle. This reinterpretation of the nondelegation doctrine, the court believed, would harmonize with the modern trend under which courts look to agencies to play a leading role in fleshing out gaps in a statutory mandate. See pp. 79–90 infra. The Supreme Court, however, curtly dismissed the idea that an agency's own standards can cure an unconstitutional delegation. That idea was "internally contradictory," according to the Court, because "the prescription of the standard that Congress had omitted ... would *itself* be an exercise of the forbidden legislative authority." The Court then upheld the Act, emphasizing the requirement that air quality standards must be set at a level that is "requisite"—that is, neither higher nor lower than necessary—to protect public health. Although this criterion did leave room for administrative lawmaking, the Court said, it "fits well within the scope of discretion permitted by our precedent." Whitman v. American Trucking Ass'ns, Inc., 531 U.S. 457 (2001).

Although *American Trucking* helps to clarify the factors that are relevant to the constitutionality of a delegation, large questions about the future of the doctrine remain open for debate. Some commentators, believing that the legislative abdication that Justice Rehnquist perceived in *Benzene* is a common phenomenon, have urged the Court to make more frequent use of the nondelegation doctrine to invalidate regulatory legislation. In the present climate, they say, Congress has too great a temptation to make use of open-ended delegations, so that it will be able to divert public blame from itself to the bureaucracy when regulatory decisions prove controversial. Furthermore, it is argued, delegation makes it all too easy for Congress to enact, or allow continuation of, regulatory schemes that work against the public interest. This theory notes the tendency of much economic regulation to transfer wealth from one private interest group to another, without any particular public benefit. Judicial toleration of vague substantive standards fosters this tendency, it is argued, by allowing major decisions to be made by administrators, without the glare of publicity that would be generated if Congress itself took on the policymaking responsibility.

While the courts have seldom articulated why they have failed to accept the challenge of Justice Rehnquist and others, three possible explanations can be suggested. First, some courts probably continue to believe that broad delegations are on the whole desirable, because they make maximum use of the flexibility that the administrative process affords. See pp. 8–11 supra. Indeed, it has been argued that broad delegations are not even necessarily undemocratic, as Rehnquist claimed. Many of them can be seen as simply shifting policymaking discretion to appointees of the President, who has his own electoral base. In other words, vague delegations can at times be defended as a means of giving an incumbent Administration the latitude it needs if it is to implement the President's electoral mandate.

Second, the courts may believe that they cannot devise a workable test with which to implement the nondelegation doctrine. It might be very difficult for judges to identify those delegations that involve "fundamental" issues or that are motivated by a congressional desire to avoid political accountability. If the standards for applying the nondelegation doctrine were too subjective, every new regulatory statute would be under serious threat of being held unconstitutional. It would be all too easy for private parties to make a credible argument, especially with hindsight, that Congress should have spoken in more detail than it did.

Finally, and perhaps most important, courts may have refrained from using the nondelegation doctrine to strike down statutes because they have found alternative methods of preventing broad grants of power from becoming instruments of administrative oppression. The next section discusses some of these methods.

D. CONSTRUCTION TO SAVE A DELEGATION

Although the requirement that delegations of lawmaking authority must contain substantive standards has been relaxed, if not abandoned, since the 1930s, courts are highly attentive to questions about the legitimate scope of agencies' powers. The tendency in modern cases is to address these questions by examining not only whether an administrative statute contains an "intelligible principle" on its face, but also the total system of controls, both substantive and procedural, that limit agency power. The issue becomes whether the statutory scheme, taken as a whole, fulfills the fundamental objective of the nondelegation doctrine—assuring adequate control and accountability in the exercise of official power. Integral to this mode of analysis is the principle that a court should construe a statute to avoid constitutional difficulties. In line with that principle, courts sometimes adopt relatively restrictive interpretations of regulatory legislation, while stating or suggesting that a more permissive reading could raise problems under the nondelegation doctrine.

A famous case that illustrates these tendencies is Amalgamated Meat Cutters v. Connally, 337 F.Supp. 737 (D.D.C.1971). Like the *Yakus* case, *Meat Cutters* involved a broad grant of discretion to the President to set limits on wages and prices throughout the national economy. The court upheld this statute in litigation that challenged President Nixon's adoption of a wage-price freeze. Although the text of the legislation gave little if any direction as to how the President's authority should be administered, the court reviewed the legislative history and the nation's experience under previous price control programs to give content to the vague statutory language. The court concluded that the statutory standard of an earlier program—that any price controls imposed must be fair and equitable—could be read into the legislation under which the President had adopted the current controls. The court also emphasized that Congress would closely monitor the program, and that judicial review was available pursuant to the Administrative Procedure Act. Finally, the court declared that the executive branch could be expected to develop its own administrative standards over time, thus supplying the requisite specificity and precision.

To the extent that the holding in *Meat Cutters* rested on standards that the executive branch itself would need to devise, its reasoning is probably no longer tenable in light of the *American Trucking* case discussed in the preceding section. However, the broader message of *Meat Cutters*—that the validity of a delegation can rest on the overall system of controls that a court can find in the regulatory framework—remains viable and finds parallels elsewhere in the case law.

1. *Implying Substantive Limitations.* Even when a statute has not been directly challenged as violating the nondelegation doctrine, courts sometimes adopt a relatively narrow view of an agency's powers, intimating that a broad view might constitute an unlawful delegation of legislative power. This device was employed to save a questionable delegation in Kent v. Dulles, 357 U.S. 116 (1958), where the Court construed the relevant statutes to prohibit the Secretary of State from denying a passport because of the applicant's political beliefs. Since the administrator's decision curtailed the constitutionally protected freedom to travel, and prior administrative practice had not included similar restraints, the Court would not presume that the agency had been granted the power in question without a clear statement of congressional intention. See also Zemel v. Rusk, 381 U.S. 1 (1965).

The narrow construction device also played a role in the two Supreme Court cases discussed in the preceding section. In *Benzene*, Justice Stevens, writing for a plurality, declined to accept Justice Rehnquist's conclusion that the Occupational Safety and Health Act was unconstitutionally vague. Instead, he maintained that the benzene rule was flawed because the agency had not found that the requirements would cure a "significant risk" in the workplace, as he claimed the Act required. Most commentators agree that this construction of the Act was rather forced. But Stevens declared that he was adopting it partly because of the possibility that, without this limitation, the Act would have violated the nondelegation doctrine. Similarly, in *American Trucking*, the Court not only upheld the Clean Air Act but also used statutory interpretation to define its limitations. In addition to reading the statute as requiring that EPA's air quality standards must go no further than "necessary," the Court endorsed the government's concession that any such standards must "reflect the latest scientific knowledge." That construction, which went beyond the statutory language, imposes a significant constraint on EPA's rulemaking power.

2. *Procedural Safeguards*. Procedural safeguards to assure fair, informed decisionmaking can be crucial to the validity of a possibly overbroad delegation. In the *Panama Refining* and *Schechter* decisions, the Court placed considerable emphasis on the fact that the statutes did not require the President to use fair and open administrative proce-

dures and explain his decisions clearly. This theme was also reflected in the *Carter Coal* case. Where governmental power has been delegated to a private group, some members of the industry may attempt to use this grant of authority to harm or exclude their competitors. Such regulation by a biased decisionmaker may be fatal to a delegation under the due process clause. See pp. 237–40 infra. Conversely, in *Meat Cutters* the presumed availability of judicial review under the APA supported the validity of the delegation, because it ensured that administrative standards could be tested for rationality and compliance with the congressional intent, and that the agency's consistency in interpreting and applying those standards in particular cases could be checked.

The notion that the availability of judicial review can help sustain a delegation also played a role, at least implicitly, in the Court's decision in Touby v. United States, 500 U.S. 160 (1991). Under a 1984 amendment to the Controlled Substances Act, the Attorney General could summarily issue a "temporary scheduling order" imposing strict regulatory controls on newly invented "designer drugs." In a prosecution of a drug manufacturer for violating such an order, the defendant argued that the statute was an invalid delegation, in part because the act provided that a temporary scheduling order "is not subject to judicial review." The Court parried this argument by holding that the act's seemingly absolute bar to judicial review referred only to *preenforcement* challenges to scheduling orders; an

individual facing criminal charges could still attack
the validity of such an order as a defense to prosecution. By adopting this somewhat strained statutory interpretation, the Court seemed to acknowledge
that a more literal reading of the act might indeed
have raised serious doubts about the constitutionality of the Attorney General's powers.

3. *Conclusion.* The courts' technique of implying
limitations to circumscribe a broad delegation obviously must be used with restraint. Substitution of
judicial for executive lawmaking does little if anything to promote one of the major objectives of the
nondelegation doctrine—to encourage Congress to
take responsibility for major policy choices. Instead,
this technique replaces one unelected decisionmaker
with another. Indeed, a judicially imposed construction may impair the efficacy of the regulatory
scheme or make it less workable.

If, however, the choice is between construction to
avoid a nondelegation problem and actual invalidation of a regulatory statute, the former has evident
advantages. A judicial holding that a delegation is
unconstitutional invites a major confrontation between the branches of government, for it may require radical restructuring or even abandonment of
an entire program. Statutory interpretations that
specify limits to regulation or require procedural
fairness are less disruptive and more easily correct-
able if the court has misread the will of Congress.

The practice of construing regulatory authority to
save a delegation also represents an effort to accom-

modate the needs of a complex modern economy. Rigid insistence on the legislative specification of detailed standards often may be unsound and unworkable. For many regulatory problems, the legislature can neither foresee what actions the agency should take, nor constantly revise the statutory mandate as conditions change. Even when the policy alternatives are reasonably clear, an attempt to write highly detailed standards in the legislature may delay the passage of desired legislation, or jeopardize its chances for enactment. The nondelegation doctrine remains available as an *in terrorem* threat—and could be used in truly extreme cases. For most situations, however, the more immediate—and more pragmatic—task for Administrative Law is to evaluate and further refine the doctrines and techniques for making bureaucratic power accountable, without destroying the effectiveness of those administrative agencies considered necessary.

E. NONDELEGATION IN THE STATES

Since many state constitutions are based on the principle of separation of powers and provide for due process of law, delegation questions also arise at the state level. As might be expected, the nondelegation doctrines that have evolved in the states are more variable than the current federal law on the subject. Some states—a relatively large proportion, judging from the reported cases—still adhere to a relatively stringent version of the doctrine and require that statutes contain detailed standards confining agency discretion. See, e.g., Thygesen v. Callahan, 74 Ill.2d 404, 24 Ill.Dec. 558, 385 N.E.2d 699 (1979). Some state courts have also been readier than federal courts to rely on nondelegation doctrine themes in holding that administrative regulations exceed the power granted to the relevant agency by the legislature. See Boreali v. Axelrod, 71 N.Y.2d 1, 523 N.Y.S.2d 464, 517 N.E.2d 1350 (1987) (overturning health council's regulations limiting smoking in public places, in part because legislature had articulated no policies to guide the agency on that subject).

One reason for this divergence between the state and federal approaches may be the fact that the scope of administrative regulation has increased much more rapidly in the federal government than in the states in recent decades. As a result, the federal courts may be more sensitive to the need for broad delegations than their state counterparts. Another reason might be the kinds of regulatory activities undertaken by the states. States often delegate some of the responsibilities for economic regulation to boards composed of members of the regulated industry itself. As in the *Carter Coal* case, due process concerns become more compelling when the administrative process is controlled by private individuals who might use government power for their own ends and who may be subject to very few of the procedural safeguards that government officials must normally observe. See, e.g., Texas Boll Weevil Eradication Found. v. Lewellen, 952 S.W.2d 454 (Tex.1997).

At the other extreme from the states that put teeth in the standards requirement are a few that place little or no emphasis on statutory standards as such. This latter approach is illustrated by Sun Ray Drive–In Dairy, Inc. v. Oregon Liquor Control Comm'n, 16 Or.App. 63, 517 P.2d 289 (1973). The court in that case reversed an administrative order refusing to treat a convenience store as a "grocery store" eligible for a liquor license. It remanded the case to the Commission with a directive not to act on the petitioner's application until the agency had adopted general rules giving content to the vague statutory standard. The *Sun Ray* decision follows the *Meat Cutters* approach of tolerating broad delegations but insisting on safeguards at the agency level. Here, the court reasoned that the development of administrative standards through rulemaking would ensure fair notice to applicants of what they must prove, would promote consistent application of the law, and would facilitate legislative and judicial oversight. It remains to be seen whether state cases will continue to adhere to this reasoning despite *American Trucking*.

F. DELEGATION OF JUDICIAL POWER

The discussion thus far has concerned delegation of *legislative* power. A distinct question is the extent to which Congress may grant an agency *judicial* power, i.e., the power to adjudicate controversies between individual litigants. A strict reading of

Article III of the Constitution, which provides that the "judicial Power of the United States" shall be exercised by judges with lifetime tenure and salary protection, would foreclose this option.

The propriety of using administrative agencies to adjudicate was long considered settled by Crowell v. Benson, 285 U.S. 22 (1932), which allowed an agency to resolve workers' compensation claims brought by maritime workers. The Court recognized that the case involved "private rights," i.e., rights between private parties, and thus closely resembled cases traditionally heard in Article III courts. Nevertheless, the Court saw no objection to administrative adjudication as long as Congress permitted full judicial review of the agency's legal conclusions and deferential judicial review of its fact findings.[1] The Court indicated that Article III was even less of a constraint in controversies involving "public rights," i.e., rights between a private party and the government.

In 1982, however, the Court raised doubts about the survival of *Crowell's* permissiveness when it held unconstitutional the system of bankruptcy courts that Congress had established in 1978. Northern Pipeline Constr. Co. v. Marathon Pipe Line Co., 458 U.S. 50 (1982) Although there was no

---

1. The Court insisted, however, that there must be de novo judicial review of certain "jurisdictional facts." Later cases have never extended this perplexing holding, and seven Justices pronounced it dead in the *Northern Pipeline* case discussed just below. A related notion, that courts must be allowed to review de novo the fact findings on which a constitutional right depends, may have more vitality today. See p. 113 infra.

opinion for the Court, the prevailing Justices expressed concern that Congress had authorized the bankruptcy judges to adjudicate a wide range of private rights questions, including rights that derived from state law rather than from Congress itself. *Northern Pipeline* was widely regarded as potentially applicable to administrative agencies as well as specialized courts.

But subsequent cases have removed many of these apprehensions. First, the Court upheld the EPA's use of an arbitrator to decide how much one pesticide manufacturer should pay another for using the latter's research data in a registration proceeding under the Federal Insecticide, Fungicide and Rodenticide Act. Thomas v. Union Carbide Agric. Products Co., 473 U.S. 568 (1985). Although this was in one sense a private rights case, the Court considered the distinction between public and private rights unhelpful. Instead, it stressed that Congress must have the flexibility to adopt innovative procedures to implement a complex regulatory scheme. Furthermore, the manufacturer that would be making the payment had in effect consented to the use of arbitration; and the Act provided for judicial review of the arbitrator's decision for fraud, misconduct, misrepresentation, or constitutional error. Later, the Court sustained the jurisdiction of the Commodities Futures Trading Commission to resolve a dispute between a commodities broker and his customer, including a counterclaim based on state law. CFTC v. Schor, 478 U.S. 833 (1986). Again the Court emphasized that the private nature of the claims should not prevent the Court from weighing a number of factors in deciding whether Congress had fatally compromised the independence of the judiciary. Given that the parties had voluntarily chosen to litigate their claims before the CFTC rather than in court, that traditional judicial review was available, and that the CFTC's jurisdiction over private rights was strictly limited to what Congress believed necessary to make the regulatory scheme effective, there was no reason to invalidate this minor transfer of Article III business.

Thus, Congress's power to delegate judicial power to agencies seems fairly secure. Nearly all administrative cases involve "public rights," which are universally considered appropriate for agency adjudication; and even though the Court has declined to embrace any bright line rules for private rights cases, *Northern Pipeline* increasingly appears to have little relevance to the administrative state. Similarly, the Seventh Amendment right to jury trial is no bar to administrative adjudication, at least in "public rights" cases Atlas Roofing Co. v. OSHRC, 430 U.S. 442 (1977). Indeed, when the Court upheld a creditor's right to jury trial in a bankruptcy trustee's suit to recover a fraudulent conveyance, it was careful to reaffirm that an administrative agency may adjudicate a dispute between private citizens if the claim is "closely intertwined with a federal regulatory program Congress has power to enact." Granfinanciera, S.A. v. Nordberg, 492 U.S. 33 (1989). But cf. Tull v. United States, 481 U.S. 412 (1987) (when government brings penalty action *in court,* jury determines defendant's liability).

If anything, the Court may have become too permissive: *Thomas* has disturbed some commentators, because the parties were allowed less judicial review than is customarily available against administrative agencies. But in any event, the current doctrine on delegation of judicial power, which avoids flat prohibitions and focuses on the net effect of a variety of factors, is broadly similar to the *Meat Cutters* approach, as well as to the balancing approach found in some of the separation of powers cases that will be examined in the next chapter.

CHAPTER II

POLITICAL CONTROLS OVER AGENCY ACTION

In a constitutional democracy, government institutions that set and enforce public policy must be politically accountable to the electorate. When the legislature delegates broad lawmaking powers to an administrative agency, the popular control provided by direct election of decisionmakers is absent. However, this does not mean that administrative agencies are free from political accountability. In many areas, policy oversight by elected officials in the legislature or the executive branch is a more important check on agency power than judicial review.

Formally, agencies are dependent on the legislature and the executive for their budgets and their operating authority. If an agency oversteps the bounds of political acceptability or society's priorities change, it may be subjected to radical restructuring. For example, in 2002 Congress consolidated functions previously exercised by twenty-two separate agencies into a single entity, the Department of Homeland Security, in order to improve coordination of the government's efforts to prevent domestic terrorism attacks. Homeland Security Act of 2002, Pub.L. 107–296, 116 Stat. 2135. A followup measure created a Director of National Intelligence with broad authority to coordinate the collection and evaluation of intelligence data. Intelligence Reform and Terrorism Prevention Act of 2004, Pub.L. 108–458, 118 Stat. 3638.

While there are numerous examples of legislatures and chief executives taking formal action to bring regulatory policy into accord with changing political realities, the network of less formal and less visible political "oversight" mechanisms is probably more important in the day-to-day functioning of the administrative process. There are numerous procedures and practices which bring the activities of the agencies to the attention of elected officials and their staffs, and in most regulatory settings the continuing dialogue that results from this process is an important determinant of public policy. Here, the role of law and legal rules has been to channel this interaction within limited boundaries—for example, by restricting *ex parte* contacts—rather than to determine final results.

Another significant dimension of agency accountability is the political acceptance of administrative policy among those who will be affected or regulated. Public dissatisfaction not only triggers the oversight of the political branches, but also may determine the practical effectiveness of an entire regulatory program. The Internal Revenue Service would require a much larger staff and different approach to enforcement if it could not count on a substantial measure of honest self-reporting and voluntary compliance by taxpayers. Thus, an accurate understanding of the methods used to assure the control and accountability of administrative agencies must begin with an appreciation of the political environment within which the agencies function.

In considering the mechanisms for assuring political control over agency policy, it is useful to keep in mind some basic differences between judicial and political methods for making regulatory bureaucracies accountable. Judicial review seeks to assure that agency action is consistent with principles expressed in constitutional mandates or properly enacted statutes. Political oversight is not limited to these formal directives; a newly elected President, for example, is expected to bring new people and new policies into the regulatory process even if the basic statutes remain the same. Moreover, judicial review usually is based on the premise that agency actions are reasoned decisions that result from a process of finding facts and applying generally accepted principles to them. Courts cannot easily review decisions that are the result of bargaining or compromise or pure policy choice. Compromise and choice among competing values are the essence of the political process, and for these kinds of issues, political methods for making and legitimizing decisions are essential. The difficulty in the administrative process is that agency decisions range across the spectrum, from pure policy choice to reasoned application of settled principles, with most of them falling somewhere in between. Thus, there is often conflict over the proper scope of judicial and political accountability.

A. LEGISLATIVE OVERSIGHT
BY FORMAL ACTION

Although the modern nondelegation doctrine puts few limits on the legislature's ability to grant broad powers to administrative agencies, Congress can always revoke or narrow the authority it has granted through subsequent legislation. At times, Congress moves quickly and explicitly to reverse or postpone controversial agency action. When large numbers of consumers complained to their congressional representatives about the National Highway Traffic Safety Administration's automobile seat belt "interlock" rule, the legislature promptly amended the agency's organic act to provide that NHTSA safety standards could not require belt systems which prevented the car from starting or sounded a continuous buzzer when seat belts were unfastened. 15 U.S.C.A. § 1410b. Similarly, the Food and Drug Administration's attempts to ban the only approved artificial sweetener, saccharin, aroused such strong popular opposition that the Congress imposed a moratorium on regulatory action, and substituted a warning label for products containing the chemical. 91 Stat. 1451 (1977).

Another important form of political control over the agencies is a statutory directive to change their traditional ways of making decisions, either by using different procedures or by taking account of new values and interests. The National Environmental Policy Act of 1969, 42 U.S.C.A. §§ 4321–61, is one of the clearest examples of significant substantive change in the agencies' mandates: for the first time, it forced all federal agencies to consider the environmental impacts of major decisions. Similarly, the Regulatory Flexibility Act, 5 U.S.C.A. §§ 601–12, requires agencies to study the economic effect of regulations on small businesses and to consider ways of minimizing those effects. And the Unfunded Mandates Reform Act of 1995, 2 U.S.C.A. §§ 1501–71, provides that any agency rule that will impose high compliance costs on other governmental units or the private sector must be accompanied by an extensive analysis of the rule's economic effect. The agency must consider alternative regulatory approaches and must adopt the least burdensome alternative that meets the objectives of the rule, or else explain why it did not.

During the 1970s, many members of Congress began to feel that the normal process of legislation was too cumbersome for effective control of administrative action. The solution they favored was increased reliance on an old device: the so-called "legislative veto." These provisions took a variety of forms, but most of them directed agencies to transmit final administrative rules to the Congress for review before they became effective. The vote of two chambers, or sometimes only one (or even a committee or a committee chairman) would be enough to kill the rule.

Just as this approach to regulatory reform was gathering speed, the Supreme Court dealt it a fatal blow in INS v. Chadha, 462 U.S. 919 (1983). Under

the Immigration and Nationality Act, a decision by
the Attorney General suspending deportation of an
alien could be nullified by vote of either House of
Congress. When the House of Representatives exercised this power in Chadha's case, he brought suit.
The Supreme Court held that this "one-house veto"
scheme violated Art. I, § 7, of the Constitution.
Under that section, no legislation can be valid unless it is passed by both houses of Congress and
signed by the President (or, if he vetoes it, repassed
by two-thirds of each house). The House's veto
should be presumed to be an exercise of legislative
power, the Court explained, and thus the Art. I, § 7
requirements applied. The veto's "legislative purpose and effect" was all the more clear, according to
the Court, because it was intended to have the force
of law and to affect Chadha's legal rights. *Chadha*
appeared to invalidate all of the nearly 200 legislative veto devices that were then on the books. That
implication was underscored two weeks later, when
the Court summarily upheld challenges to two other
legislative vetoes, involving rulemaking proceedings. United States Senate v. FTC, 463 U.S. 1216
(1983); Process Gas Consumers Group v. Consumer
Energy Council, 463 U.S. 1216 (1983).

The *Chadha* opinion has been severely criticized
as formalistic. Commentators have questioned the
Court's premise that Congress can act only in a
legislative capacity. It was not self-evident that the
procedural requirements of Art. I, § 7 were applicable to a congressional device—created by a duly
enacted statute—that was only intended to con-

strain the executive branch's use of delegated authority. And although the Court assumed that the legislative veto had altered Chadha's rights, it would have been equally logical to conclude that his rights were at all times contingent on the nonoccurrence of a legislative veto. A more practical analysis, it is argued, would have paid more attention to the need of the people's representatives to exert more control over policymaking by the unelected bureaucracy.

The ruling may appear in a more sympathetic light, however, if one assumes that the Court was motivated by functional concerns. Prior studies of the legislative veto had suggested that it tended to bring out some of the less admirable aspects of congressional decisionmaking. The abbreviated procedure and the purely negative character of the vote seemed to encourage Congress to override well-considered agency decisions thoughtlessly—as apparently happened in Chadha's case—or on the basis of lobbyists' influence rather than deliberation. Moreover, since agencies issue far too many rules for the entire legislature to review in a meaningful fashion, the legislative veto actually tended to reinforce the power of oversight committees and their staffs, which themselves are often unrepresentative of Congress as a whole.

Congress's impulse to expand its control over administration by creating special structural devices could not be suppressed indefinitely, however. In 1996 Congress adopted a broad scheme for legislative review of agency rules, known as the Congressional Review Act (CRA), 5 U.S.C.A. §§ 801–08. With very limited exceptions, this scheme requires agencies to submit all newly issued rules to Congress before they can take effect. Congress then has the option of using expedited procedures to adopt a joint resolution to disapprove the rule. Presumably, the constitutional objection that proved decisive in *Chadha* will not threaten this system, because a joint resolution is enacted through the same constitutional formalities as are required for a statute. Nevertheless, the 1996 Act has made the rulemaking process more unwieldy in certain ways. It prevents "major rules" (those which impose the most significant costs on the economy) from going into effect until sixty days after their submission to Congress. The law also states that when a rule is disapproved by joint resolution, it "shall be treated as though such rule had never taken effect"; this provision could cause hardships for citizens who relied on a rule while it was in effect. It remains to be seen whether these and other practical drawbacks of the 1996 legislation will be outweighed by the benefits of strengthened oversight of the rulemaking process by popularly elected legislators. Probably, the impact of the law, for good or ill, will remain fairly limited. To date, Congress has invoked the full CRA procedure only once and under unusual circumstances. The process was used to invalidate a regulation by which the Occupational Safety and Health Administration had sought to protect employees from ergonomic (repetitive-motion) injuries. The rule had been issued during the last days of the Clinton Administration, and the incoming President, George W. Bush, was more than willing to sign a joint resolution of disapproval. Pub.L. 107–5, 115 Stat. 7 (2001).

Regulatory "reform" aside, much congressional review of agency actions occurs as part of the routine legislative process. Indeed, since Congress retains the power of the purse, it has ample opportunity to influence implementation of regulatory statutes when it can muster the will. There are two required stages for congressional approval of agency funding. First, there must be a legislative *authorization* for appropriations, which is usually contained in the basic delegation of power to the agency. The authorization for a particular program may expire after a fixed period of years, or it may be permanent. Similarly, it may set a ceiling on future appropriations, or permit the appropriation of such sums as are necessary to carry out the purposes of the statute. For example, when the Federal Trade Commission instituted a series of sweeping consumer protection proposals that many members of Congress believed were unnecessary or ill conceived, the legislature used its budgetary powers to prohibit the FTC from taking final action on the pending rules until new statutory controls on the agency's authority could be enacted. See FTC Improvements Act of 1980, 94 Stat. 374 (1980), amending 15 U.S.C.A. § 41 et seq. On the other hand, when the Environmental Protection Agency came under political attack for being too lenient with those responsible for toxic waste dumps, Congress responded with numerous "hammer" provisions. These provisions required the agency to ban certain practices or impose specified performance standards by a fixed date unless it could find that the statutory limits were unnecessary to protect health or the environment. Hazardous and Solid Waste Amendments of 1984, 98 Stat. 3221 (1984).

More commonly, funding controls are imposed in the annual *appropriations* process. Each year, agencies must submit budget requests, which are reviewed by the President (acting through the Office of Management and Budget) and are transmitted to the appropriations committees of the House and Senate. These committees then hold hearings and report bills allocating funds among the various agencies and programs, which must be voted on by both houses of Congress. Generally, the appropriations committees are responsible for "fiscal" oversight of agency spending, while the authorizing committees are primarily concerned with "legislative" oversight or substantive policy. In practice, however, the two functions tend to overlap, and appropriations measures can become vehicles for legislative intervention into highly specific areas of regulatory policy. In 1990, for example, Congress used an appropriations act to modify, on a temporary basis, the applicability of several environmental statutes to thirteen specific forests in the Pacific Northwest, so that the Interior Department would be free to allow logging there despite possible harm to spotted owls that inhabited the forests. The

Supreme Court upheld the provision, rejecting environmentalists' claims that the law intruded on the courts' powers by interfering with ongoing litigation over the future of the forests. Robertson v. Seattle Audubon Society, 503 U.S. 429 (1992). As *Robertson* illustrates, the legislature's power to intercept active litigation by changing the underlying law is broad. (Once a court case becomes final, however, Congress may not enact a statute that would retroactively change the law applicable to it. That step would improperly supplant the judicial power. Plaut v. Spendthrift Farm, Inc., 514 U.S. 211 (1995).)

Circumscribing this wide sphere of oversight activity are separation of powers principles such as those animating the *Chadha* decision. The Supreme Court reaffirmed its commitment to those principles in Metropolitan Wash. Airports Auth. v. Citizens for the Abatement of Aircraft Noise, 501 U.S. 252 (1991). There the Court held unconstitutional a statutory scheme in which administrative decisions regarding management of the airports in the District of Columbia area could be vetoed by an oversight board staffed by members of the House and Senate transportation committees. According to the Court, the Board had to be seen as an agent of Congress itself. It made no difference whether the board's functions were characterized as "legislative" (in which case the formalities of bicameralism and presentment to the President would be essential) or "executive" (in which case Congress could not perform them at all). Regardless of labels, therefore, when Congress wants to take legally effective action, it must utilize the full enactment process of Art. I, § 7.

The Line Item Veto Act, another congressional attempt to work around the restrictions of Art. I, § 7, met a similar fate in Clinton v. City of New York, 524 U.S. 417 (1998). The Act provided that the President, immediately after signing an appropriations bill, could notify Congress that he intended to "cancel" specific expenditures in the bill. The cancellations would take effect unless the legislation overrode them in a "disapproval bill"—a new piece of legislation enacted through the Art. I, § 7 process. The Court struck down the Act, regarding it as a means by which the President could, in effect, amend an appropriations statute unilaterally. Although, as the dissenters in *New York* pointed out, this arrangement was actually not very different from other laws that confer discretionary spending authority on the executive branch, the Court's holding may have been prompted by awareness that the Act was an effort to bestow on the President, without a constitutional amendment, a power that is tantamount to a kind of authority that many governors possess under their state constitutions.

B. INFORMAL LEGISLATIVE OVERSIGHT

In addition to its formal legislating and funding powers, Congress has broad authority to investigate implementation of statutory programs and to expose corrupt or ineffective administration. Primary responsibility for investigating the efficiency and effectiveness of the agencies is lodged in the House Government Reform and Senate Governmental Affairs committees, but any committee that has jurisdiction over some aspect of the agency's program may conduct investigations. By mobilizing public and political pressure on the agency and by raising the threat of future legislation, investigative oversight can greatly affect agency behavior.

Congressional demands for information can often come into conflict with the executive branch's interest in the confidentiality of its internal deliberations. The doctrine of executive privilege, which has roots in the Constitution, gives agencies a limited right to withhold information for this reason. See generally United States v. Nixon, 418 U.S. 683 (1974). However, the scope of the privilege is ill-defined, because disputes over executive privilege are ordinarily resolved through political compromise rather than court litigation.

To facilitate the oversight process, Congress normally requires agencies to report back periodically on their activities. Most reports are submitted on an annual basis, but occasionally Congress will request a special report. Agencies may also submit special reports on their own initiative, particularly if the agency needs additional legislative authority to deal with a particular problem.

Congress has also created several permanent organizations to assist it with its legislative and oversight responsibilities. Studies of agency activities by the Congressional Research Service, for example, can trigger more formal oversight mechanisms, or induce the agencies to modify their practices. The support agency that is most influential in the legislative oversight process is the Government Accountability Office (previously General Accounting Office), headed by the Comptroller General. The GAO was originally created to conduct financial audits of the agencies' use of public funds, but in recent years it has taken on considerable responsibility for program review and evaluation. The Supreme Court made clear in Bowsher v. Synar, 478 U.S. 714 (1986), that there are limits beyond which the GAO may not go if it is to avoid infringing on the constitutional powers of the executive branch. See pp. 60–62 infra. However, the location of those limits remains unsettled. See Walker v. Cheney, 230 F.Supp.2d 51 (D.D.C.2002) (limiting GAO's authority to subpoena documents from executive branch entities, largely because of separation of powers concerns); see also pp. 164–65 infra.

Another method by which the legislature influences agency activities is through the institution of congressional "casework," which is the general name given to legislators' attempts to assist their constituents in dealing with the bureaucracy. Ideally, congressional casework puts the legislator in the role of an "ombudsman" checking up on the quality of administration and helping citizens to obtain fair treatment from the agencies. It can also help the representatives identify problem areas which are appropriate for oversight hearings or statutory correction. In its less-than-ideal manifestations, however, casework can become an attempt by a legislator to pressure the bureaucrats into making an improper decision in favor of a constituent, or a means of rewarding campaign contributors (as illustrated by the Keating Five ethics scandal of the early 1990s), or a paper shuffle in which the citizen's complaint is simply "bucked" back to the agency topped by a form letter from the legislator.

Since legislative oversight is basically political in nature and often operates through pressure or bargaining, it may come into conflict with legal or constitutional requirements for agency decision-making. This is particularly true in formal adjudications, where an agency passes upon the legality of private conduct in a trial-type setting. In Pillsbury Co. v. FTC, 354 F.2d 952 (5th Cir.1966), a congressional oversight committee subjected the chairman of the Federal Trade Commission to prolonged and hostile questioning regarding a legal interpretation that the Commission had issued in an interlocutory order during a pending adjudication. The court held that this intrusion into the agency's decisionmaking process had deprived the respondent of a fair adjudication. Even when the decision is not made in so formal a fashion, however, some kinds of congressional oversight may be improper. The "Three Sisters Bridge" case, D.C. Federation of Civic Ass'ns v. Volpe, 459 F.2d 1231 (D.C.Cir.1971), is an example of legal limits on political intervention. There, the powerful chairman of a House appropriations committee brought pressure to bear on the Secretary of

Transportation to grant approval of a controversial bridge construction project. The court concluded that the Secretary's consideration of this pressure in making his decision was grounds for reversal. In its basic grant of authority to the Secretary, the Congress as a whole had directed him to consider the project "on its merits" and to make a reasoned analysis of the facts. Thus, political pressures were technically irrelevant to that kind of decision; oversight activities by one congressman or one committee could not override the will of the Congress as a whole as expressed in the underlying legislation. In Sierra Club v. Costle, 657 F.2d 298 (D.C.Cir.1981), however, the court distinguished *D.C. Federation.* A Senator from a coal mining state had forcefully expressed his constituents' concerns to the EPA during a rulemaking proceeding to set limits on emissions from coal-fired power plants. Since there was no hard evidence that the Senator had brought irrelevant considerations into the deliberations and since rulemaking is by its nature a political process, the EPA rules were upheld.

C. CONTROL OVER PERSONNEL

1. APPOINTMENT OF OFFICERS

Like the Congress, the President has a variety of powers and techniques he can use to oversee and influence the operations of administrative agencies. One of the President's most important instruments of control is his power to appoint federal officers. The Appointments Clause of the Constitution (Art.

II, § 2, cl. 2) contains some fairly specific guidance on the staffing of federal administrative agencies. It provides that the President generally appoints all "Officers of the United States," with the advice and consent of the Senate. These appointees normally share the President's policy preferences and feel some commitment to advancing his priorities.

Congress tested the limits of the Appointments Clause in 1974 when it passed a statute creating the Federal Election Commission. The statute required that four of the FEC's six voting members would be appointed by the Speaker of the House and the President *pro tempore* of the Senate. The Supreme Court struck down this legislation in Buckley v. Valeo, 424 U.S. 1, 118–43 (1976). The Court explained that the constitutional term "Officers of the United States," identifying those officeholders who must be chosen pursuant to the Appointments Clause, includes all appointees exercising significant authority pursuant to the laws of the United States, such as rulemaking, adjudication, or enforcement functions. Thus the FEC, a typical agency wielding all of those powers, was clearly covered by the clause. The Court noted, however, that it would have reached a different result if the FEC had merely been assigned powers of an investigative and informative nature. (The so-called 9/11 Commission, which inquired into security lapses that facilitated the terrorist attacks of September 11, 2001, was an example of such an agency. The President appointed its chairman, but congressional leaders appointed the other members. Pub.L. 107–306, 116 Stat. 2408 (2002).)

A significant limitation on the President's appointment power is found in a proviso to the Appointments Clause itself: "Congress may by Law vest the Appointment of such inferior Officers, as they think proper, in the President alone, in the Courts of Law, or in the Heads of Departments." This proviso came into play in a celebrated case concerning the constitutionality of the Ethics in Government Act. The Act authorized a federal court of appeals to appoint a special prosecutor, or "independent counsel," to investigate allegations of criminal wrongdoing by high officials of the Executive Branch. The Court upheld the statute, finding that the independent counsel was an "inferior officer" and thus could properly be appointed by one of the "Courts of Law," rather than by the President. Morrison v. Olson, 487 U.S. 654 (1988). The Court concluded that the independent counsel fell within that category because she was removable by the Attorney General (although only under strictly limited conditions) and because her duties were limited to handling a single case and would terminate at the end of that case. The Court cautioned, however, that in some situations judicial appointment of an executive officer would create a fatal "incongruity"—for example, if a court were charged with appointing officials in the Agriculture Department. The Ethics in Government Act was not vulnerable on that ground, however, because courts have appointed prosecutors in various circumstances for many years. *Morrison* did not spell out any general test for identifying an "inferior officer," but a later case clarified that the term refers to an official whose work "is directed and supervised at some level by" a presidential appointee. Thus, judges of the Coast Guard Court of Criminal Appeals could be appointed by the Secretary of Transportation rather than the President. Edmond v. United States, 520 U.S. 651 (1997).

When an agency hires someone to become a mere "employee," who will not wield "significant authority" under federal law, his appointment need not comply with the Appointments Clause at all. The scope of this limitation was at issue in Freytag v. Commissioner, 501 U.S. 868 (1991). That case involved a challenge to the appointment authority of the chief judge of the Tax Court, an administrative tribunal specializing in tax disputes. A statute empowered the chief judge to appoint "special trial judges," who usually act as adjuncts to the regular judges of the court but also adjudicate a few classes of cases themselves. The Supreme Court found that the special trial judges were "inferior officers," not employees, and thus had to be appointed pursuant to Article II. The Court went on to uphold the chief judge's appointment power, reasoning that the Tax Court is one of the "Courts of Law" mentioned in the Appointments Clause. At the same time, however, the Court insisted that the chief judge could not be classified as head of a "Department" for purposes of the Clause, because that term applies only to "executive divisions like the Cabinet-level departments." In short, even though the constitutional challenge in *Freytag* failed, the reasoning of the case indicates that the Court has been seriously concerned about the possibility of excessive diffusion of the appointment power.

2. REMOVAL OF OFFICERS

Except in the clauses dealing with impeachment, the Constitution does not address the circumstances under which agency personnel may be removed from office. There is, however, substantial case law on this subject, applying generalized separation of powers notions. Indeed, these cases are the source of one of the central puzzles of administrative law: the concept of the "independent agency." Independent agencies tend to be multimember boards and commissions, such as the SEC, FCC, and NLRB. A major difference between these agencies and the "executive agencies" (a category that includes the familiar Cabinet departments) is that the heads of independent agencies do not serve "at the pleasure of the President." Their governing statutes may provide, for example, that commissioners are appointed for a fixed period of years that does not correspond with the President's term of office. There may also be statutory provisions protecting the commissioners from arbitrary removal during their terms of office.

The paradox inherent in this situation is easy to state. The independent agencies perform functions that one would normally associate with the executive branch, yet they are not under the full control of the President, in whom Article II of the Constitution vests "the executive Power." On the other hand, if they are not part of the executive branch, there seems to be no constitutional basis for them to exist at all. Thus, independent agencies are sometimes described as "arms of Congress" or as members of a "headless fourth branch."

For a long time, two cases dominated discussion of these matters. The first, involving the dismissal of a postmaster at a time when the Post Office was still a Cabinet department, suggested that Congress could not limit the President's removal power without violating Article II. Myers v. United States, 272 U.S. 52 (1926). The opinion, written by Chief Justice (and former President) Taft, reasoned that the President needed the power to fire any public officer at will if he was to fulfill his constitutional duty to "take Care that the Laws be faithfully executed." However, a decade later the Court limited *Myers.* The issue came to a head when President Roosevelt sought to remove a chairman of the Federal Trade Commission who was unsympathetic to some of the New Deal programs that the FTC was responsible for administering. The statute provided that FTC commissioners were to serve for a fixed term of years and that they could be removed during their term only for "inefficiency, neglect of duty, or malfeasance in office." The President did not claim that the recalcitrant chairman was guilty of any of these offenses; he simply wanted to change the policy direction of the agency. When the discharged chair-

man brought suit to challenge the legality of his
removal, the Supreme Court held that the statutory
removal-for-cause provision was a constitutionally
proper limit on the President's removal power.
Humphrey's Executor (Rathbun) v. United States,
295 U.S. 602 (1935). The Court distinguished *Myers*
as a case involving a "purely executive" officer. As
such, it did not apply to officers of the FTC, which
"occupies no place in the executive department"
and "acts in part quasi-legislatively and in part
quasi-judicially."

The Court's desire to shield "quasi-judicial" officers from executive domination has obvious appeal.
Adjudication of individual disputes is often thought
to call for independent, apolitical judgment. The
Court relied on this rationale in Wiener v. United
States, 357 U.S. 349 (1958), to prevent a member of
the War Claims Commission from being dismissed
without cause. The *Wiener* holding was striking
because the statute said nothing about removal of
commissioners. Because the commissioners were expected to "adjudicate according to law," the Court
felt that it could *infer* a congressional desire to
protect them from arbitrary removal.

Other aspects of the *Humphrey's Executor* reasoning, however, have been roundly criticized. To the
extent that an agency exercises "quasi-legislative"
or policymaking powers, a substantial measure of
political responsiveness and accountability to elected officials seems highly desirable. More fundamentally, it is not possible to pigeonhole functions as
neatly as the Court seemed to assume. As the

nondelegation cases illustrate, there is considerable overlap between "quasi-legislative" and "executive" power, and no good way to draw the line. In practice, scholars have found no consistent difference separating the work of the independent commissions from that of the Cabinet departments.

The Court explicitly abandoned the analysis of *Humphrey's Executor* in 1988, when it decided Morrison v. Olson, 487 U.S. 654 (1988), also discussed at pp. 52–53 supra. The Court recognized that the duties of the independent counsel were clearly "executive" in nature. Nevertheless, the Court upheld the provision in the Ethics in Government Act allowing the independent counsel to be removed only for "good cause." The proper inquiry, the Court said, was whether removal restrictions "impede the President's ability to perform his constitutional duty." The good cause standard in the Act did not constitute such an impediment, especially in light of the limited nature of the independent counsel's responsibilities and the congressionally perceived need for her to function independently The Court added that the good cause standard was equivalent to the statutory protections enjoyed by many independent agency heads. The clear implication was that the removal protections applicable to traditional independent agencies would also survive scrutiny under the *Morrison* test.

There were suggestions in the years leading up to *Morrison* that *Humphrey's Executor* should be overruled, so that all agencies would be under the complete control of the President. After *Morrison* the constitutionality of the independent agency appears to be secure. Indeed, even before the decision, Presidents were generally cautious about trying to make independent agencies adhere to Administration policy. What *Morrison* does appear to change is the theory on which the independent agencies are justified. The Court acknowledged Congress's power to innovate, pursuant to the necessary and proper clause, so long as the President's "ability to perform his constitutional duty" is not impaired. In the political arena, however, reappraisals of the value of "independence" in particular contexts are always possible. Indeed, Congress allowed the independent counsel provisions of the Ethics in Government Act to expire in 1999. This decision reflected disillusionment with what was seen as excessive zeal, without effective political controls, on the part of a number of independent counsel who had investigated officials in both Democratic and Republican administrations, including most conspicuously the multiple criminal investigations into the conduct of President Clinton. This is one instance in which the political community ultimately concluded that, although persons who must probe possible misconduct within an administration need freedom of action, they themselves must not be so "independent" as to lack political accountability for their choices.

As a practical matter, the distinction between independent and executive agencies should not be overemphasized. Even fixed terms of office and removal-for-cause statutes do not pose serious obstacles to the President's ability to influence regulatory policy through the appointments process. Since regulators' terms of office are typically staggered in the multimember agencies and many commissioners do not serve out their terms, a newly elected President almost always has the opportunity to make key appointments early in his administration. Moreover, if the President formally requests an administrator's resignation, even an "independent" commissioner is not very likely to resist or to face the prospect of a removal-for-cause controversy. Indeed, the President can sometimes hasten the departure of an embattled commissioner by simply failing to rally to the official's defense. In 2002, for example, when a controversial SEC chairman came under fire for mishandling his agency's response to corporate accounting scandals, a studious silence from the White House led directly to the chairman's resignation. The President also has the statutory power to designate one of the commissioners of an independent agency to serve as chairman and to "demote" the chairman back to the rank of commissioner without cause. Since the chairman of a regulatory agency has the primary responsibility for managing its operations, including the hiring of new personnel, a change in agency leadership often results in policy changes.

On the other hand, Presidents sometimes have to put up with high-ranking executive officials whom they have the legal right to fire, because a dismissal would be politically costly, particularly if the administrator has the support of a powerful constituency. Finally, it should be noted that both executive and

independent agencies follow roughly the same procedures and are reviewed in the same fashion by the
courts. Thus, the distinction between the two has
little relevance to the vast majority of the principles
of administrative law.

3. THE CONGRESSIONAL ROLE

In light of *Buckley v. Valeo,* discussed at pp. 51–
52 supra, Congress cannot make appointments to
the agencies itself. It can, however, set qualifications for various offices. One type of restriction is a
statutory provision requiring that a multimember
commission be politically balanced; for example, no
more than three of the five members of the SEC
may be members of one political party. The Senate
also must decide whether to "advise and consent"
to the President's appointees. Confirmation controversies in the Senate have become intense, especially during the current period of strong ideological
divisions. Individual Senators often extract significant policy concessions as the price of allowing a
nomination to come to a vote. Senators may also
use confirmation hearings for more intangible purposes: to air their concerns about regulatory matters and to elicit policy commitments from nominees.

Except by impeachment, Congress also has no
power to remove agency officials, as the Court held
in Bowsher v. Synar, 478 U.S. 714 (1986). The
Gramm–Rudman–Hollings Act provided that if Congress and the President failed to agree on fiscal

policies that would hold federal budget deficits down to a specified target figure, across-the-board reductions in program funding would go into effect. Final responsibility for calculating these reductions rested with the Comptroller General, an official who is removable by joint resolution of Congress. The Supreme Court found the Act unconstitutional, declaring that separation of powers principles prevent Congress from taking "an active role ... in the supervision of officers charged with the execution of the laws it enacts." Thus, Congress cannot remove an executive official except for impeachable offenses. Although the Comptroller General normally performs legislative support functions, see pp. 47–48 supra, the responsibilities he might have to exercise in implementing the new Act were "executive" in nature; he could not be asked to fulfill those responsibilities under threat of a congressional ouster.

Like *Chadha, Bowsher* has been criticized for relying on an overly formal model of the congressional role in the checks and balances system. It would have been hard for the Court to make a case in pragmatic terms that *any* threat of congressional removal of an "executing" official disrupts the balance of power among the branches. (In the case of the Comptroller General, the threat was only abstract; the removal power had never been exercised.) Some of the Court's language was surely overbroad: the exclusion of Congress from any "supervision," if taken literally, would even condemn routine congressional oversight activity. On a more

concrete level, however, *Bowsher* can be understood
as reflecting a feeling that the Comptroller General's role under the Act was an improper attempt by
Congress to exert influence over the budget reduction process without taking the political risks that
substantive budget-cutting legislation would have
entailed. By its holding, the Court ensured that one
or more elected officials (Congress, the President, or
both) would ultimately be accountable for making
the quintessentially political choices about how
much to fund various programs. Notwithstanding
the *Bowsher* holding, however, Congress is by no
means as impotent in practice as it is in constitutional theory. Every agency needs a minimum degree of legislative support if it is to maintain its
programs and obtain funding for them. When legislators' confidence in an administrative official drops
too far, a resignation is likely to follow.

D. OTHER EXECUTIVE OVERSIGHT

In the day-to-day functioning of the administrative process, the President's power of persuasion
and the other less drastic tools of executive oversight are usually more significant factors than the
threat of removal. Exercise of these oversight powers often takes the form of an executive order, a
formal directive from the President to federal agencies or officials. For example, Presidents George
H.W. Bush and Bill Clinton each issued orders
instructing agencies to minimize litigation by making liberal use of settlement and alternative dispute

resolution. Depending upon the context, a particular executive order may be based either on an inherent constitutional power of the President, or on an express or implicit delegation from Congress.

Much of the work of executive oversight takes place within the organizations which comprise the Executive Office of the President, commonly referred to as "The White House." The Executive Office of the President includes not only the President's personal advisors, who comprise the White House Office, but also permanent organizations like the National Security Council and the Council of Economic Advisers. See 3 U.S.C.A. § 101. The most important of these units to the regulatory agencies is the Office of Management and Budget (OMB). As its name suggests, OMB has primary responsibility for formulating the annual executive budget which the President transmits to the Congress. In performing this task, OMB receives budget requests from the individual agencies and modifies them in accordance with the Administration's priorities. 31 U.S.C.A. § 16. Similarly, OMB reviews the agencies' requests for substantive legislation, including agency officials' proposed testimony before congressional committees, for consistency with the Administration's position. Both of these "clearance" procedures typically give rise to extensive negotiations between OMB staff and agency officials. Usually a compromise solution is reached, but major disagreements are sometimes resolved by the President. In addition, the Paperwork Reduction Act, 44 U.S.C.A. § 3501 et seq., provides that OMB must approve any new information demand that an agency wishes to impose on the private sector. Initially the courts interpreted this authority as applying only to information that the government seeks for its own purposes, Dole v. United Steelworkers of America, 494 U.S. 26 (1990), but in 1995 Congress extended the Act by authorizing OMB to review rules such as consumer product labeling regulations, which require companies to disclose information to the public.

Since 1971, the White House has attempted to exert direct supervision and control over major rulemaking proceedings through a regulatory analysis program. This technique was first formalized in the Ford and Carter Administrations, but reached fullblown form when President Reagan issued Executive Order 12,291, 46 Fed.Reg. 13,193 (1981). The order instructed agencies, "to the extent permitted by law," to take regulatory action only if "the potential benefits to society for the regulation outweigh the potential costs to society." They were also to prepare a "regulatory impact analysis" or assessment of anticipated costs and benefits for any proposed rule that was likely to have a significant economic impact. An entity within OMB, the Office of Information and Regulatory Affairs (OIRA), would then conduct its own review of the agency's cost-benefit analysis, and the agency could not issue the rule without OIRA's clearance. A related directive, Executive Order 12,498, 50 Fed.Reg. 1036 (1985), required executive agencies to submit their anticipated regulatory programs to OIRA each year.

This "regulatory planning process" was intended to give OIRA and the agency heads themselves an opportunity to consider carefully at the outset whether the ideas being developed by the agency's staff were intrinsically sound and were consistent with the Administration's priorities. The two presidential orders applied only to *executive* agencies, although some independent agencies voluntarily participated in the oversight program.

When President Clinton took office, he replaced the two Reagan orders with Executive Order 12,-866, 58 Fed.Reg. 51,735 (1993), which retained the basic features of the existing program but also instituted some changes. It modified the cost-benefit analysis principles of the former regime, softening the deregulatory thrust of the Reagan order and acknowledging more explicitly the limitations of quantitative analysis. It also provided that if OIRA and a rulemaking agency were unable to resolve their differences over a proposed rule, the disagreement could be referred to the President or Vice President for resolution. In addition, although most of the order remained applicable only to executive agencies, the regulatory planning process was explicitly extended to independent agencies. President George W. Bush adhered to the same basic order, modifying it only by removing the Vice President's role from the process. Executive Order 13,258, 67 Fed.Reg. 9385 (2002).

To date, the courts have not directly ruled on the legality of Executive Order 12,866 or its predecessors. The legal case for the order rests on the supervisory power that inheres in the President's status as head of the executive branch. The Constitution (Art. II, § 2, cl. 1) specifically authorizes him to "require the Opinion, in writing, [of department heads] upon any Subject relating to the Duties of their respective Offices." Moreover, because of the President's electoral base, his participation in the process can be seen as legitimizing a rule. See Sierra Club v. Costle, 657 F.2d 298 (D.C.Cir.1981). The countervailing consideration is that both agencies and the President must execute the laws enacted by Congress. Thus, it is generally agreed that OIRA must not administer the regulatory analysis program in a manner that would prevent an agency from fulfilling the duties assigned to it by the legislature. Since the order by its terms applies only "to the extent permitted by law," it leaves questions about the allowable scope of the program to be resolved on a case-by-case basis.

The strongest objections to the oversight program have been political rather than legal. In the early years of the program, critics complained about delays and procedural unfairness in the oversight process. Some of these grievances, however, have been redressed through subsequent reforms. See pp. 341–42 infra. A deeper objection to presidential oversight is that it effectively takes power away from the agency that has the greatest expertise in the relevant subject area. Of course, this result is inherent in OIRA's role, but supporters of that role reply by pointing to the practical advantages of the oversight program. They stress the President's unique vantage point as a national leader who can coordinate conflicting governmental objectives and resist the parochial demands of a department's particular constituency. They also cite OIRA's expertise in sophisticated policy analysis techniques. In any event, OIRA has in recent years usually managed to avoid public confrontations with rulemaking agencies, in part by using its planning and consultative capabilities to bring its policy views to the agency's attention at early stages of the rulemaking process. In its present form, therefore, executive oversight appears to be operating relatively smoothly and public complaints about the program have largely subsided. On balance, OIRA seems to be making a valuable contribution to the rulemaking process and is likely to remain an influential part of the regulatory scene for the indefinite future.

One other tool of executive oversight, which is often overlooked, is the President's power to control litigation affecting the agencies through the Department of Justice. See 5 U.S.C.A. § 3106; 28 U.S.C.A. § 516. Although there are significant exceptions, most agencies lack the statutory authority to litigate on their own behalf. Rather, they must obtain representation from the Department of Justice, and the Department's refusal to advocate or defend a particular agency policy may mean that the agency's decision has no practical effect. Cf. FEC v. NRA Political Victory Fund, 513 U.S. 88 (1994) (case dismissed because Justice Department had not authorized the appeal). This concentration of authority enables the Department to reconcile the competing litigation interests of multiple agencies and to insist that agencies' briefs conform to the President's policy priorities. In 1986, for example, the Department, backed by the Reagan White House, filed a brief in the Supreme Court opposing court-ordered affirmative action decrees in Title VII employment discrimination suits, even though the Equal Employment Opportunity Commission, its client agency in that case, had asserted a contrary position in the lower courts. See Local 28, Sheet Metal Workers v. EEOC, 478 U.S. 421, 444 n.24 (1986).

Over and above this wide array of formal presidential oversight techniques, the White House policy staff routinely examines and exerts influence on major rulemaking proceedings. This type of control has been particularly prominent during the Clinton and George W. Bush Administrations. Should this trend toward direct presidential management of the regulatory process hold up, pressures for strengthened controls on presidential decisionmaking are likely to result.

E.   THE FUTURE OF SEPARATION OF POWERS

Since the 1980s, administrative lawyers have witnessed an extraordinary revival of litigation raising fundamental separation of powers issues—issues that courts had scarcely reexamined since the 1930s. But the courts have not analyzed these issues in a consistent manner. Cases such as *Chadha*,

Bowsher, and *Clinton v. New York* have perceived absolute constitutional limitations on the lawmaking process; they posit that liberty can be best preserved if the courts will strictly enforce the division of responsibilities implied by the tripartite structure of the Constitution. In contrast, *Morrison* seemed to assume that courts can best decide on a case-by-case basis whether a given innovation will disrupt the balance of powers among the branches: the question became whether the challenged action would disable any branch from performing its core functions or would allow any branch (including the agency itself) to acquire so much power that there would be insufficient checks against possible abuses. Scholars describe these two styles of reasoning as "formalist" and "functionalist," respectively. The functionalist premises of *Morrison* became evident when the Court ruled that the Ethics in Government Act as a whole did not violate separation of powers principles: the Court reasoned that the Act did not significantly enhance the powers of Congress or the courts at the expense of the executive branch, nor did it unduly weaken the Presidency.

Other cases have adopted analogous functional reasoning. In Mistretta v. United States, 488 U.S. 361 (1989), the Court considered the constitutionality of the United States Sentencing Commission, which Congress had created to write guidelines that would establish, within narrow limits, the allowable sentences for most federal criminal offenses. The structure of the Commission was unconventional, because the statute referred to it as "an independent commission in the judicial branch" and some of its members were federal judges. In upholding this unusual arrangement, the Court reasoned that the statute did not unduly strengthen the judicial branch: the judiciary had traditionally been deeply involved in criminal sentencing, and there was historical precedent for judicial branch rulemaking and for individual judges to perform nonjudicial government functions. On the other hand, the statute did not unduly weaken the judicial branch: the fact that the President could appoint judges to the commission, and remove them for good cause, posed only a negligible threat of compromising the impartiality of the courts as they performed their normal adjudicatory functions. Functional arguments of this kind also underlie much of the case law that governs a related separation of powers issue: whether particular powers can be delegated to agencies in the first place. See the discussion of *Meat Cutters* and *Schor* at pp. 22–24, 32–33 supra.

In the years ahead, new questions of political oversight will surely arise: how closely the President may supervise the agencies (both executive and independent), and what supervisory role remains for Congress. No doubt the courts will continue to rely heavily on the constitutional text. Occasionally, as *Buckley* illustrates, that type of argument can be nearly conclusive. But it seems likely that courts will usually be receptive to more functional arguments as well. In context, this means that arguments about the value of political supervision will have to be weighed against arguments for keeping some matters "out of politics." This flexible approach surely gives rise to a lack of predictability in constitutional law, as its critics contend; but, at least some of the time, the Court seems to regard uncertainty as a price that it must pay if it is to accommodate new structural arrangements in the administrative state.

CHAPTER III

THE SCOPE OF JUDICIAL REVIEW

The courts' review of agency action (or inaction) furnishes an important set of controls on administrative behavior; indeed, these are the controls that are most often at issue in administrative law. Unlike the political oversight controls, which generally influence entire programs or basic policies, judicial review regularly operates to provide relief for the individual person who is harmed by a particular agency decision. Judicial review also differs from the political controls in that it attempts to foster reasoned decisionmaking, by requiring the agencies to produce supporting facts and rational explanations. Thus, judicial oversight may work at cross-purposes with the oversight activities of the political branches, which depend heavily on pressure, bargaining, and compromise rather than on reasoned analysis. Yet judicial review can also serve as an essential supplement to political controls on administration: one of its major functions is to assure that the agency is acting in accord with the will of the political branches, as expressed in the enabling legislation. At the same time, judicial review may contribute to the political legitimacy of bureaucratic regulation, by providing an independent check on the validity of administrative decisions.

Like the regulatory process, judicial review has evolved over a period of years into a complex and not completely coherent system. A series of statutory, constitutional, and judicial doctrines have been developed to define the proper boundaries on judicial oversight of administration. In some areas, the courts may lack institutional competence to review an administrative action because the decision in question is political, or the plaintiff is asking the court to render an advisory opinion; in other instances, the court may decline to intervene until the administrative process has had a chance to run its course. On the whole, however, the trend in the recent judicial decisions and in modern statutes like the APA is to make judicial review more widely and easily available. This trend, and its limits, will be examined in Chapter 10 of this text.

Where judicial review is available, the question then becomes: how far can the court go in examining the agency decision? Technically, this issue is known as "scope of review" and, as Professor Davis has observed, the scope of review for a particular administrative decision may range from zero to a hundred percent. That is, the reviewing court may be completely precluded from testing the merits of an agency action, or it may be free to decide the issues de novo, with no deference to the agency's determination. Usually, however, the function of the reviewing court falls somewhere between these extremes.

Inherent in judicial review are many functional limitations. It is designed only to maintain minimum standards, not to assure an optimal or perfect decision. Thus, above the threshold of minimum fairness and rationality, the agencies may still make unsatisfactory decisions or use poor procedures. Even a judicial reversal may have little impact on administrative policy, if there are strong bureaucratic or political reasons for the agency to persist in its view. On remand, the agency may simply produce a better rationalization for its action, or reach the same result using different procedures, or misinterpret the court's directives (perhaps intentionally). And, of course, there are many decisions in which judicial review is not even sought. Judicial review is expensive and slow, and the outcome is never certain. These factors often combine to prevent parties from bringing even a meritorious claim, particularly when the person aggrieved is not wealthy or does not have a large financial stake in the outcome. Yet, despite the "limited office" of judicial review, it is generally regarded as the most significant safeguard available to curb excesses in administrative action.

A. LAW, FACT, AND DISCRETION

To understand the complex assortment of administrative law doctrines on judicial review, one must begin with the realization that most administrative decisions result from a series of determinations on the agency's part. Typically, an agency *interprets the law* it is supposed to implement; it *finds facts* about the situation it will address; and it *uses discretion* in applying the law to the factual situation that it has found to exist. Each of these types of determinations, when contested, calls for a different kind of inquiry by a reviewing court.

These same categories are reflected in 5 U.S.C.A. § 706, the Administrative Procedure Act's scope of review provision. Section 706(2) lists a variety of grounds on which an agency decision can be reversed. Two clauses deal exclusively with questions of law: whether the Constitution has been violated (§ 706(2)(B)), and whether the agency has exceeded its statutory authority (§ 706(2)(C)). Two other clauses deal exclusively with fact issues: § 706(2)(E) codifies the "substantial evidence" test, which is most often applied in proceedings in which there has been a formal, trial-type hearing; and § 706(2)(F) provides for de novo fact review (a rarity in administrative law). Section 706(2)(A) contains the APA's "arbitrary and capricious" test, which, depending on the context, can involve legal, factual, or discretionary issues. Finally, § 706(2)(D) permits a court to reverse an agency because of procedural error. (Procedural issues are discussed in subsequent chapters of this book; the present chapter is concerned exclusively with judicial review of substantive issues.)

A general rule of thumb is that a reviewing court owes less deference to an agency's legal conclusions than to the agency's factual or discretionary determinations. Some of the reasons for this distinction

can be briefly stated. The courts' relative independence in declaring the law is a natural outgrowth of
their traditional role in the American legal system;
in administrative law, as in other subject areas, the
judiciary claims to be "the final authority on issues
of statutory construction." Chemical Manufacturers
Ass'n v. NRDC, 470 U.S. 116 (1985). This posture of
judicial independence, however, has to coexist with
the reality that Congress regularly delegates broad
authority to administrative agencies. Sometimes
Congress does so explicitly; at other times it delegates by merely leaving a statutory term openend-
ed, in the expectation that the agency will flesh out
the legislation. In either situation, broad judicial
deference to the administrator's discretionary
choices enables an agency to exercise the kind of
creativity that the legislature intended. In line with
this reasoning, a court's review of the merits of an
agency action typically entails two tasks, performed
in sequence: first, to ensure, through a relatively
vigorous examination of the agency's legal conclusions, that the agency did not exceed the outer
bounds of the delegation; and second, to ensure,
through a more deferential examination of the
agency's factual and discretionary determinations,
that the delegated power was exercised in a rational
fashion.

This sequence of inquiries is similar to the manner in which a court reviews a jury verdict in civil
litigation. There, the court will decide on its own
("as a matter of law") whether an issue should have
been submitted to the jury at all, whether the

instructions were properly worded, and whether the trial was conducted fairly. If the court finds no errors in these respects, its review of the jury's fact findings is more limited—essentially a question of reasonableness. In like fashion, a court's most intensive scrutiny during judicial review of administrative action is typically directed at questions of whether the agency acted within its authority, considered proper factors in reaching its decision, and complied with all required procedures. If it did, the agency's remaining determinations, relating to its findings of fact and exercise of discretion, should (at least in theory) be reviewed more deferentially.

This analogy to civil litigation is imperfect, because an agency's capacity to act in a deliberative, legally sophisticated fashion is much greater than a jury's. It can write opinions to explain its actions, generate and follow its own precedents, and structure its discretion through rules and standards. Thus, a court can, and often will, hold the agency to observe high standards of "reasoned decisionmaking." This also means, however, that the agency can itself play a lawmaking role, rivaling the court's role. Questions about the manner in which these two branches of government should share normsetting authority have been a major source of debate during the modern history of administrative law.

Some of the respective institutional strengths of courts and agencies suggest further justifications for the above division of labor. For example, the judiciary's ability to interpret constitutional and statutory requirements is commensurate with that of the agencies, and judges also have the advantage of being comparatively disinterested. An agency may tend to misinterpret a jurisdictional limitation in order to expand its power and authority, for example, and close judicial attention to legal issues can counteract this tendency toward bureaucratic empire building. On the other hand, when the agencies are dealing with highly technical issues of fact or policy—whether the airborne pollutants generated by leaded gasoline are absorbed by human beings in sufficient quantities to pose a health hazard, or whether emergency core cooling systems on nuclear reactors are adequate to prevent releases of radiation in certain hypothesized accidents—one would expect the courts, staffed by generalist lawyers, to be less well equipped to make the basic decision. Even if the issue is as simple as whether a welfare recipient has outside sources of income, the agency fact-finder who has heard the testimony and observed the demeanor of the witnesses may be in a better position to assess their credibility and decide where the truth lies.

Considerations of economy and efficiency are also pertinent. When a court announces an interpretation of the law, it sets forth a standard that an agency can apply in future cases of the same general type. A one-time decision of this kind consumes few judicial resources. But if, in every individual case, the court were obliged to duplicate the agency's work in finding facts and applying the law to them, the burden on the courts would be enormous and the delays intolerable. The costs to the participants and the government would also be formidable.

Despite these theoretical and practical factors suggesting that courts should review legal issues more intensively than factual and discretionary issues, the differences in rigor among the various standards of review should not be exaggerated. While courts regard themselves as the final authorities on legal questions, they do give significant deference to administrators' views in resolving those questions. On the other hand, judicial review of factual findings and exercises of discretion, although basically quite deferential, includes a significant supervisory role for the courts. Indeed, this latter type of review has become particularly probing in the modern era. Moreover, whatever the doctrinal rules may say, each of the prevailing standards of judicial review in administrative law is highly flexible, giving the courts ample room to maneuver in the interests of justice as they may define it. Notwithstanding these cautionary considerations, however, distinctions among law, fact, and discretion are vital starting points if one is to make sense out of contemporary case law on scope of review.

B. LEGAL ISSUES: IN GENERAL

In most areas of our legal system, the courts enjoy unquestioned preeminence in deciding issues of law, but in administrative law there is a strong tradition of deferring to the legal views of agencies. The doctrinal principles governing this area evolved in a gradual, perhaps erratic, fashion. An early milestone was NLRB v. Hearst Publications, Inc., 322 U.S. 111 (1944). There the Board ruled that "newsboys" who sold Hearst newspapers on street corners were "employees" within the meaning of the National Labor Relations Act, and hence entitled to bargain collectively under the Act. The Supreme Court upheld that ruling, but not by finding on its own authority that the newsboys were "employees." Instead, the Court said that its function as a reviewing court was "limited," because "the question [was] one of specific application of a broad statutory term." This holding can be understood as resting on a conclusion that Congress had delegated to the Board the responsibility to determine what types of workers would qualify as "employees" under diverse circumstances. The *Hearst* decision did not, however, oust the judiciary from its law-declaring role entirely. On the contrary, the Court began its analysis by considering whether the NLRB's understanding of its duty was consistent with the congressional mandate. The Court answered this question on its own authority, agreeing with the Board that the correct inquiry was whether the newsboys suffered from economic conditions of a kind that deserved labor law protection, not whether they would have been deemed "employees" at common law. Only because the Board had applied proper legal standards, in the Court's view, did the Court proceed to the second stage in its inquiry, where its function was "limited." In short, *Hearst* effectively endorsed a model of decisionmaking in which administrators would wield significant norm-setting authority, but only within judicially drawn boundaries.

The Court took a further step towards deference to agencies' interpretations in what is now the leading case on the subject, Chevron U.S.A., Inc. v. NRDC, 467 U.S. 837 (1984). *Chevron* involved a challenge to the EPA's "bubble" policy, a plan designed to reduce the costs to manufacturers of installing pollution controls. The legality of the plan hinged on the validity of an EPA rule that defined the Clean Air Act term "stationary source" to refer to an entire manufacturing plant, rather than an individual device within the plant. The Court upheld the rule, prescribing two inquiries that a reviewing court should conduct when reviewing an agency's construction of a statute that it administers. The first was whether "Congress has directly addressed the precise question at issue." If so, the court would have to "give effect to the unambiguously expressed intent of Congress." However, if the statute were to prove "silent or ambiguous with respect to the specific issue," the remaining question was whether the agency's answer was "permissible"—or, as the Court also phrased it, a "reasonable interpretation." Here, Congress itself "did not have a specific intention" regarding the bubble approach, and the EPA's use of that approach was "a reasonable policy choice for the agency to make."

To some extent, the *Chevron* reasoning was simply a restatement of *Hearst*, recognizing that, within judicially defined boundaries, an agency should have latitude to exercise its delegated authority, subject to only limited oversight by the courts. In other respects, however, the *Chevron* opinion broke new ground. Rather than determine on a case-by-case basis whether to follow the delegation reasoning of *Hearst*, the Court spoke broadly of a test that a court should "always" apply when it reviews an agency's construction of a statute that it administers. Moreover, the logic of the *Chevron* test indicated that, to whatever extent the statute remained ambiguous with respect to a particular controversy, the reviewing court should *presume* that Congress has delegated to the agency the task of filling in the gap in some reasonable way. As the Court remarked, the drafters of the legislation may have actually decided to make such a delegation, or they may have left an ambiguity through inadvertence or inability to reach agreement, but "[f]or judicial purposes, it matters not which of these things occurred."

The Court's strong support in *Chevron* for judicial deference to agencies' interpretations of statutes has given rise to extensive debate. Defenders of the decision have argued that such deference is supported by a number of policies, including the following: (1) Agencies tend to be familiar with, and sophisticated about, the statutes they administer; they understand the relationships among various provisions, the practical implications of adopting one interpretation as opposed to another, etc. (2) As unforeseen problems develop in the administration of a complex regulatory scheme, the agency needs flexibility if it is to make the program function effectively. (3) As *Chevron* noted, an agency has ties to the incumbent administration, and thus is politically accountable for its choices in a way that a court cannot be. (4) Deference promotes uniformity in the law, because it makes reviewing courts scattered across the country less likely to adopt differing readings of a statute; instead, the view taken by a single centralized agency will usually control. Skeptics have responded to these arguments by recalling traditional justifications for judicial review—for example, that administrative agencies cannot be trusted to be the final arbiters of their own power, that the courts' independence is a necessary check, and that courts are at least as competent as agencies in matters of legal interpretation.

Perhaps reflecting this clash of views, cases have applied *Chevron* in a variety of ways over the years. In one group of decisions, courts have upheld agency interpretations with little elaboration, simply declaring that a statute is ambiguous and the agency's view is not unreasonable. It is sometimes hard to tell how closely the court examined the parties' contentions before drawing this conclusion. Other cases, however, have taken full advantage of the flexibility that is built into the *Chevron* doctrine. When carefully applied, the formula leaves open a number of avenues for active court intervention, as the following discussion explains.

1. *Framing Issues That Congress Has "Directly Addressed."* Generally, the first task in applying the *Chevron* test is to identify the "precise question" that Congress may have "directly addressed." The most straightforward argument a challenger can make is that the statute categorically prohibits the agency from taking the action in question, but this is not the only possible option. Many statutory delegations of power "directly address" an agency by instructing it to take account of particular factors or interests in making its decisions. One issue for the court to resolve during review, therefore, will be whether the agency applied the legally permissible factors. A classic case in which this sort of judicial inquiry led to reversal is Addison v. Holly Hill Fruit Prods., 322 U.S. 607 (1944): The Court remanded a regulation of the Wage–Hour Administrator classifying companies on the basis of size, because the underlying statute had required the Administrator to classify them on the basis of geography only.

Furthermore, ambiguity is usually a matter of degree. Enabling legislation that is acknowledged to be vague in some respects may nevertheless contain enough specificity to convince a court that a statutory term cannot possibly mean what the agency claims it means. For instance, in a well-known post-*Chevron* case, the Immigration and Nationality Act provided that an alien was eligible for discretionary relief from deportation if she could show that she had a "well-founded fear of persecution" in her native land. The Board of Immigration Appeals interpreted this phrase to mean that the alien must show a "clear probability" of persecution. The Court rejected that interpretation, noting that the Act elsewhere used the "clear probability" test as a basis for *automatic* relief from deportation. According to the Court, the language, history, and structure of the Act unequivocally demonstrated that Congress intended the discretionary provision to be less demanding than the automatic one. INS v. Cardoza–Fonseca, 480 U.S. 421 (1987); see also City of Chicago v. Environmental Defense Fund, 511 U.S. 328 (1994) ("EPA's interpretation ... goes beyond the scope of whatever ambiguity [the legislation] contains.").

Ultimately, there is no single preferred way to frame the "precise question" presented in a given review proceeding. The challenger is entitled to a free choice of statutory theories against which the agency action will be measured—but the challenger has the burden of showing that the statute "clearly" supports some such theory (as opposed to being ambiguous on that score).

2. *Resolving Questions Using "Traditional Tools."* Once a court has identified an issue that Congress may have "directly addressed," it must decide whether the statute contains a "clear" answer to that question. Sometimes judges find such an answer in the language of the statute. In MCI Telecomms. Corp. v. American Tel. & Tel. Co., 512 U.S. 218 (1994), for example, the FCC announced that it would exempt all long-distance telephone carriers, except the most dominant one (AT & T),

from having to submit tariffs to the agency specifying the rates they would charge. The Commission relied on its statutory power to "modify" the filing requirements of the Communications Act. Quoting from dictionary definitions, however, the Court concluded that the word "modify" connotes moderate change, and the agency's wholesale dismantling of its rate regulation program for the smaller carriers was too sweeping to qualify as a "modification." Of course, as the Court's 5–3 vote in *MCI* suggests, statutory clarity is often in the eye of the beholder. In *Chevron* terms, a court's conclusion that the legislature's intent is "clear" seems to mean only that the court finds the challenger's theory very convincing, not that the theory must be beyond debate.

Not all rejections of agency interpretations rely as heavily on the "plain meaning" of the statutory language as the *MCI* opinion did. *Chevron* itself said that courts may draw upon "traditional tools of statutory construction," and in our legal system courts have traditionally inquired into the intent of Congress by looking at the overall structure of a statute, related provisions, the legislative history, and the underlying purposes of the statute. For example, in FDA v. Brown & Williamson Tobacco Corp., 529 U.S. 120 (2000), the Court invalidated FDA regulations that would have restricted the marketing of tobacco products to young people. The agency's jurisdiction extends to "drugs" or "devices" that are "intended to affect the structure or any function of the body," and the Court assumed for argument's sake that this wording was broad enough to apply to tobacco products. Nevertheless, the Court reasoned, the statutory context militated against jurisdiction, because the regulatory scheme contemplates that any product regulated by the agency must be safe and effective for its intended use. Tobacco, however, had not been shown to be safe for any use; thus, a finding that the FDA had jurisdiction over these products would require the agency to ban them outright, a result that even the agency did not seek. Moreover, the FDA had for years assured Congress that it lacked jurisdiction over tobacco products. In the Court's view, the legislature had relied on and effectively ratified these assertions when it adopted several limited regulatory measures itself, such as laws requiring warning labels on cigarette packages.

Contextual considerations do not always overcome the deference policy of *Chevron*, however. For example, the Endangered Species Act prohibits "taking" a protected species without a permit, and it defines "take" to include "harm." A regulation of the Secretary of the Interior provided that modification of the habitat of a species could qualify as a "harm." A group of landowners sued for a declaration that the regulation was unlawful. They argued that the word "take" most naturally suggests the direct use of force against an animal, and that other words in the Act's definition of "take," such as "shoot," "kill," and "capture," confirmed that interpretation. The Court, however, decided that, in light of the ambiguity in the word "take" and the history and purposes of the Act, as well as the breadth of the Act's delegation and the Secretary's expertise, the regulation was sufficiently reasonable to survive scrutiny under *Chevron*. Babbitt v. Sweet Home Chapter of Communities for a Great Oregon, 515 U.S. 687 (1995).

Courts also draw freely on canons of construction in administrative cases. For example, they may say that an otherwise tenable agency interpretation must be rejected because it would raise a serious constitutional question. See Solid Waste Agency of Northern Cook County v. U.S. Army Corps of Eng'rs, 531 U.S. 159 (2001) (construing Clean Water Act narrowly, in part to avoid possible Commerce Clause problems); see also INS v. St. Cyr, 533 U.S. 289 (2001) (construing immigration statute as prospective only, in part because of a canon that disfavors retroactive legislation). As usual in matters of statutory construction, however, the courts' use of canons in regulatory cases is highly discretionary. Thus, the judicial policy of deferring to administrative interpretations can still outweigh the constitutional avoidance canon in a given case. See, e.g., Rust v. Sullivan, 500 U.S. 173 (1991) (relying on *Chevron* to uphold HHS "gag rule" limiting abortion counseling by doctors in federally funded clinics, despite the constitutional concerns implicated by such a restriction on speech).

3. *Unreasonable Interpretations.* As noted above, the *Chevron* opinion indicated that, even where the applicable statute does not "clearly" foreclose an administrative interpretation, a reviewing court

need not uphold the agency's view unless it is "reasonable." By adding this condition, *Chevron* apparently meant to say that, once the court has decided that an agency acted within the terms of its delegated authority, it must go on to determine whether the agency implemented that authority in a reasoned fashion. In AT & T Corp. v. Iowa Utilities Bd., 525 U.S. 366 (1999), for example, the Court invalidated an FCC rule that required local telephone companies to make their facilities available to competitors on an unlimited basis. The Court said that the FCC's interpretation of the Act was unreasonable, because it did not adequately consider the Act's criteria for granting access; the Commission had failed to prescribe an access policy that was "rationally related to the goals of the Act." In practice, this second step in the *Chevron* formula seems equivalent to, or at least overlaps, the "reasoned decisionmaking" inquiry that courts conduct when they decide whether an agency action is arbitrary and capricious (see pp. 102–04 infra). (One source of confusion is the Court's tendency to use the word *interpretations* to describe the agency determinations that courts review at this step in the *Chevron* analysis; they could be more precisely described as *applications* of the statutory criteria that the court will have found sustainable during the first step.) Of course, this phase of *Chevron* review is intended to be particularly deferential, because by definition it relates to the agency's exercise of discretion. Indeed, judicial rejections of agencies' statutory interpretations occur much more frequently at the first step of *Chevron* review than at the second.

4. *Summary.* In practice, the *Chevron* doctrine has proved to be more complex and subtle than was initially anticipated. To many minds, the case remains closely associated with the theme of judicial deference to administrators; yet *Chevron* has by no means prevented courts from maintaining significant discipline over agency action. Admittedly, the manner in which *Chevron* review will play out in any particular case is often unpredictable; given the plasticity of statutory interpretation principles in our legal system, the situation could hardly be otherwise. At the very least, however, *Chevron* has provided courts with something they never had prior to the modern era: a more or less orderly framework within which the inevitable controversies over statutory meaning in administrative law cases can be worked out.

C. LEGAL ISSUES: EXCEPTIONAL CASES

In a number of situations, courts do not use the *Chevron* test to review agency interpretations of law. Some of these exceptions are more widely accepted than others.

1. *Lack of Discretionary Authority.* In a classic early case, the Court examined the deference due to interpretations of the Administrator of the Fair Labor Standards Act. Skidmore v. Swift & Co., 323 U.S. 134 (1944). Because the responsibility to decide

cases under that Act rested solely with the courts, the Administrator's interpretations of the Act could not bind the courts. Even so, said the Court, he did conduct investigations under the Act and initiate injunction actions. Accordingly, the interpretive guidelines that he issued under the Act were "entitled to respect" from the judiciary, in light of the knowledge and experience that shaped them and the need for uniform standards governing the public and private sectors. The weight of any given pronouncement would "depend on the thoroughness evident in its consideration, the validity of its reasoning, its consistency with earlier and later pronouncements, and all those factors which give it power to persuade, if lacking power to control." Modern decisions have adhered to the logic of *Skidmore* in other situations in which a regulatory scheme does not authorize an agency to adopt interpretations that have the force of law. Such interpretations do not qualify for *Chevron* deference (which is designed to facilitate agencies' exercises of discretionary authority), but are nevertheless accorded deference under the "respect" standard of *Skidmore* insofar as they have "power to persuade." Gonzales v. Oregon,   U.S. ___, 126 S.Ct. 904 (2006); EEOC v. Arabian American Oil Co., 499 U.S. 244 (1991).

2. *Insufficient Format.* In recent cases, the Court has extended the uses of the *Skidmore* standard of review in more controversial directions. According to these cases, the applicability of the *Chevron* standard of review depends in part on

factors such as the "format" or type of pronouncement in which an interpretation has been articulated. Thus, in Christensen v. Harris County, 529 U.S.
576 (2000), the Court said that opinion letters and
other "interpretations contained in policy statements, agency manuals, and enforcement guidelines—all of which lack the force of law—do not
warrant *Chevron*-style deference." At most, such
statements are "entitled to respect" under *Skidmore*, according to their "power to persuade." The
Court elaborated on this theme at length the following year in United States v. Mead Corp., 533 U.S.
218 (2001). The dispute in *Mead* concerned a tariff
classification in which the Customs Service determined that Mead's day planners, which came in
three-ring binders, were "bound diaries" and thus
were subject to a tariff. The Court held that the
ruling was entitled to *Skidmore* deference but not
Chevron deference. The Court explained that the
critical question was whether circumstances indicated that "Congress would expect the agency to be
able to speak with the force of law." Congress
would be most likely to hold that expectation where
the interpretation is rendered through "a relatively
formal administrative procedure tending to foster
the fairness and deliberation that should underlie a
pronouncement of such force." The *Mead* opinion
emphasized, however, that it was not establishing
any bright-line rules to determine when *Chevron*
deference should apply. And in Barnhart v. Walton,
535 U.S. 212 (2002), the Court reaffirmed its desire
for flexibility, remarking that a definition of "dis-

ability" expressed in informal pronouncements by the Social Security Administration could qualify for *Chevron* deference in light of "the interstitial nature of the legal question, the related expertise of the Agency, the importance of the question to administration of the statute, the complexity of that administration, and the careful consideration the Agency has given the question over a long period of time."

Despite some mixed signals in this series of cases, their upshot seems to be that formal adjudication and notice-and-comment rulemaking will normally entitle an agency to *Chevron* deference, but interpretive rules, policy statements, and opinion letters normally will not. The applicability of *Chevron* to informal adjudication is unsettled and seems to depend on the circumstances of individual cases. For example, *Mead* reaffirmed a decision that had accorded *Chevron* deference to a letter ruling in which the Comptroller of the Currency had allowed small banks to sell annuities, NationsBank of North Carolina, Inc. v. Variable Annuity Life Ins. Co , 513 U.S. 251 (1995). Yet an EPA order that blocked construction of a pollution-emitting facility did not trigger *Chevron*, evidently because the order relied on analysis contained in agency internal guidance memoranda. Alaska Dep't of Envtl. Conservation v. EPA, 540 U.S. 461 (2004).

The future of the *Mead* line of cases is difficult to project. No consensus yet supports the Court's thesis that an interpretation that otherwise falls within an agency's discretionary authority should be denied *Chevron* deference if it was adopted with minimal (but lawful) procedure or has not yet been expressed in a binding format. On a more practical level, one should recognize that the differences between the *Chevron* and *Skidmore* standards of review are elusive at best. Given that considerable flexibility is already built into each of these two standards, it remains to be seen whether the payoffs resulting from the Court's efforts to fine-tune the process of choosing between the two standards will ultimately be judged sufficient to justify the complexity that *Mead* has injected into judicial review litigation.

A less controversial *Chevron* exception based on "format" is the Court's refusal to accord *Chevron* deference to an agency interpretation that is advanced for the first time in a litigation brief. Bowen v. Georgetown Univ. Hosp., 488 U.S. 204 (1988). This limitation follows readily from the doctrine that discretion should be exercised only by agency decisionmakers, not appellate counsel, see pp. 108–109 infra, and perhaps also from apprehensions that government litigants have too great a temptation to advance questionable legal arguments that may help them prevail in a pending court action. (However, when an agency adopts an interpretation using the full notice-and-comment process, it can qualify for *Chevron* deference even if the advent of litigation provided the impetus for the regulation. *Barnhart v. Walton*, supra.)

3. *Issues That Are Inappropriate for Administrative Resolution*. Some types of issues fall outside the

scope of *Chevron* because the courts assume that Congress would not have left them to the judgment of an administrative agency. For example, courts do not apply *Chevron* to interpretive questions arising under the APA, the Freedom of Information Act, and other generic administrative law statutes; these measures address agency action in general, so no single agency's reading can be controlling. Collins v. NTSB, 351 F.3d 1246 (D.C.Cir.2003). Nor does *Chevron* apply to matters that by their nature must be resolved by courts, such as an individual's criminal liability, Crandon v. United States, 494 U.S. 152, 177 (1990) (Scalia, J., concurring), or the powers of federal courts themselves, see Adams Fruit Co. v. Barrett, 494 U.S. 638 (1990) (availability of private right of action in court); Murphy Exploration and Prod. Co. v. U.S. Dep't of Interior, 252 F.3d 473 (D.C.Cir.2001) (limitations period for judicial review statute).

The years immediately following *Chevron* saw debate over whether that case's review standard should apply to an agency's interpretation of its own jurisdictional boundaries. See Mississippi Power & Light Co. v. Mississippi ex rel. Moore, 487 U.S. 354 (1988). This proposed exception to the *Chevron* doctrine has not taken hold, probably because statutory constraints on *what* an agency may regulate are not very different analytically from statutory constraints on *how* it may regulate. Nevertheless, the Court has said that it may "hesitate" to conclude that Congress would delegate "a policy decision of [great] economic and political magnitude to

an administrative agency." FDA v. Brown & Williamson Tobacco Corp., 529 U.S. 120 (2000) (citing
this hesitation as one reason to reject the FDA's
assertion of authority to regulate tobacco products).

4. *Stare Decisis.* In a series of cases decided in
the 1990s, the Court asserted that, once it had
adopted one interpretation of an ambiguous statute,
it would adhere to that construction as a matter of
precedent, even if an agency that administers the
statute later endorsed a different reasonable construction of the statute. See, e.g., Neal v. United
States, 516 U.S. 284 (1996). Recently, however, the
Court has apparently developed second thoughts
about this stance. In National Cable & Telecomms.
Ass'n v. Brand X Internet Services, 545 U.S. ____,
125 S.Ct. 2688 (2005), the Court ruled that "[a]
court's prior judicial construction of a statute
trumps an agency construction otherwise entitled to
Chevron deference only if the prior court decision
holds that its construction follows from the unambiguous terms of the statute and thus leaves no
room for agency discretion." This holding seems to
amount to an abandonment of the stare decisis
"exception," because it gives prior judicial precedent only the force that one would expect from a
reading of *Chevron* itself.

5. *Nonstatutory Issues.* Finally, *Chevron* principles are not directly applicable when a court con-
strues a legal norm other than a statute. When
addressing constitutional questions, judges rarely
display any deference at all to administrative

views. On the other hand, when reviewing agencies' interpretations of their own regulations, courts have traditionally recited a formula that seems comparable in stringency to the *Chevron* test itself: they will accept the agency's reading unless it is "plainly erroneous or inconsistent with the regulation." Auer v. Robbins, 519 U.S. 452 (1997); Bowles v. Seminole Rock & Sand Co., 325 U.S. 410 (1945). Although this principle seems to be in tension with *Mead* (because agencies' constructions of their regulations are usually expressed in documents that do not themselves have the force of law), the Court has continued to cite *Auer* as authoritative. Gonzales v. Oregon, ___ U.S. ___, 126 S.Ct. 904 (2006). Nevertheless, the *Oregon* opinion carved out a narrow exception to *Auer*: if a regulation merely quotes statutory language, the agency is entitled to no more deference in interpreting the regulation than it would have enjoyed if it were interpreting the statute itself. The controversy in that case concerned the Attorney General's view that the Controlled Substances Act prohibits states from adopting assisted suicide laws. The Court held that, because the Attorney General possessed no authority under that Act to define legitimate medical practices, his reading of the Act was not entitled to *Chevron* deference; accordingly, his interpretation of a regulation that "parroted" the statutory language was not entitled to substantial deference either.

D. SUBSTANTIAL EVIDENCE REVIEW

When an agency's legal premises survive judicial scrutiny, the reviewing court must go on to consider whether to sustain the agency's factual findings. The APA contains three standards of review that potentially can govern this inquiry, and the court must apply one of these standards unless a statute or historical practice clearly dictates otherwise. Dickinson v. Zurko, 527 U.S. 150 (1999) (evidence of early use of a stricter test in patent cases was not "clear" enough to permit any departure from the APA framework in such cases). The "substantial evidence" test, 5 U.S.C.A. § 706(2)(E), comes into play in "a case subject to sections 556 and 557 of this title or otherwise reviewed on the record of an agency hearing provided by statute." In other words, it is triggered if the agency decision was made after a trial-type, on-the-record hearing (a "formal adjudication" or "rulemaking on a record"). In most other proceedings, the facts are reviewed under the "arbitrary and capricious" test of § 706(2)(A), although in a handful of cases the court finds the facts for itself in a de novo trial, as provided in § 706(2)(F). This section explains the substantial evidence test, the most traditionally recognized and easily comprehended of the three. This discussion will provide the groundwork for an analysis of the other two standards, which are considered at pp. 111–15 infra.

A court applying the substantial evidence test is supposed to assess the reasonableness of the agency's factfinding, and not find the "right" or "true" facts itself. The test is sometimes analogized to appellate review of jury verdicts: in this view, substantial evidence is "enough to justify, if the trial were to a jury, a refusal to direct a verdict when the conclusion sought to be drawn from it is one of fact for the jury." NLRB v. Columbian Enameling & Stamping Co., 306 U.S. 292, 300 (1939). Another frequently quoted formulation states that substantial evidence is "such relevant evidence as a reasonable mind might accept as adequate to support a conclusion." Consolidated Edison Co. v. NLRB, 305 U.S. 197, 229 (1938). These verbal glosses on the text of the APA are admittedly not very helpful in applying the substantial evidence test to particular cases. Perhaps the most that can be said is that a court reviewing agency action under the substantial evidence test should make sure that the agency has done a careful, workmanlike job of collecting and evaluating the available data—or, as Judge Leventhal put it, that the agency has taken a "hard look" at the important factual issues. When the action being reviewed is a rule rather than an order, however, other complications enter the picture, as discussed at pp. 122–24 infra.

In reviewing agency findings under the substantial evidence test, the court is obliged to consider the "whole record." Universal Camera Corp. v. NLRB, 340 U.S. 474 (1951). That is, the court is not supposed to look only for evidence that supports the agency's decision; it is required to consider all of the relevant evidence for and against the agency's findings, and determine whether they are within the zone of reasonableness. In the federal system, and in many states as well, uncorroborated hearsay can constitute substantial evidence. See, e.g., Richardson v. Perales, 402 U.S. 389 (1971) (hearsay reports of examining physicians were substantial evidence for denial of disability claim, even though opposed by live testimony on behalf of the claimant). The old "legal residuum rule," which required that there be a residuum of legally competent evidence to support agency findings, is now generally regarded as an overly technical doctrine which can work substantial injustice when hearsay is the only, or best, available evidence. See Carroll v. Knickerbocker Ice Co., 218 N.Y. 435, 113 N.E. 507 (1916) (workers' compensation claim denied because the only evidence that the injuries had been sustained on the job was statements by the injured worker, who had died as a result of his injuries).

Another question that can arise when courts review agency findings under the substantial evidence test is how the court should view an agency's reversal of an administrative law judge's initial decision. Section 557(b) of the APA gives the agency heads broad power to find the facts de novo when they are reviewing an initial decision. See pp. 273–75 infra. At the same time, however, § 557(c) declares that the initial decision is part of the official record of the proceeding, and the substantial evidence test requires the reviewing court to consider the "whole record." The *Universal Camera* decision relied on these provisions in explaining the proper role of the

ALJ's decision during judicial review: The substantial evidence test applies to the agency's decision, not the ALJ's. However, since the ALJ's decision is part of the record, the reviewing court must consider it in evaluating the evidentiary support for the final agency decision. Thus, a contrary initial decision may undermine the support for the agency's ultimate determination. In this context, the weight to be accorded the ALJ's findings may depend upon the kind of issues that are involved in the proceeding. When the case turns on eyewitness testimony, as the *Universal Camera* case did, the initial decision should be given considerable weight: the ALJ was able to observe the demeanor of the witnesses and assess their credibility and veracity first hand. See, e.g., Penasquitos Village, Inc. v. NLRB, 565 F.2d 1074 (9th Cir.1977). On the other hand, if the decision depends primarily upon expert testimony or policy considerations, the ALJ's decision may deserve little deference; the agency heads may be the best equipped to deal with this kind of testimony, and the reviewing court should be less concerned about their reversal of the ALJ.

Of course, the substantial evidence test becomes meaningful only in conjunction with a substantive standard against which the agency's fact findings will be evaluated. An agency can sometimes lighten its evidentiary burdens, in effect, by interpreting the governing statute in a way that makes the requirements for a prima facie case very lenient. This device will be effective if (but only if) the court finds that the agency's interpretation of the statute is reasonable and consistent with the statutory purpose, as required by *Chevron*. See, e.g., NLRB v. Transportation Mgmt. Corp., 462 U.S. 393 (1983) (in "mixed motive" discharge cases, Board may put burden on employer to disprove causation in fact). Agencies often use rulemaking for this purpose. See pp. 294–98 infra.

E. ABUSE OF DISCRETION REVIEW

Once the reviewing court has found that the agency correctly understood the law and adopted a rational view of the facts, it must still consider whether the action was "arbitrary, capricious, an abuse of discretion, or otherwise not in accordance with law." 5 U.S.C.A. § 706(2)(A). This inquiry is sometimes nicknamed review for "arbitrariness," sometimes review for "abuse of discretion," and sometimes "rational basis" review. (Although § 706(2)(A) also supplies the standard for judicial review of agency fact findings in cases that are not governed by the substantial evidence test, see pp. 111–15 infra, the following discussion deals only with arbitrariness review in its nonfactual dimensions.)

In Citizens to Preserve Overton Park, Inc. v. Volpe, 401 U.S. 402 (1971), the Court described arbitrariness review as an inquiry into "whether the decision was based on a consideration of the relevant factors and whether there has been a clear error of judgment." This formula still shows up in the case law,[1] but in modern practice the emphasis in arbitrariness review has shifted towards scrutiny of the *quality of an agency's reasoning*. A court will typically ask whether an exercise of discretion rests on an analysis that is at least plausible in light of the record, the parties' contentions, and the constraints of the underlying statute. Theoretically, this sort of review is supposed to be quite deferential, and it frequently is. At times, indeed, abuse of discretion review can seem rather perfunctory. When a court feels that an agency has reached a credible result and that the parties have raised no troubling issues, it might uphold the action with only minimal discussion.

Sometimes, however, modern abuse of discretion review becomes quite probing. A classic articulation of this approach was written by Judge Leventhal in Greater Boston Television Corp. v. FCC, 444 F.2d 841, 850–52 (D.C.Cir.1970): the court will intervene if it "becomes aware, especially through a combination of danger signals, that the agency has not really taken a 'hard look' at the salient problems, and has not genuinely engaged in reasoned decision-making." Although the phrase "hard look"

---

1. An agency's duty to consider "relevant factors" does not mean, however, that it necessarily must take into account the policies of statutes that it has no responsibility for administering, even if those statutes seem pertinent to the subject matter. For example, the PBGC, in overseeing an employer's obligations under the Employee Retirement Income Security Act, is not required to consider the policies of the labor and bankruptcy laws, although the concerns of all three statutory schemes are somewhat overlapping. Pension Benefit Guaranty Corp. v. LTV Corp., 496 U.S. 633 (1990).

originally meant the careful scrutiny that an *agency* was expected to give to the issues, today it is more commonly used to refer to the detailed and intensive inquiry that the *courts* often conduct as they review exercises of administrative discretion. Such an inquiry is clearly susceptible of abuse by the courts, which might easily use a critique of an agency's reasoning process as an excuse to overturn a policy judgment with which they simply happen to disagree. Notwithstanding its dangers, however, the hard look doctrine, also known as the "reasoned decisionmaking" standard, is widely employed. It has been especially prominent in review of rulemaking, as will be seen in a later section. See pp. 116–19 infra.

The case law has established a number of specific situations in which a reviewing court can properly hold that an agency has abused its discretion, including the following:

First, even when an administrator's discretionary decision is in accord with governing statutes, it may be unlawful if it is inconsistent with the agency's own rules. Since a legislative regulation has the "force of law," it is normally binding on an agency in the same way that a statute is. This point was at issue in litigation resulting from the famous "Saturday Night Massacre" incident. The Justice Department had issued formal regulations providing that the Watergate Special Prosecutor would not be removed from his duties "except for extraordinary improprieties on his part." Nevertheless, Acting Attorney General Bork followed President Nixon's directive to dismiss the prosecutor without cause. The court held that this violation of a valid administrative regulation made the firing illegal. Nader v. Bork, 366 F.Supp. 104 (D.D.C.1973). The court did not actually reinstate the prosecutor (in part because a successor had already been appointed), but its legal reasoning was later adopted by the Supreme Court in a closely related context. United States v. Nixon, 418 U.S. 683 (1974).

Second, departure from agency precedents embodied in prior adjudicative decisions can constitute an abuse of discretion, if the reasons for the failure to follow precedent are not adequately explained. See, e.g., Atchison, T. & S.F. Ry. v. Wichita Bd. of Trade, 412 U.S. 800 (1973); Shaw's Supermarkets, Inc. v. NLRB, 884 F.2d 34 (1st Cir.1989). Differential treatment of parties who are similarly situated raises questions as to whether the agency is administering its program in a fair, impartial, and competent manner. However, reviewing courts have refrained from requiring agencies to follow precedent mechanically. Since conditions in a regulated industry may change rapidly and the agency often needs some latitude to adjust and develop its policies, rigid adherence to precedent would sometimes frustrate the objectives of the regulatory program. Furthermore, when one administration replaces another, it may have a legitimate desire to alter existing policies to fulfill what it sees as its political mandate. Thus, when a reviewing court finds that a particular administrative decision is inconsistent with the agency's own precedents, it will remand the matter to the agency for a fuller statement of reasons instead of reversing outright. If the agency supplies a reasonable explanation for its new direction, its action should survive review.

Third, an agency can abuse its discretion by breaching certain principles of judge-made law. Equitable estoppel is one such area, although the Supreme Court has confined this doctrine within very narrow limits. See pp. 193–95 infra. Res judicata and collateral estoppel may also limit an agency's discretion. In United States v. Stauffer Chem. Co., 464 U.S. 165 (1984), Stauffer secured a court decision rejecting an EPA interpretation of the Clean Air Act. When the agency tried to relitigate the identical issue against Stauffer in another court, the Supreme Court held that the agency was precluded by collateral estoppel. On the other hand, in United States v. Mendoza, 464 U.S. 154 (1984), the Court held that collateral estoppel may not be asserted against the United States by persons who were not parties to the earlier case. The Court explained that to allow such "nonmutual" collateral estoppel "would substantially thwart the development of important questions of law by freezing the first final decision rendered on a particular legal issue."[2]

2. *Mendoza*'s suggestion that the law should develop gradually, through litigation in multiple forums, has been read as indirectly supporting the practice of "nonacquiescence," by which an agency declines to give stare decisis effect to lower court decisions with which it disagrees. Too much nonacquiescence, however, would interfere with the courts' ability to prevent an agency from violating its statutory mandate. The prac-

Fourth, a court will sometimes hold that a particular remedy is too severe, if the agency has not explained satisfactorily why it did not choose a less drastic sanction. See, e.g., Jacob Siegel Co. v. FTC, 327 U.S. 608 (1946) (remanding case in which FTC ordered company to abandon allegedly deceptive brand name but did not seriously consider whether an informational label would have been adequate). More specifically, courts may intervene when an agency applies a new holding retroactively, if they think that the public interest in enforcement is outweighed by the unfairness of imposing a sanction for conduct that the respondent had reasonably believed to be lawful. See, e.g., Epilepsy Found. of Northeast Ohio v. NLRB, 268 F.3d 1095 (D.C.Cir. 2001); Retail, Wholesale & Dep't Store Union v. NLRB, 466 F.2d 380 (D.C.Cir.1972). Still, review of an agency's remedial decisions tends to be fairly deferential; usually courts are reluctant to second-guess the agency's choice of sanctions, which falls close to the core of the executive branch's enforcement discretion. See Butz v. Glover Livestock Comm'n Co., 411 U.S. 182 (1973) (upholding strict sanction).

F. FINDINGS AND REASONS

The review standards for legal, factual, and discretionary determinations, as set forth in the pre-

tice is generally upheld, but is considered questionable when an agency adheres to its legal position in a case that could only be reviewed in a circuit that has already rejected the agency's stance. When the Social Security Administration made frequent use of the latter kind of nonacquiescence in the administration of its disability benefits program in the 1980s, it was widely criticized.

ceding three sections, all presuppose that the court will examine the agency's reasoning with a good deal of care. In practice, however, agencies often take action without explaining, or explaining adequately, the grounds on which they have made their determinations. To overcome this difficulty, the courts have developed the device of remanding administrative actions to the agency for fuller explanation. See, e.g., Northeast Md. Waste Disposal Auth. v. EPA, 358 F.3d 936 (D.C.Cir.2004); United States v. Dierckman, 201 F.3d 915 (7th Cir.2000); Armstrong v. CFTC, 12 F.3d 401 (3d Cir.1993). The courts often remark that they do not need great detail; the basic requirement is that the agency reveal enough of its reasoning to permit meaningful judicial review. (At times, however, it appears that no amount of explanation would suffice, because the court is using a remand for "reconsideration" as a diplomatic way of expressing its disapproval of the agency's substantive policy.)

Actually, a focus on the agency's reasoning is inescapable, because it is axiomatic that a discretionary agency action may be upheld *only* on the strength of the agency's own rationale. In the leading case, the Supreme Court remanded an SEC order disapproving a corporate reorganization plan, because the Commission had reasoned from incorrect legal premises. SEC v. Chenery Corp., 318 U.S. 80 (1943) *(Chenery I)*. In doing so, however, the

Court indicated that it might uphold the SEC's position if the Commission justified it on a lawful basis; and when the SEC issued a revised opinion, the Court did exactly that. SEC v. Chenery Corp., 332 U.S. 194 (1947) *(Chenery II)*. The reason why a reviewing court may not affirm on a basis other than the agency's is that only the agency has authority to make discretionary determinations that Congress has delegated to it.

Several important corollaries follow from the *Chenery* principle. First, "courts may not accept appellate counsel's post hoc rationalizations for agency action," Burlington Truck Lines v. United States, 371 U.S. 156, 168–69 (1962), because discretionary judgments on regulatory policy should be made by agency heads, not the attorneys who defend their decisions in court. Second, if a court finds that an agency's announced rationale for an action is impermissible, it may not uphold the action on the ground that the agency was actually following a different, permissible rationale without saying so. Allentown Mack Sales & Service, Inc. v. NLRB, 522 U.S. 359 (1998). Third, if an agency takes an action that it mistakenly believes to be legally required, the court must remand for further consideration, even if the agency would have had discretion to take the action, because the agency might have chosen differently if it had known that the law permitted it to do so. FCC v. RCA Communications, Inc., 346 U.S. 86 (1953); Prill v. NLRB, 755 F.2d 941 (D.C.Cir.1985).

Although under *Chenery* the courts must carefully scrutinize administrative opinions, they generally will not probe for motives hidden beneath the surface of those opinions. The principle was established in lengthy litigation involving ratesetting by the Secretary of Agriculture. Initially, the Court authorized the district court to investigate allegations that the Secretary had issued his decision without reading the briefs or considering the evidence. After remand, however, the Court reconsidered, declaring that "it was not the function of the court to probe the mental processes of the Secretary in reaching his conclusions if he gave the hearing that the law required." Morgan v. United States, 304 U.S. 1, 18 (1938) *(Morgan II)*. The Court stated this point even more forcefully when the *Morgan* controversy came before it for a fourth time several years later. Just as a judge cannot be deposed or cross-examined about his decisions, "so the integrity of the administrative process must be equally respected." United States v. Morgan, 313 U.S. 409, 422 (1941) *(Morgan IV)*. Without this presumption of regularity, agency officials would constantly be called away from their duties to answer questions about their decisions.

Special problems arise, however, when an agency acts without issuing any explanation at all for its decision. In that situation, said the Supreme Court in Citizens to Preserve Overton Park, Inc. v. Volpe, 401 U.S. 402 (1971), the reviewing court could make a factual inquiry into the agency's rationale, either by obtaining affidavits from the officials who made the decision or by calling them into court to testify. Alternatively, the court could remand the action to the agency for the necessary explanation— a solution which the Court now views as "preferred," PBGC v. LTV Corp., 496 U.S. 633 (1990). On the other hand, *Overton Park* made clear—and Camp v. Pitts, 411 U.S. 138 (1973), reaffirmed— that where an agency *does* provide a contemporaneous explanation for its decision, the *Morgan* rule is still good law; the administrative opinion must be taken as a bona fide expression of the agency's reasoning unless the challenger makes a "strong showing of bad faith or improper behavior" (a standard that is seldom met). The net effect of these cases is to give agency decisionmakers a strong incentive to write opinions to accompany their actions, even when procedural law does not compel them to do so.

G. REVIEW ON THE ADMINISTRATIVE RECORD

Most of the scope of review principles discussed in preceding sections were originally developed for courts to use when an agency acts after formal, trial-type proceedings. For cases in which there is no such formality, including most rulemaking cases, additional principles must be examined. Since the substantial evidence test normally does not apply, the court could potentially turn to either of two other provisions of § 706 as the basis for reviewing the agency's fact findings: it could review the facts de novo, without any deference to the agency's findings (§ 706(2)(F)); or it could review the agency's findings pursuant to the arbitrariness standard (§ 706(2)(A)).

Citizens to Preserve Overton Park, Inc. v. Volpe, 401 U.S. 402 (1971), definitively established the relative scope of these two clauses. The Court held that an informal action, such as the Secretary of Transportation's highway funding decision, must be reviewed for abuse of discretion under § 706(2)(A), on the basis of "the full administrative record that was before the Secretary at the time he made his decision." Although the Court asserted that the APA required this approach, scholars agree that the concept of an exclusive "administrative record" for review of informal agency actions was not contemplated by the framers of the APA. Prior to *Overton Park,* any facts that the courts needed in order to review such actions were typically developed through judicial trial.

At the same time, the Court accomplished a drastic narrowing of § 706(2)(F). Relying on what is generally agreed to have been a misreading of the legislative history of the APA, the *Overton Park* opinion asserted that independent judicial factfinding pursuant to clause (2)(F) is available in only two circumstances: where "the action is adjudicatory in nature and the agency factfinding procedures are inadequate," or where "issues that were not before the agency are raised in a proceeding to enforce nonadjudicatory agency action." Scholars have puzzled about what these phrases might mean; but the debate has little practical significance, because judicial decisions finding *either* of the two conditions applicable are virtually nonexistent. De novo review of the facts underlying agency actions has essentially vanished from administrative law, except in the handful of situations in which a statutory or constitutional guarantee outside of the APA requires such treatment. For example, the Court early held that an individual facing deportation has a constitutional right to an independent judicial decision as to whether he is a citizen. Ng Fung Ho v. White, 259 U.S. 276 (1922). Congress has since codified this holding. 8 U.S.C.A. § 1105a(a)(5). A case from the same era called for de novo review of whether a ratesetting order was confiscatory. Ohio Valley Water Co. v. Ben Avon Borough, 253 U.S. 287 (1920). This holding may still be valid, but it is unimportant, because the constitutional limits on ratemaking have become very lenient today. See also p. 31 supra.

The *Overton Park* holding that review would take place on an "administrative record" was soon extended to informal rulemaking cases. Under the prior practice, courts were willing to presume the existence of facts supporting the validity of an administrative rule, unless the challenging party proved at trial that the rule was arbitrary. Pacific States Box & Basket Co. v. White, 296 U.S. 176 (1935). Since any litigation over the factual basis of the rule would occur in court, agency decisionmakers did not take time *during* the rulemaking proceeding to compile a "record" for judicial review. After *Overton Park*, however, both agencies and regulated parties came to realize that they would have to make their case at the administrative level, because the reviewing court would disregard any evidence submitted subsequently. See United States v. Nova Scotia Food Prods. Corp., 568 F.2d 240 (2d Cir.1977) (in proceeding to enforce FDA rule, courts refused to examine new evidence casting doubt on need for rule).

In an informal rulemaking proceeding, the administrative record will generally consist of the notice of proposed rulemaking, the final rule and accompanying statement of basis and purpose, the comments filed by the public, and any unprivileged working papers prepared by the agency itself. The rule will pass muster under the arbitrary and capricious test if this record contains evidence that could lead a reasonable person to accept the factual premises of the regulation (taking into account the evidence submitted by opponents of the rule).[3] The agency's obligation to assemble such evidence has turned modern rulemaking into a more formalized, adversarial process than the framers of the APA anticipated. However, *Overton Park*'s administrative record concept was an essential step in the development of "hard look" review of rulemaking. Intensive scrutiny of an agency's reasoning process

3. However, the agency need not supply complete record support for scientific conclusions and other propositions that are inherently unprovable. See pp. 119–21 infra. Also, under some circumstances an agency can dispense with proof by invoking the doctrine of official notice. See pp. 300–05 infra.

would scarcely be meaningful if the agency did not have to defend its exercise of discretion by reference to facts that were actually before it at the time the rule was written.

H. REVIEW OF RULES

On a general level, most of the scope of review principles described above are fully applicable to judicial review of rules. Like all other forms of agency action reviewed under the APA, rules must be consistent with the agency's statutory mandate (§ 706(2)(C)), the Constitution (§ 706(2)(B)) and procedural requirements (§ 706(2)(D)). They also must not be "arbitrary and capricious" (§ 706(2)(A)), a standard that is breached if the agency lacked support in the administrative record for its factual assumptions, or otherwise misused its discretion.[4]

However, courts have had to struggle to apply these standards satisfactorily in the rulemaking context. In those situations, many of the central issues concern policy judgments and "legislative facts," which often are not susceptible of "proof" in the same way as the facts in a typical adjudicative proceeding are. Moreover, the issues involved in the rulemaking proceeding can be highly technical, notably in the newer fields of health and safety regulation. Finally, an informal rulemaking record is fundamentally different from the adjudicative records

4. In the rare case of a rule issued after a trial-type hearing, the substantial evidence test (§ 706(2)(E)) would apply to review of the agency's fact findings.

that judges have traditionally reviewed. As Judge McGowan noted, an informal rulemaking record "is indistinguishable in its content from [materials collected in] the proceedings before a legislative committee hearing on a proposed bill—letters, telegrams, and written statements from proponents and opponents, including occasional oral testimony not subjected to adversary cross-examination." In reviewing this kind of record, there is a risk that the judges will "vote their policy preferences in the same manner as does the legislator" and "thereby risk nullification of the principle that democracies are to be run in accordance with the majority will." Carl McGowan, Congress and the Courts, 62 A.B.A.J. 1588, 1589–90 (1976). Thus, courts have had to develop a method of review that would enable them to prevent abuses of power in the rulemaking process, but that would not permit them to make essentially legislative or political judgments.

1. *Hard Look Review.* In Automotive Parts & Accessories Ass'n v. Boyd, 407 F.2d 330 (D.C.Cir. 1968), the court faced up to some of these complications. Judge McGowan stated that judicial review of rulemaking "need be no less searching and strict [than in a case of formal adjudication], but because it is addressed to different materials, it inevitably varies from the adjudicatory model. The paramount objective is to see whether the agency, given an essentially legislative task to perform, has carried it out in a manner calculated to negate the dangers of arbitrariness and irrationality. . . ." To that end,

the agency's statement of basis and purpose (the written explanation accompanying the rule) must "enable us to see what major issues of policy were ventilated by the informal proceedings and why the agency reacted to them as it did." In other words, the court would examine whether the agency had engaged in what Judge Leventhal was soon to call "reasoned decisionmaking," including whether the agency explained its position cogently and thoroughly, and whether it responded to significant criticisms by participants in the rulemaking proceeding. The term "hard look," which is also used to describe this type of inquiry, is not a distinctive standard of review, but rather an informal description of the scrutiny that (at least theoretically) is regularly used in abuse of discretion review generally.

The Supreme Court gave its most explicit approval to the developing case law insisting on reasoned decisionmaking in Motor Vehicle Mfrs. Ass'n v. State Farm Mut. Auto. Ins. Co., 463 U.S. 29 (1983). In 1981, the Department of Transportation rescinded ed a 1977 rule requiring the installation of "passive restraints" in automobiles—either airbags or automatic seatbelts. The agency explained this action by saying that "detachable" automatic seatbelts, the industry's favored method of meeting the requirement, would not necessarily promote safety, because consumers would detach them. The *State Farm* Court found two flaws in this explanation. First, the agency's doubts about the effectiveness of automatic seatbelts ignored the factor of inertia:

consumers who would not bother to fasten manual belts might well allow self-fastening belts to remain in place. The agency had to address this crucial point. Second, even if those belts were ineffective, the agency did not explain why it had not fallen back on a requirement of airbags or "nondetachable" seatbelts instead.

The Court in *State Farm* was careful to point out that the alternatives ignored in the rescission decision had previously been endorsed by the agency itself, and that the administrator was reversing a settled course of action. It also emphasized that a rule is not arbitrary simply because there is no direct evidence in support of the agency's conclusion. But the agency must analyze the evidence that is available and "provide a rational connection between the facts found and the choice made." Generalizing, the Court declared: "Normally, an agency rule would be arbitrary and capricious if the agency has relied on factors which Congress has not intended it to consider, entirely failed to consider an important aspect of the problem, offered an explanation for its decision that runs counter to the evidence before the agency, or is so implausible that it could not be ascribed to a difference in view or the product of agency expertise."

The judicial assertiveness inherent in this formula remains characteristic of modern hard look review. In the years since *State Farm*, courts of appeals have often remanded rules after discerning such problems as a conclusory or illogically reasoned statement of basis and purpose, Tripoli Rocketry Ass'n v. BATF, 437 F.3d 75 (D.C.Cir.2006); failure to address a statutorily required factor, Public Citizen v. FMCSA, 374 F.3d 1209 (D.C.Cir.2004); failure to respond to significant arguments submitted during the public comment period, Appalachian Power Co. v. EPA, 249 F.3d 1032 (D.C.Cir.2001); reliance on factually insupportable assertions, United States Telecom Ass'n v. FBI, 276 F.3d 620 (D.C.Cir.2002); or failure to explain the rejection of a salient alternative regulatory strategy, Public Citizen, Inc. v. Mineta, 340 F.3d 39 (2d Cir.2003). To be sure, the great majority of administrative rules do survive judicial review for abuse of discretion. Nevertheless, the threat of reversal on this basis imposes significant discipline on agencies, particularly since the relevant criteria involve judgment calls, and the agency may not be able to predict how stringently a given panel of judges will apply them. Indeed, some scholars regard the intrusiveness of today's judicial review as an impediment to the rulemaking process itself. See pp. 350–52 infra.

2. *Scientific Uncertainty.* Despite the ambitions of hard look review, reviewing courts realize that their capacity to evaluate regulations in highly technical areas is limited. The problems in this area surfaced in Ethyl Corp. v. EPA, 541 F.2d 1 (D.C.Cir. 1976) (en banc), which upheld an EPA rule reducing the use of lead additives in gasoline on the ground that the additives created a health hazard. Judge Bazelon, in a concurring opinion, argued that judicial review of the facts should be extremely restrained, because "substantive review of mathe-

matical and scientific evidence by technically illiterate judges is dangerously unreliable." At most, reviewing courts could assure rationality indirectly, by making sure that the agency had strictly complied with applicable procedural requirements and had exposed its factual premises to public scrutiny. Judge Leventhal, however, cautioned against judicial abdication: court review of the substance of agency rules, even in technical areas, was crucial to the legitimacy of agency rulemaking. Yet even Leventhal joined the opinion of the majority, written by Judge Wright, which demonstrated keen awareness of the importance of judicial restraint in such cases. First, the court interpreted the Clean Air Act permissively: the EPA's mandate to regulate emissions that "will endanger" public health was satisfied if the agency showed a significant risk of harm, not necessarily proof of actual harm. Second, the court showed a willingness to defer to the agency's fact-finding, so long as it was not based on "hunches" or "wild guesses." Judge Wright concluded: "Where a statute [delegating rulemaking authority] is precautionary in nature, the evidence difficult to come by, uncertain, or conflicting because it is on the frontiers of scientific knowledge, ... and the decision that of an expert administrator, we will not demand rigorous step-by-step proof of cause and effect."

The Supreme Court has also called for judicial restraint in this area. In the *Benzene* case, although the plurality read the statute to require a showing of significant risk before toxic substances could be regulated, it also concluded that the Secretary was not required to support his finding "with anything approaching scientific certainty"; the finding of risk need only be supported by "a body of reputable scientific thought." Industrial Union Dep't, AFL–CIO v. American Petroleum Inst., 448 U.S. 607 (1980). (The dissenters would have allowed even more leeway to the Secretary.) Similarly, in Baltimore Gas & Elec. Co. v. NRDC, 462 U.S. 87 (1983), the Court remarked that "a reviewing court must generally be at its most deferential" when an agency is "making predictions, within its area of special expertise, at the frontiers of science." Accordingly, the Court sustained an NRC rule that permitted licensing boards to ignore the possibility of environmental harm from long-term storage of spent nuclear fuel, despite considerable uncertainty about whether a safe method of storing nuclear waste would ever be found.

3. *Remedies*. If the court finds a rule invalid, it will almost always remand it for further consideration. Under *Chenery* principles, the court cannot specify what alternative rule, if any, the agency should adopt. See pp. 108–09 supra. Usually, when remanding a rule, a court also sets it aside. Recent decisions, however, have sometimes left a rule in effect during remand proceedings. Fox TV Stations, Inc. v. FCC, 280 F.3d 1027 (D.C.Cir.2002); Central Maine Power Co. v. FERC, 252 F.3d 34 (1st Cir. 2001). This practice of "remand without vacation" enables a court to protect reliance interests and prevent disruption in a regulatory program while the agency is considering how best to respond to the

court's concerns. The legality of this practice has been questioned because of its seeming conflict with § 706 of the APA, which provides that a court "shall ... set aside" agency action that is found to violate any of the Act's review standards. See Checkosky v. SEC, 23 F.3d 452 (D.C.Cir.1994). Nevertheless, courts have continued to employ the technique, which can arguably be defended as an exercise of equitable remedial discretion, which the APA should be presumed not to have repealed. In deciding whether to use remand without vacation in a particular case, courts usually consider factors such as the seriousness of the rule's deficiencies (which bears on the likelihood that the agency can rehabilitate the rule through further explanation or procedures) and the degree of disruption that would result from short-run invalidation. *Fox TV*, supra; Allied–Signal, Inc. v. U.S. NRC, 988 F.2d 146 (D.C.Cir.1993).

4. *Substantial Evidence Review*. In several regulatory statutes enacted in the early 1970s, such as the Occupational Safety and Health Act, Congress provided that agency rules should be reviewed under a substantial evidence test. This trend evidently resulted from a desire for particularly probing judicial review; historically, the substantial evidence test had been regarded as significantly more rigorous than the arbitrariness test, which ordinarily governs rulemaking. But this approach created an "anomaly," Judge McGowan later wrote, because these new rulemaking statutes generally contemplated "informal" (notice-and-comment) rulemak-

ing, while the substantial evidence test has traditionally been understood as a test for judging the evidence in a record compiled during a trial-type hearing. Industrial Union Dep't, AFL–CIO v. Hodgson, 499 F.2d 467 (D.C.Cir.1974). He went on to say that, no matter how the standard of review was phrased, a court could not be expected to demand solid factual support for predictive or scientific fact findings, let alone for policy judgments. Congress now seems to have ceased creating this type of statutory provision—partly because it has become more aware of the inherent limits of the judicial function, as explained by Judge McGowan, and partly because the "hard look" that courts provide under the arbitrariness test has become just as intrusive as the rigorous review that Congress had hoped to achieve through a substantial evidence test. See National Lime Ass'n v. EPA, 627 F.2d 416, 452 (D.C.Cir.1980) (in 1977 revision of Clean Air Act, substantial evidence test for rulemaking was rejected as unnecessary).

Some cases continue to assert that a statute that applies the substantial evidence test to rules requires unusually rigorous review. E.g., AFL–CIO v. OSHA, 965 F.2d 962 (11th Cir.1992). Increasingly, however, courts see a "convergence" between the arbitrariness test and the substantial evidence test. As Judge (now Justice) Scalia explained in Association of Data Processing Serv. Orgs. v. Board of Govs., 745 F.2d 677 (D.C.Cir.1984), the real difference between the two tests is that in substantial evidence review the court seeks support for factual findings in the record of a formal hearing, while in arbitrariness review it does not. But, he continued, this does not mean that an agency needs more factual support to pass one test than to pass the other. The *Data Processing* analysis is likely to prevail in the long run. Traditionally, the substantial evidence test was regarded as a more stringent standard because it occurred on a record. But now that informal actions are reviewed on the "administrative record," that functional distinction has lost its force. Moreover, agencies are now using informal rulemaking to implement policies that formerly would have been handled through trial-type proceedings, and courts perceive no reason why this shift in procedure should result in a diminished scope of review on substantive issues. In any event, the debate over which test is stricter is somewhat fruitless. Both tests really contemplate a standard of "reasonableness," which no one can define with precision. Under either test, ultimately, the court is likely to be influenced by a variety of subtle factors, such as the nature and complexity of the issues involved, the consequences of an erroneous determination, the agency's reputation for competence and fairness, and the judge's philosophy of judicial review.

I. AGENCY INACTION AND DELAY

The APA's definition of "agency action" includes "failure to act." 5 U.S.C.A. § 551(13). Nevertheless, when courts are asked to review administrative inaction, they are usually much more deferential than when affirmative acts are challenged, and sometimes they refuse review altogether. This attitude reflects an understanding of the practical point that an agency has limited resources and must set priorities in a manner that courts cannot easily supervise. One example of this self-restraint is Heckler v. Chaney, 470 U.S. 821 (1985), in which the Court held that an agency's refusal to initiate an enforcement proceeding is "presumptively unreviewable." See pp. 369–71 infra. Moreover, courts have asserted that they will overturn an agency's refusal to commence a rulemaking proceeding "only in the rarest and most compelling of circumstances," American Horse Protection Ass'n v. Lyng, 812 F.2d 1 (D.C.Cir.1987), although whether they have actually shown as much self-restraint as those words suggest is debatable. Similarly, an agency may bring an enforcement action against one suspected violator without immediately pursuing similarly situated competitors; this enforcement strategy will withstand judicial review in the absence of a "patent abuse of discretion." Moog Industries, Inc. v. FTC, 355 U.S. 411 (1958); see F.T.C. v. Universal–Rundle Corp., 387 U.S. 244 (1967) (similar ruling).

The APA specifically addresses judicial review of inaction in § 706(1), which provides that the reviewing court shall "compel agency action unlawfully withheld or unreasonably delayed." In a unanimous opinion in Norton v. Southern Utah Wilderness Alliance, 542 U.S. 55 (2004) (*SUWA*), the Supreme Court identified two significant limitations on the scope of this section. The plaintiffs in *SUWA* were environmentalists who contended that the Bureau of Land Management was not doing enough to prevent the intrusion of off-road vehicles into federal lands that were candidates for designation as wilderness areas. The Court held, first, that § 706(1) may only be used to require an agency to take a "discrete" or particularized action. Thus, the lower court could not simply enter a general order commanding BLM to fulfill its statutory obligation to manage the lands so as to preserve their potential to be designated as wilderness. Second, a court may not use § 706(1) to compel an action unless that action is *legally required*. Thus, although BLM's own land use plan provided that the agency "will conduct" an intensive monitoring program in a specific mountain area, the lower court could not direct BLM to comply with that provision. These land use plans were designed to be provisional and dependent on the availability of funding, and neither Congress nor the agency considered them binding commitments.

The second of these *SUWA* limitations follows straightforwardly from the language of § 706(1), which refers to "unlawfully" withheld action. The first limitation, however, was more surprising. Federal courts have in the past occasionally undertaken to oversee an agency's administration of a broad program—normally upon a showing that the agency was entirely failing to live up to its statutory obligations. E.g., NAACP v. Secretary of HUD, 817 F.2d

149 (1st Cir.1987). *SUWA* seems to signal that the Court will not tolerate similar ventures in the future.

After a proceeding has been launched, participants may ask the courts to intervene if the agency does not render a decision within a reasonable period of time. Courts resolve unreasonable delay claims through a "rule of reason," balancing hardships to the agency and to the complaining party. In re American Rivers & Idaho Rivers United, 372 F.3d 413 (D.C.Cir.2004); Telecommunications Research & Action Center v. FCC, 750 F.2d 70 (D.C.Cir.1984). Here again, however, courts try to remain sensitive to the agencies' problems of resource allocation, and so their responses usually take the form of exhortation rather than direct compulsion. In addition, the Court in *SUWA* remarked in a footnote that "a delay cannot be unreasonable with respect to action that is not required." If this cryptic comment is read to mean that a court may not redress administrative delay except where Congress has directly required an agency to act, such as with a statutory deadline, the availability of relief will become even more limited than in the past.

J. CONCLUSION

In the final analysis, the scope of review standards examined in this chapter—both those of the APA and those created by case law—leave a great deal of discretion in the hands of individual judges.

Phrases like "substantial evidence" and "arbitrary and capricious" can never be defined with precision, and courts have their own reasons for wanting to keep the governing standards rather vague. One explanation for this preference is that judges like to have flexibility to respond to the equities of individual fact patterns. Another explanation is that the courts disagree among themselves about the proper degree of deference that they should give to various administrative decisions. This disagreement, in turn, can be traced to differing assessments of the ultimate utility of judicial review in the control of agency action.

To some minds, judicial review should be highly prized for its contribution to the rule of law: it is the best means to ensure that agencies' policies adhere to the terms of their statutory mandates, and that individuals receive fair and evenhanded treatment in the implementation of those policies. On the other hand, overly intrusive judicial review is sometimes criticized for its undemocratic character. When courts use their review powers aggressively, they may undermine the agencies' ability to make legitimate responses to the will of the public. As the Court in *Chevron* observed, "federal judges— who have no constituency—have a duty to respect legitimate policy choices made by those who do."

Defenders of judicial review also emphasize that it can serve a quality control function, remedying carelessness and corner-cutting at the administrative level. Moreover, courts can supply a generalist perspective that single-mission agencies often lack.

However, those who are more skeptical about the value of judicial review point out that administrative agencies possess technical sophistication and experience that courts simply cannot duplicate. They also note that the courts, with their limited sources of information, do not always grasp the realities of program administration that lurk in the background of some agency policy choices.

Supporters of judicial review also argue that the courts' openness to a wide variety of suitors is one of their strengths. Groups that obtain aid from the courts sometimes represent interests that the agency should have heeded at an earlier stage. And courts are often the only hope for individuals who lack access to the mechanisms of political oversight. Critics see the courts as too often serving as pawns in interest groups' campaigns of delay and obstructionism, sabotaging the coherence of orderly program administration. History records many incidents in which an agency simply gave up on a project because it was exhausted by efforts to overcome judicial roadblocks.

In the years ahead, these and other competing arguments will undoubtedly shape the continuing development of scope of review doctrine, as courts endeavor to maintain meaningful controls over administrative actions without usurping the functions that Congress intended the agencies to perform.

CHAPTER IV

ACQUIRING AND DISCLOSING INFORMATION

Without information, administrative agencies could not regulate industry, protect the environment, prosecute fraud, collect taxes, or issue grants. Good decisions require good data, and if an agency does not fully understand the nature of the problems confronting it or the consequences of possible actions, its programs are likely to be either unduly burdensome or ineffective. Indeed, one of the strongest arguments for "deregulating" major sectors of the economy is the claim that agencies often cannot learn enough about the regulated industry to make sound policy.

Much of the information needed to make the administrative process work is freely available from published sources, voluntary submissions by regulated persons and organizations, citizen complaints, and studies conducted by agency staff or outside parties. Frequently, however, the necessary information can be obtained only from members of the regulated industry or other private parties who are not willing to give it to the government. A substantial legal battle may then develop. Personal privacy and freedom from governmental intrusion have long been considered fundamental elements of liberty, and these interests are constitutionally protected by the Fourth Amendment's prohibition of unreasonable searches as well as the Fifth Amendment's ban on compulsory self-incrimination. The growth of regulatory and benefit programs in recent years has greatly increased the government's demand for sensitive private information, and the computerization of files has heightened popular fears that agencies may misuse personal data.

Beyond these legitimate concerns about abuse of official power, however, there are some strong practical incentives for regulated persons and firms to resist disclosure. Withholding requested information is often an effective way of avoiding unwanted regulation or delaying it; even if the agency ultimately succeeds in forcing disclosure, conditions may have changed sufficiently to make the data useless or irrelevant. Moreover, some of the data sought by the regulatory agencies may be commercially valuable material such as trade secrets, and companies may fear that information will "leak" from the agencies' files to their competitors. Cost is also an important factor in many situations where private parties refuse to provide information voluntarily.

Just as agencies thrive on information, citizens have a vital need for information *from* the agencies. Many of the procedural protections found in judicial and administrative proceedings are designed to give interested persons a fair opportunity to discover, present, and challenge relevant information. In addition, disclosure of information about the government serves the interest of public and political accountability, by revealing areas where administration is ineffective and reform is necessary. Because of several disclosure statutes enacted during the 1960s and subsequently, a great deal of the business of government in the United States is open to public view, and much of the data on which agency decisions rest is available for the asking to interested citizens.

A. AGENCY INVESTIGATIONS IN CONTEXT

The power to compel private parties to submit information, like other administrative powers, must be based upon a valid legislative delegation of authority, and the agency must observe the standards and procedures specified in the relevant statutes. Traditionally, however, Congress has granted the agencies wide discretion to investigate and compel disclosure of information; many statutes impose only minimal constraints on the agency's use of compulsory process. Another source of legal limitations on agency data gathering is the Constitution. Because the government's attempts to gather information can threaten constitutionally protected privacy interests, the agency's activities must be measured against the requirements of the Fourth and Fifth Amendments.

Application of these constitutional guarantees has often proved difficult, however, because the agencies engage in widely diverse activities, and the constitutional protections, which were designed primarily to deal with criminal law enforcement proceedings, cannot be mechanically applied to all agency activities. Administrative inquiries may be directed towards an eventual criminal prosecution, as in the case of an IRS tax fraud investigation, but they may also be designed to support a civil penalty, or a cease and desist order, or the setting of rates for the future, or the formulation of general policy. Moreover, much of the work of the regulatory agencies takes place outside of formal proceedings. The Equal Employment Opportunity Commission mediates discrimination complaints; the Food and Drug Administration negotiates "voluntary" recalls of potentially hazardous food products; the Federal Reserve Board exercises continuing supervision over banks. The agency's (and the public's) need to compel disclosure of information may vary in each of these settings, and so also may the potential harm to the regulated if that power is unchecked.

Another source of difficulty is the fact that agencies use a variety of techniques for gathering data, and these techniques vary in their burdensomeness and intrusion on protected interests. In some Federal Trade Commission investigations, for example, the Commission can issue subpoenas for documents or testimony, or it can demand to inspect records in the office where they are kept, or it can require companies to fill out special "report orders"; in other instances, the FTC can issue "civil investigative demands" that are subject to different standards and procedures; and presiding officers in adjudicative proceedings can issue discovery orders much like those used in federal courts. Other agencies, particularly those enforcing health and safety regulations, have the power to inspect facilities and seize suspicious goods. As might be expected, the courts' attempts to adapt the constitutional protections to the administrative process have produced a large and not entirely consistent body of law.

A threshold question in disputes over agency access to information is how the party who is presented with an agency demand for records or other data may contest the legality of the request. In many agencies, rules or statutes explicitly provide a procedure similar to the motion to quash a subpoena that is used in the courts. When such a procedure is available, the party served with a subpoena must present her objections before the agency, or she may be barred from raising them in the courts under the doctrine of exhaustion of administrative remedies. McClendon v. Jackson Television, 603 F.2d 1174 (5th Cir.1979); see also pp. 391–97 infra.

While courts can enforce their own subpoenas directly by use of the contempt power, most agencies cannot; they must bring an enforcement action and obtain a court order directing compliance with the subpoena. In this enforcement action, the party who is resisting disclosure may present her objections to the subpoena, and the court will review the legality of the agency's use of compulsory process. If the court upholds the subpoena, it will issue an order enforcing it, and a violation of this order is punishable as contempt of court. Thus, a party resisting an agency subpoena typically does not incur any risk of penalties or legal liability until after court review. On the other hand, some statutes do provide that a party who refuses to comply without just cause is subject to fines or criminal penalties from the time the agency subpoena is issued. See, e.g., Securities Exchange Act, 15 U.S.C.A. § 78u(c) (failure to comply with SEC subpoena is a misdemeanor). These immediate sanctions are rarely enforced, however, and a party can usually obtain judicial review of administrative subpoenas with no risk that substantial penalties will accrue. Of course, if the subpoena is directed to a third party, the "target" may have no remedy because she may not even know that she is under investigation. See SEC v. Jerry T. O'Brien, Inc., 467 U.S. 735 (1984) (SEC has discretion not to notify target).

B. SUBPOENAS: GENERAL PRINCIPLES

When a private party contests an agency's demand for records, testimony, or other information, the reviewing courts will test the legality of the agency's demand by applying general principles that have evolved to control the use of compulsory process. These basic standards can be divided into four categories.

1. *The Investigation Must Be Authorized by Law and Undertaken For a Legitimate Purpose.* Because administrative agencies can exercise only those

powers that the legislature has delegated to them, the first inquiry is whether the relevant statutes have conferred the power to conduct the investigation in question. See 5 U.S.C.A. § 555(c) (compulsory process may not be issued or enforced "except as authorized by law"). In practice, however, this jurisdictional limit on administrative investigations is generally easy to satisfy. Both the substantive delegation of regulatory power to the agency and the grant of investigative authority may be drafted in such broad terms that the reviewing court will find it difficult to conclude that the investigation is *ultra vires*. Even when the issue of agency jurisdiction is arguable or unclear, the court is likely to perceive several reasons to let the investigation go forward. First, an injured party will generally have an opportunity to challenge the scope of the agency's power on review of a final decision. Second, a judicial attempt to fix the boundaries of agency jurisdiction at the preliminary stage of subpoena enforcement may be premature, because the issues may be more clearly defined if review is postponed until there is a final administrative decision. Third, the question may become moot if the agency ultimately decides not to exercise regulatory power over the complaining party. Thus, the courts generally conclude that the question of statutory coverage is to be determined by the agency in the first instance. See, e.g., Oklahoma Press Pub. Co. v. Walling, 327 U.S. 186 (1946).

A jurisdictional argument may succeed where the agency's lack of authority over the complaining party is apparent from the face of the complaint. Thus, a court enjoined a state attorney general from conducting an antitrust investigation of major league baseball clubs that had voted to drop two Florida teams from their ranks, because the business of professional baseball is completely exempt from federal and state antitrust laws. Major League Baseball v. Crist, 331 F.3d 1177 (11th Cir.2003). Another situation in which reviewing courts are likely to take a close look at agency demands for information is where the complaining party can make a convincing showing that the investigation was undertaken in bad faith for some improper purpose such as harassing or persecuting the respondent. United States v. Powell, 379 U.S. 48 (1964). However, if the administrator has a colorable basis for requesting the information in question, the complaining party will have to satisfy a substantial burden of pleading and proof in establishing an improper motive. Id.

2. *The Information Sought Must Be Relevant to the Agency's Regulatory Responsibilities, But Not Necessarily to a Specific Suspected Violation.* The Fourth Amendment prohibits the issuance of search warrants unless there is probable cause to believe that a specific violation of law has occurred, and during the early years of administrative regulation a similar standard was applied to administrative subpoenas. The leading case was FTC v. American Tobacco Co., 264 U.S. 298 (1924), where the Court strictly construed the FTC's investigative authority in order to avoid the constitutional question: if the

statute did not require "[s]ome evidence of the materiality of the papers demanded," it might well violate the Fourth Amendment.

A few years later, however, the Court relaxed this seemingly stringent requirement. In Endicott Johnson Corp. v. Perkins, 317 U.S. 501 (1943), the Secretary of Labor had requested payroll data from a government contractor for the purpose of determining whether certain factories were covered by the minimum wage law. The Court concluded that the issue of whether the factories were covered should not be litigated in the subpoena enforcement proceeding; so long as "[t]he evidence sought by the subpoena was not plainly incompetent or irrelevant to any lawful purpose of the Secretary in the discharge of her duties under the Act," the district court should grant enforcement.

The constitutional basis for this result was further explained in Oklahoma Press Pub. Co. v. Walling, 327 U.S. 186 (1946). There, the Court distinguished actual searches and seizures, like those commonly used in criminal law enforcement, from the "figurative" or "constructive" search that takes place when a regulatory agency demands to see the records of a regulated company. The *Oklahoma Press* opinion emphasized that there was a long history of legislative provisions requiring corporations to maintain records that were open to public and government scrutiny, while individuals had been protected against "officious intermeddling" in their affairs. In essence, the threat to legitimate expectations of privacy was less in the regulatory setting, while the public interest in access to corporate records was strong. In many fields of regulation, the only evidence of possible violations of law may be the records of regulated companies. In this situation, a strict probable cause requirement could make enforcement impossible. The Supreme Court recognized this necessity in United States v. Morton Salt Co., 338 U.S. 632 (1950), when it analogized the agency's investigative power to a grand jury's: an agency with a proper legislative authorization "can investigate merely on suspicion that the law is being violated, or even just because it wants assurance that it is not." Furthermore, many agencies' responsibilities extend beyond the enforcement of existing laws and rules. When administrators are delegated the power to make policy through rule-making or are authorized to report to the Congress on matters that may require legislation, they will often need to obtain information from unwilling private parties. Rigid application of the probable cause standard could undermine the quality of agency policymaking. See also Donovan v. Lone Steer, Inc., 464 U.S. 408 (1984) (reaffirming *Oklahoma Press*). It is important to remember, however, that although the constitutional standard of relevance has become easy to satisfy, particular statutes may impose more rigorous requirements on agency investigations. An EEOC subpoena, for example, may only inquire into matters that are "relevant to [a] charge under investigation." 42 U.S.C.A. § 2000e–8(a); see EEOC v. Shell Oil Co., 466 U.S. 54 (1984).

3. *The Investigative Demand Must Be Sufficiently Specific and Not Unreasonably Burdensome.* The Fourth Amendment's prohibition of unreasonable searches and seizures has also been modified in its application to administrative investigations. As the Court noted in the *Oklahoma Press* case, this requirement implies that the subpoena must adequately describe the materials sought; however, the sufficiency of the specifications is "variable in relation to the nature, purposes, and scope of the inquiry." Other factors bearing on the reasonableness of the subpoena are the cost of assembling and copying the requested materials; the disruption of the data source's business or activities that will result from compliance with the agency's request; the repeated or excessive nature of the agency's demands for data; and the risk of competitive harm if trade secrets or other commercially valuable information is released by the agency. While claims of unreasonable burden are frequently made, they are rarely successful. At most, the reviewing court may inquire whether there is adequate assurance, through protective orders or other procedural devices, that the respondent will be protected against the loss of proprietary information.

4. *The Information Sought Must Not Be Privileged.* The extent to which constitutional, common law, or statutory privileges limit the agencies' powers of compulsory process has been the subject of continuing debate. Much of the controversy has concerned the Fifth Amendment's privilege against self-incrimination. The extent of this protection is

discussed in the next section. Other testimonial privileges, such as the common law protection for husband-wife and lawyer-client communications, as well as the more recent state statutes such as those protecting journalists and their sources or accountants and their clients, have rarely been litigated in the administrative context. Agency statutes and regulations are usually silent on this point. In Upjohn Co. v. United States, 449 U.S. 383 (1981), however, the Court held that a taxpayer could assert both the attorney-client privilege and the work product privilege in resisting enforcement of an IRS summons. But see University of Pennsylvania v. EEOC, 493 U.S. 182 (1990) (no privilege for peer review materials); United States v. Arthur Young & Co., 465 U.S. 805 (1984) (no accountant-client privilege).

C. SELF–INCRIMINATION

When an agency seeks to compel a witness to testify, its attempts may conflict with the Fifth Amendment's assurance that no person "shall be compelled in any criminal case to be a witness against himself." Although the agency that is seeking the testimony will not have the power to impose criminal sanctions itself, a witness may fear that the information she provides will later be used against her in a criminal prosecution. When there is a risk that criminal sanctions will be imposed, the witness may refuse to answer questions that could incriminate her or provide a link in a chain of evidence against her. However, there are some significant limitations on the use of the privilege in administrative investigations or hearings.

1. *The Threatened Penalty Must Be Criminal Rather Than Civil in Nature.* In many regulatory areas, the sanction the witness fears may be labeled a "civil penalty," a "forfeiture," or some similar term rather than a crime. When this occurs, the court must determine whether the statutory penalty is sufficiently punitive in purpose or effect to be considered criminal. See Flemming v. Nestor, 363 U.S. 603, 613–21 (1960). In making this determination, the court will consider a variety of factors, such as whether the penalty is designed to promote retribution and deterrence rather than to compensate for damage, and whether the sanction in question is excessive in relation to its claimed purpose. United States v. Ward, 448 U.S. 242 (1980) (requirement that persons responsible for oil spills in navigable waters must report the spills to appropriate government agencies was not a violation of Fifth Amendment despite civil penalties of $5000 for each spill); see also Kennedy v. Mendoza–Martinez, 372 U.S. 144, 168–69 (1963).

2. *The Privilege Is Available Only to Natural Persons and Cannot Be Asserted on Behalf of Corporations or Associations.* Since the purpose of the self-incrimination privilege is to protect individuals from the government's use of the "third degree" and similar coercive tactics to extract confessions of personal wrongdoing, a corporation has no Fifth Amendment privilege. Thus, the officers of corpora-

tions and other business associations may not withhold testimony that might incriminate their firms. Bellis v. United States, 417 U.S. 85 (1974). A related principle, known as the collective entity rule, provides that a corporate officer who has custody of the firm's records must produce them in response to a subpoena, even though this response might incriminate the custodian herself. "[T]he custodian's act of production is not deemed a personal act, but rather an act of the corporation." Braswell v. United States, 487 U.S. 99 (1988).

3. *The Privilege Attaches Only to Compelled Testimonial Utterances and Not to Other Communications.* To receive Fifth Amendment protection, a communication must be coerced and must be testimonial in nature. Thus, in Couch v. United States, 409 U.S. 322 (1973), a subpoena for documents that were in the hands of the taxpayer's accountant did not violate the taxpayer's privilege, because it did not compel the taxpayer to do anything.[1] Conversely, in Fisher v. United States, 425 U.S. 391 (1976), the Court concluded that taxpayers could be required to produce the work papers their accountants had created in preparing their tax returns. Such papers would contain testimonial declarations by the accountants, not by the taxpayers. The Court

1. Similarly, even if the documents sought are personal records that are in the possession of the individual and contain handwritten notations, the agency may still be able to obtain them by using a search warrant rather than a subpoena. Here, also, the individual is not compelled to testify against herself, and so the Fifth Amendment does not apply. Andresen v. Maryland, 427 U.S. 463 (1976).

extended *Fisher* in United States v. Doe, 465 U.S. 605 (1984), holding that the contents of even the respondent's own business records were unprivileged: since he had prepared these records voluntarily (in the ordinary course of business), their contents did not constitute *compelled* testimony.

The Court did recognize in *Fisher* that the very act of producing records can be self-incriminating, because the response in effect admits that the subpoenaed documents exist and are genuine. On the facts of that case, the Court did not believe that production of the accountants' work papers would be the equivalent of testifying to damaging information: "The existence and location of the papers are a foregone conclusion, and the taxpayer adds little or nothing to the sum total of the government's information by conceding that he in fact has the papers." Where, however, compliance with a subpoena would effectively admit to the existence and authenticity of numerous documents of which the government is otherwise unaware, the act of production may have testimonial aspects that come within the privilege. *United States v. Doe,* supra (privilege claim upheld). Similarly, a defendant's act of collecting and producing documents, in response to a subpoena, can be deemed "testimonial" if it provides the government with leads that direct prosecutors' attention to incriminating information. United States v. Hubbell, 530 U.S. 27 (2000).

A separate limitation on Fifth Amendment rights, which has special importance in administrative law, is the so-called required records doctrine. This doctrine recognizes that, under many regulatory programs, individuals must keep business records and make them available for inspection by an administrative agency. In a sense, such individuals can be considered custodians of public records. Thus, an order compelling the production of such records does not necessarily infringe the privilege against self-incrimination. In Shapiro v. United States, 335 U.S. 1 (1948), the Court applied this reasoning to uphold, against Fifth Amendment challenge, an order requiring a grocer to produce his sales records, which he had maintained in compliance with a price control statute. The required records doctrine does not apply, however, where the reporting requirement, instead of being imposed in "an essentially non-criminal and regulatory area of activity," is directed at a "selective group inherently suspect of criminal activities." Marchetti v. United States, 390 U.S. 39 (1968). Thus, in *Marchetti*, the Court struck down a requirement that bookmakers must provide information about their activities to the Internal Revenue Service in connection with an occupational tax on wagering. Since bookmaking was a criminal offense under state and federal laws, enforcement of this requirement would have forced all bookmakers either to violate the law by not registering or to incriminate themselves. See also Haynes v. United States, 390 U.S. 85 (1968) (invalidating statute that required persons to report their unlawful possession of firearms). The required records doctrine also may not apply to record-keeping obligations that sweep so universally that an individual has essentially no

choice about whether to become subject to regulation. Smith v. Richert, 35 F.3d 300 (7th Cir.1994)
(forced disclosure of personal income tax records
would violate Fifth Amendment). Notwithstanding
these limitations, however, a wide range of administrative reporting requirements have been sustained
under the logic of the *Shapiro* case. See, e.g., Baltimore City Dept. of Social Services v. Bouknight, 493
U.S. 549 (1990) (upholding, under *Shapiro,* juvenile
court order directing mother to produce allegedly
abused child who was subject to a judicially approved protective custody order).

4. *The Privilege Can Be Defeated by a Grant of
Immunity From Prosecution.* Even if the Fifth
Amendment has been validly invoked by the subject
of an administrative investigation, the agency can
still compel the individual to testify by granting her
immunity from prosecution. Under 18 U.S.C.A.
§ 6004, the agency must find that the testimony is
"necessary to the public interest," and it must
obtain the approval of the Attorney General before
immunizing the witness. A grant of immunity will
not prevent the government from bringing a criminal prosecution based on independent evidence, see
Kastigar v. United States, 406 U.S. 441 (1972), and
it will not protect the witness against use of the
information in a noncriminal administrative proceeding, see Roach v. NTSB, 804 F.2d 1147 (10th
Cir.1986).

D. SEARCHES AND INSPECTIONS

Many agencies gather information through direct observation. Administrative inspections cover a wide range of activity, including safety tests of commercial equipment and personal cars, sanitary inspections of restaurants and hotels, environmental monitoring of factory emissions, and fire and health checks of apartments and homes. Although they are occasionally used for law enforcement purposes, the primary function of administrative inspections is to prevent and correct undesirable conditions. Physical inspections or tests may also take the place of formal hearings. The Administrative Procedure Act provides an exception to the Act's trial-type hearing procedures when an adjudicative decision "rest[s] solely on inspections [or] tests." 5 U.S.C.A. § 554(a)(3). Regardless of the reason for which it is undertaken, however, an administrative inspection must not violate the Fourth Amendment's prohibition of unreasonable searches and seizures, nor its requirement that search warrants may be issued only upon a showing of probable cause. Evidence seized in violation of these requirements can be excluded in a subsequent criminal prosecution. (The exclusionary rule does not, however, prevent admission of the evidence in *administrative* proceedings. Pennsylvania Bd. of Probation v. Scott, 524 U.S. 357 (1998); INS v. Lopez–Mendoza, 468 U.S. 1032 (1984).)

Much of the litigation on administrative searches has involved the application of the warrant clause to agency inspections. At one time administrative inspections were considered exempt from the constitutional warrant requirement. Thus, a health inspector did not need a search warrant to enter a house in search of a source of rats that had been infesting the neighborhood, if the authorizing statute imposed reasonable safeguards such as a requirement that the inspector adequately identify himself and conduct his inspections only during normal business hours. Frank v. Maryland, 359 U.S. 360 (1959). Prior judicial authorization for this kind of limited investigation was unnecessary, because the strong public interest in sanitation and the historic acceptance of such inspections outweighed the individual's interest in privacy. However, this view was rejected in two later inspection cases, Camara v. Municipal Court, 387 U.S. 523 (1967) (apartment building), and See v. Seattle, 387 U.S. 541 (1967) (commercial warehouse). Although routine fire and health inspections may be less hostile and less intrusive than the typical police search for evidence of a crime, the Court reasoned, "[i]t is surely anomalous to say that the individual and his private property are fully protected by the Fourth Amendment only when the individual is suspected of criminal behavior." Moreover, health and fire codes are frequently enforced by criminal processes. Thus, the individual's privacy interests were entitled to the protection of the warrant requirement.

At the same time, the Court in *Camara* and *See* recognized that inspections are essential to effective enforcement of health and sanitary standards and that the concepts of probable cause developed in criminal law enforcement could not be mechanically applied to these administrative searches. In place of the criminal law standard requiring a showing of probable cause to believe that a violation had occurred and that fruits, instrumentalities, or evidence of a crime would be recovered at the place specified, the Court established the rule that an administrative search warrant could issue when "reasonable legislative or administrative standards for conducting an area inspection are satisfied." The standards would vary according to the nature of the regulatory program, and they might be based upon factors such as "the passage of time, the nature of the building ... , or the condition of the entire area, but they will not necessarily depend upon specific knowledge of the condition of the particular dwelling."

The *See* decision left open the possibility that warrants would not be required for administrative searches in situations where a license was required to conduct the business in question and the grant of a license was effectively conditioned on the applicant's consent to warrantless searches. Two later cases confirmed that warrantless searches were permissible in industries subject to a licensing system that involved intensive regulation. Colonnade Catering Corp. v. United States, 397 U.S. 72 (1970) (licensed retail liquor establishment); United States v. Biswell, 406 U.S. 311 (1972) (firearms dealer).

This trend toward judicial approval for warrantless administrative inspections was interrupted by the Supreme Court's decision in Marshall v. Barlow's, Inc., 436 U.S. 307 (1978). The Occupational Safety and Health Administration, defending a statute that explicitly authorized it to conduct warrantless searches, argued that surprise inspections of workplaces were both necessary for effective protection of workers, and reasonable within the meaning of the Fourth Amendment. The Court, however, described the *Colonnade–Biswell* exception to the warrant requirement as a narrow one, applicable only when the target of the search was part of a "pervasively regulated" industry that has been subject to a "long tradition of close supervision." For all other inspections, a warrant was still necessary. As in *Camara* and *See,* the warrant would not require "specific evidence of an existing violation"; it could be based on reasonable legislative or administrative standards, including "a general administrative plan for the enforcement of the Act derived from neutral sources such as ... dispersion of employees in various types of industries across a given area." In the Court's view, the warrant requirement would protect employers against arbitrary or harassing invasions of their privacy, and give them notice of the proper scope of the inspection.

In more recent decisions, however, the Court has aggressively expanded the *Colonnade–Biswell* exception to the warrant requirement for "closely regulated" businesses. In Donovan v. Dewey, 452 U.S. 594 (1981), the Court upheld a statute autho-

rizing warrantless inspections in the mining industry. Although there was no "long tradition" of
regulation throughout this industry, as in *Colonnade*, the Court noted that the legislation created a
"comprehensive and defined" regulatory scheme
that would make mine operators aware that they
would face periodic inspections. The Court also
based its decision on the gravity of the social problem (health and safety hazards in mines); the legislature's determination that surprise inspections
were essential to detect violations; and the existence
of statutes and regulations that defined the circumstances in which inspections could be conducted, so
that individual inspectors would not wield unchecked discretion. Using essentially the same reasoning, the Court later held that police had validly
conducted a warrantless search of an automobile
junkyard, pursuant to a New York statute that
"closely regulated" the vehicle dismantling business
in order to curb automobile theft. New York v.
Burger, 482 U.S. 691 (1987). In fact, however, the
scope of the state's regulation in *Burger* was slight,
consisting of minimal registration and record-keeping duties; and the constraints that the statute
placed on the police's discretion were also minor.

To judge from recent cases, therefore, Congress
can apparently subject a wide variety of industries
to warrantless searches. The Court has perhaps
effectively limited the reach of *Barlow's* to agencies
like OSHA, which has jurisdiction over almost the
entire range of workplaces in American society. Of

course, even when an agency is subject to the *Barlow's* rule, the scope of the protection afforded by the warrant requirement will largely depend on the diligence of reviewing courts in scrutinizing agency requests for warrants. Experience in the field of criminal law enforcement suggests that some courts may be willing to grant approvals routinely, with only a perfunctory review of the agency's justification.

Administrative inspections also may fall within exceptions to the warrant requirement that have evolved in the context of criminal law enforcement. If the individual consents to the search of the premises, no warrant is required. *Barlow's,* supra. The consent may be valid even if permission to search is a condition to receiving important benefits. Wyman v. James, 400 U.S. 309 (1971) (requirement that recipients of welfare benefits consent to home visits by caseworkers not a violation of the Fourth Amendment). Nor is a warrant necessary if the evidence gathered by the inspector is in "plain view" from roadways or other public space. Air Pollution Variance Bd. of Colorado v. Western Alfalfa Corp., 416 U.S. 861 (1974) (emissions from smokestack visible from public areas of factory grounds); Dow Chem. Co. v. United States, 476 U.S. 227 (1986) (inspection of industrial complex by aerial photography). But see Kyllo v. United States, 533 U.S. 27 (2001) (warrant required for observation of thermal images, which could only be detected through special heat sensors).

E. DISCLOSURE OF AGENCY RECORDS

The public interest in a liberal disclosure policy is generally strong. Effective public and political oversight requires detailed knowledge of agency activities; and without disclosure of records in the government's possession, citizens may be unable to determine whether the agency is ignoring violations of law. Moreover, when administrative powers are exercised in secrecy, they can readily be abused to subvert fundamental rights. The exposure during the 1970s of the FBI's extensive efforts to suppress political dissent graphically illustrates this risk. In addition, disclosure of unpublished "secret law" can serve the public interest by helping citizens know whether their conduct is likely to lead to enforcement action. But disclosure of government data also carries with it some very substantial risks. Premature release of information about pending investigations can impede the enforcement of regulatory laws by alerting wrongdoers to hide or destroy evidence, or by discouraging potential witnesses from cooperating with investigators. Public disclosure can invade personal privacy and damage the reputations of persons or firms before they have had a chance to establish their innocence. It may also destroy commercially valuable trade secrets, or give competitors an unjustifiable advantage.

In contemporary administrative practice, these conflicting concerns are addressed through a series of information disclosure statutes. The most important of these is the Freedom of Information Act (FOIA), 5 U.S.C.A. § 552, which was enacted in 1966 and has been amended several times since. FOIA's major provision directs each agency to release identifiable records in its possession to "any person" who requests them, unless the material in question falls within one of the exemptions listed in the Act. Id. § 552(a)(3).[2] When the government refuses a request, the citizen may obtain de novo review in a district court, with the burden on the government to justify the withholding. The court may examine the requested agency records "in camera" (privately) to determine whether they should be released; and if the court finds that only a portion of the document is exempt, it may order release of the remainder. Id. § 552(a)(4)(B). Parties who sue successfully under the Act may recover their costs and attorneys' fees. Id. § 552(a)(4)(E).

Some of the primary users of FOIA are the organized constituency groups that are sufficiently concerned about regulatory policy to conduct continuous monitoring of agency activities. The most familiar—and often the most numerous and influ-

2. Other FOIA provisions require agencies to publish their rules and statements of general policy in the Federal Register, 5 U.S.C.A. § 552(a)(1), and to make available for public inspection their final opinions, interpretations, staff manuals, and instructions that affect an individual's rights. Id. § 552(a)(2). Pursuant to 1996 amendments to FOIA, these materials are also generally accessible from agency websites. When an agency fails to comply with these requirements, the undisclosed pronouncements may not be relied on or used against citizens who did not have actual notice of them.

ential—of these constituency groups are the regulated industries and their trade associations, but environmental, consumer, and other "public interest" groups have also become a significant factor in the administrative arena. By following agency activities and learning the basis of proposed actions, these constituency groups can often use persuasion or pressure to mold regulatory policy at the early stages of a proceeding, when participation is most effective. In many regulatory areas, FOIA, supplemented by personal contact within the agencies, functions as a kind of informal "discovery" system that constituency groups use in preparing to make their "case" to the agency.

Section 552(b) of FOIA lists nine categories of information that are exempt from disclosure, and most litigation under the Act has concerned the scope of one or more of these categories. The exemptions were designed to permit the withholding of records only when disclosure would harm some important governmental function or private interest, and the reviewing courts have usually construed them narrowly. The nine exemptions are often known by their subsection numbers; for example, the provision that permits agencies to deny requests for classified information that must be kept secret in the interest of national security, 5 U.S.C.A. § 552(b)(1), is usually called "Exemption 1." Case law on the exemptions is voluminous, and only a few illustrative issues can be treated here.

Exemption 5 of FOIA, § 552(b)(5), permits an agency to withhold information "which would not be available by law to a [private] party ... in litigation with the agency." The provision is interpreted as preserving the evidentiary privileges that the government has traditionally enjoyed in litigation, such as the attorney-client and work product privileges. Particularly significant is the so-called "deliberative process privilege," which protects internal deliberative documents that contain advice or recommendations. The rationale for this privilege is that the threat of eventual disclosure might inhibit candid discussion within the agencies. See EPA v. Mink, 410 U.S. 73 (1973) (evaluative portions of policy memoranda are exempt, although segregable factual portions are not). This privilege, however, exempts only *predecisional* documents. When an agency reaches a final decision and writes a memorandum explaining it, the document cannot be considered part of the deliberative process; it is part of the law itself, and must be disclosed. For example, requesters are entitled to obtain memoranda of the General Counsel of the NLRB explaining why he did *not* commence an unfair labor practice proceeding. NLRB v. Sears, Roebuck & Co., 421 U.S. 132 (1975). However, a General Counsel's memorandum explaining why he *will* commence a proceeding is protected as work product, because its release could reveal his litigation strategy. Id.

The government's interest in effective law enforcement is acknowledged in Exemption 7, § 552(b)(7), which protects against forced disclosure of "records or information compiled for law enforcement purposes" when the release could cause such harms as revealing the identity of a confidential source or endangering any individual's physical safety. (A separate subsection of FOIA, § 552(c), reinforces these safeguards.) Exemption 7 also authorizes the withholding of investigatory records when disclosure "could reasonably be expected to interfere with enforcement proceedings." Thus, in NLRB v. Robbins Tire & Rubber Co., 437 U.S. 214 (1978), the Court upheld the Board's policy of refusing to give access to witness statements gathered during unfair labor practice investigations. The Court noted that disclosure would permit employers or unions to coerce potential witnesses into changing their testimony, or not testifying at all. In addition, some persons might refuse to provide information to investigators if they knew that their statements would become public documents. In light of these possibilities, it was not necessary for the Board or the courts to conduct a burdensome case-by-case inquiry into the harm that was likely to result from a particular disclosure of witness statements; the agency could treat them as exempt on a generic basis.

Other FOIA provisions protect the privacy rights of individuals whose personal data is incorporated into agency records. Exemption 6, § 552(b)(6), authorizes agencies to withhold personnel and medical records if disclosure would constitute a "clearly unwarranted invasion of personal privacy," and a comparable provision in Exemption 7 is designed to prevent invasions of privacy through the release of investigatory records. Both of these provisions enable the reviewing court to balance the threat to the data subject's privacy interests against the public's interest in access to the data in question. For example, in Dep't of the Air Force v. Rose, 425 U.S. 352 (1976), the government relied on Exemption 6 in denying a request for access to summaries of disciplinary actions taken under the Honor Code at the Air Force Academy. The Supreme Court, however, refused to uphold this blanket denial, stressing that the language of the exemption compels disclosure unless the invasion of privacy is "clearly unwarranted." The Court remanded so that the district court could consider, through in camera inspection, whether the cadets' privacy could be protected if the case summaries were released with identifying details edited out. This solution, the Court suggested, would respect privacy interests and at the same time allow some public scrutiny of the Air Force's administration of the Honor Code.[3]

Another private interest that could be threatened by indiscriminate release of government files is the commercial value of trade secrets and other proprie-

3. A separate source of protection for individuals is the Privacy Act, 5 U.S.C.A. § 552a. It applies to all agency systems of records in which files can be retrieved by the individual's name or identifying number. The Act permits the individual citizen to inspect government agencies' files relating to her and to seek correction of erroneous or incomplete records. In addition, the Act requires agencies to publish notice of all "routine uses" of personal information, and it provides damages and injunctive relief for the record subject if the agency makes unauthorized disclosures of her file. This is one of the few situations in which Congress has provided injured persons with a damage remedy for the government's misuse of information.

tary information. Exemption 4 of FOIA, § 552(b)(4), allows the agencies to withhold "trade secrets and commercial or financial information obtained from a person and privileged or confidential." A leading case holds that commercial information is "confidential" within the meaning of this clause if its disclosure would be likely "(1) to impair the Government's ability to obtain necessary information in the future; or (2) to cause substantial harm to the competitive position of the person from whom the information was obtained." National Parks & Conservation Ass'n v. Morton, 498 F.2d 765 (D.C.Cir.1974).[4] Further protection is provided by the Trade Secrets Act, 18 U.S.C.A. § 1905, which makes it a crime for government officials to disclose trade secrets.

During the early years of FOIA, however, companies submitting proprietary information often felt unprotected. Even if the material requested under FOIA were exempt from disclosure, the agency might still decide to release it as a matter of discretion. They also feared that the Trade Secrets Act would not be a very powerful deterrent in this situation, because the Justice Department would be unlikely to prosecute a bureaucrat for releasing documents to the public. These apprehensions were

4. Subsequently the same court modified the *National Parks* test by restricting its application to information that the government obtains through compulsion. Information that industry voluntarily submits to the government falls within Exemption 4 if it is of a type that is not customarily released to the public. Critical Mass Energy Project v. NRC, 975 F.2d 871 (D.C.Cir. 1992) (en banc).

fueled by anecdotal evidence that some firms had in fact been injured when their competitors obtained valuable proprietary information by simply filing a FOIA request. During the 1970s, suppliers of business information began initiating court actions—soon dubbed "reverse FOIA" suits—to prevent the government from disclosing such data.

One of these "reverse FOIA" plaintiffs scored a partial victory in Chrysler Corp. v. Brown, 441 U.S. 281 (1979). There, several Chrysler employees had sought copies of affirmative action compliance reports submitted by the company to the Department of Defense Logistics Agency; Chrysler in turn sued to enjoin the release of these reports on the ground that they were exempt from disclosure under FOIA. The Court rejected the company's claim that the exemptions to the Freedom of Information Act were mandatory; FOIA is a disclosure statute, and it does not affect the agencies' discretion to release material that falls within the statutory exemptions. But, the Court continued, this discretion is not unbounded. A decision to release exempt documents is a final agency action subject to judicial review under the APA, and the reviewing court must decide whether the administrative determination was "arbitrary, capricious, an abuse of discretion, or otherwise not in accordance with law." See pp. 102–07 supra. Since a disclosure that violated the Trade Secrets Act would not be "in accordance with law," the reviewing court could prohibit disclosure.

The Court did not attempt to define the scope of the Trade Secrets Act in *Chrysler*. Subsequently, however, the D.C. Circuit has held that the Trade Secrets Act is as broad as Exemption 4 is; therefore, that Act *requires* agencies to withhold any commercial information that Exemption 4 *permits* them to withhold. CNA Financial Corp. v. Donovan, 830 F.2d 1132 (D.C.Cir.1987). Another safeguard, Executive Order 12,600, 52 Fed.Reg. 23,781 (1987), issued by President Reagan, instructs agencies that when they are considering granting a FOIA request for information that arguably could be withheld under Exemption 4, they must notify the company that supplied the information and permit it to present objections. These developments have doubtless served to deter agencies from granting FOIA requests for business information. That result is not necessarily a matter for regret, however, because the basic purpose of the Act was to promote openness and accountability in government operations, not to help one firm gain commercial advantage over another.

F.　OPEN MEETINGS

Just as the Freedom of Information Act calls upon agencies to adhere to standards of openness and accountability when they act on requests for written materials, the Government in the Sunshine Act of 1976, 5 U.S.C.A. § 552b, requires officials to follow similar principles when they hold live proceedings. Under the latter act, most meetings of the multimember regulatory agencies must be open to public scrutiny. Meetings must usually be publicly announced at least a week before they are held; and when an agency holds a closed meeting, it must keep a recording or transcript that it can release to the public if a court later decides that the meeting should have been conducted openly. The Act does not apply to agencies headed by a single individual, such as a Secretary. It also contains a list of exemptions closely resembling the FOIA exemptions. Id. § 552b(c). As in FOIA cases, however, courts sometimes respond skeptically to agency pleas for secrecy. See, e.g., Common Cause v. NRC, 674 F.2d 921 (D.C.Cir.1982) (agency's strategy meetings to decide how it will present budget requests to OMB are not always exempt).

The merits of the Sunshine Act are controversial. The appeal of conducting "government in the sunshine" is obvious; but critics contend that the open meetings requirement impairs the quality of agency deliberations, because in a private session commissioners are more likely to raise tentative ideas, explore compromises, and interact in a truly collegial manner. To date the Supreme Court has not addressed the scope of the exemptions. It has, however, made clear that the Act applies only to meetings that an agency holds as it proposes to take official action on specific proposals or issues—not to exploratory background sessions, or to gatherings organized by outside groups. FCC v. ITT World Communications, Inc., 466 U.S. 463 (1984).

Still another disclosure statute is the Federal Advisory Committee Act of 1972 (FACA), 5 U.S.C.A.App. 2, which governs the activities of advisory committees. Typically, these committees are groups of private citizens who are asked to provide an agency with advice and recommendations regarding a particular issue or program. Some advisory committees are comprised of technical experts, like the scientific committees that advise the EPA on proposals to cancel the registrations of pesticides as safety or environmental hazards. Others may be designed to represent diverse political constituencies, as in the presidential committee that was appointed to investigate the nuclear reactor accident at Three Mile Island: it was composed not only of scientists and technicians, but also environmentalists, industry members, and citizens from the community where the accident occurred. Under FACA, advisory committees must hold their meetings in public (subject to the same exemptions that apply to meetings of multimember agencies under the Sunshine Act). The Act resulted in part from a congressional belief that the advisory committees had proliferated excessively, wasting taxpayer dollars and enabling favored private interests to wield undue influence over the early stages of executive policymaking. The sponsors assumed that broader public scrutiny of the committees' activities would ameliorate these problems and might induce agencies to create fewer such committees in the future.

FACA is drafted in such broad terms, however, that the courts have felt compelled to limit its reach through creative construction. On its face the Act applies to all groups that are "established or utilized" to advise the executive branch. The Supreme Court has cautioned, however, that this language must not be read too literally, lest FACA be held to constrain informal consultations that Congress could not have meant to regulate. Public Citizen v. U.S. Dep't of Justice, 491 U.S. 440 (1989) (FACA does not apply to ABA committee that advises Justice Department on Supreme Court nominees). Similarly, a FACA exemption for groups composed exclusively of "full-time officer[s] or employee[s]" of the government was held to apply to a task force headed by the First Lady of the United States. The court adopted this strained construction because of doubts that the Act could constitutionally be applied to this panel. Ass'n of American Physicians & Surgeons v. Clinton, 997 F.2d 898 (D.C.Cir.1993).

A decade later, when public interest groups brought suit to compel FACA disclosures by an energy policy task force headed by the Vice President, the courts carried this reasoning further. The Supreme Court cautioned that the very process of litigating such a case raised sensitive separation-of-powers concerns and could result in unwarranted interference with the executive branch. Consequently, the Court said, the lower courts must display restraint in authorizing discovery against senior Administration officials, even if the government has not presented a formal claim of executive privilege. Cheney v. U.S. District Court, 542 U.S. 367 (2004). On remand, moreover, the D.C. Circuit decided that the task force had been composed exclusively of federal employees and, thus, was not subject to FACA. Although energy company executives had worked with the task force, their participation was irrelevant, because they had possessed "neither a vote nor a veto." In re Cheney, 406 F.3d 723 (D.C.Cir.2005) (en banc).

CHAPTER V

THE INFORMAL
ADMINISTRATIVE PROCESS

The Administrative Procedure Act sets forth several procedural models for federal agency decision-making, but these APA models do not even apply to the largest and probably most important category of agency actions—the informal administrative process. Only when an agency is formulating policy through legislative rulemaking (5 U.S.C.A. § 553), or when the statute being implemented requires that the decision in question be made after a formal trial-type hearing (5 U.S.C.A. §§ 554, 556–57), does the APA prescribe minimum procedures to be used. See pp. ___–___, ___–___ infra. Generally speaking, the remaining administrative decisions comprise the legal category of "informal action."

The term "informal" is somewhat misleading, because many of the activities that technically fall within this category are subject to significant legal controls. Agencies often impose procedural constraints on their own discretion by issuing rules of practice, staff manuals, or instructions to the public. These procedural requirements may create opportunities for interested persons to be heard, and they may be legally binding, so that a failure to observe them can be reversed by a reviewing court.

166

Moreover, the due process clauses of the Constitution require the agencies to meet basic standards of fairness when they affect the life, liberty, or property of individuals. The application of procedural due process to informal administrative action is treated in Chapter 6. The discussion in this chapter provides context and background for that analysis, by reviewing the most common types of informal administrative decisions.

In addition to procedural checks on discretion, informal action is usually subject to judicial review. Thus, courts can generally determine whether the agency has acted within the bounds of its statutory jurisdiction, has properly exercised its discretion, and has developed a reasonable factual basis for its action. There may also be a variety of nonlegal controls on discretion, such as statistical "quality control" checks to reduce error rates, supervision by higher-level officials, oversight by the legislative and executive branches, and publicity from the media.

In short, informal action often is subject to signif icant safeguards against abuse or overreaching. Nevertheless, certain characteristics of informal agency processes give special cause for concern. Many informal programs, such as those dispensing welfare or veterans' benefits, process a high volume of cases. In this situation, the difficult or unusual case may get less attention than it deserves, and pressure to move cases along may overcome the desire to decide them correctly. The risks of error and arbitrariness are compounded when the program affects relatively powerless classes of clients who are unable to make effective use of any procedures that are available to them. Moreover, some kinds of informal action have far less visibility than formal proceedings generally do; media exposure of corruption or incompetence in these fields is unlikely and effective political oversight is a rarity.

Even when these problems come to light, the judiciary's capacity to address them is limited, because the courts have no inherent power to devise procedures that they believe will promote fairness in informal adjudication. The Supreme Court confirmed this restriction on judicial creativity in Pension Benefit Guaranty Corp. v. LTV Corp., 496 U.S. 633 (1990). There, the PBGC ordered LTV to resume responsibility for pension obligations that LTV had surrendered while in bankruptcy proceedings. A lower court set aside the PBGC's decision, because the agency had "neither apprised LTV of the material on which it was to base its decision, [given] LTV an adequate opportunity to offer contrary evidence, proceeded in accordance with ascertainable standards . . ., nor provided [LTV] a statement showing its reasoning in applying those standards." The Supreme Court reinstated the PBGC decision. No statute, including the APA, required the procedures in question, nor was any due process violation alleged, and the reviewing court had no authority to impose further obligations on its own. The Court implied that it was merely deferring to Congress, which had specified the proper procedures for informal agency adjudications in § 555 of the APA. Yet § 555 has such limited scope that the main explanation for the *LTV* holding must be the Court's aversion to unconstrained judicial activism in the realm of administrative procedure.

A. SETTLEMENT, NEGOTIATION, AND ALTERNATIVE DISPUTE RESOLUTION

Since many agencies have a huge caseload of claims, hearings, and penalty actions to resolve each year, settlements are a vital part of the administrative process. Like trial courts, most agency adjudicative systems would become hopelessly backlogged if all the cases filed had to go through a full hearing. In recognition of this fact, the agencies have developed a diverse array of settlement practices and procedures. Several factors contribute to the prevalence of settlements in administrative practice. Regulated industries have to live with the agencies that oversee their operations, and the company accused of a violation may be reluctant to earn the reputation of being uncooperative by resisting when it is in the wrong. At the same time, an agency that has become familiar with the respondent through continuing supervision or prior dealings may have access to ample information establishing the violation. Finally, the costs of litigation, including the harm to the company's reputation among consumers and the uncertainty resulting from prolonged litigation, often create a powerful incentive to settle a pending charge.

Negotiated settlements increase the efficiency of the administrative process, but they may do so at the expense of other interests. In contrast to the typical negotiated compromise between two private litigants, the agency adjudication usually has a strong public interest dimension: the rights and interests of consumers, competitors, or other parties who are not directly represented can be greatly affected by the agency's decision. Decisions made without full testing of the facts and adversary debate on matters of law and policy may reach questionable results, and persons who are indirectly affected may feel that these decisions are less fair to them than actions taken after trial-type hearings. In recognition of these risks, many agencies have codified their settlement procedures in their rules of practice, including the allowance of an opportunity for interested members of the public to comment on proposed settlements. This approach has been extended by statute to the settlement of civil antitrust cases brought by the Department of Justice. 15 U.S.C.A. § 16.

Usually, consent negotiations can take place either before or after the issuance of a formal complaint. The respondent signing a consent order agrees to comply with the order's remedial requirements, but it does not formally admit that it has committed a violation of the applicable laws. As a result, the party signing the consent settlement would not be estopped from denying legal liability if a private party, such as a competitor or a customer, later brought a civil damage action against the respondent based on the same set of facts. This opportunity to avoid a formal adjudication of wrongdoing is often a major incentive for the respondent to settle. The respondent must comply with the terms of the consent agreement itself, usually under threat of contempt sanctions, but disagreements about the meaning of the agreement sometimes arise. In those situations, because such agreements are the product of negotiation, they "are construed basically as contracts, without reference to the legislation the Government originally sought to enforce but never proved applicable through litigation." United States v. ITT Continental Baking Co., 420 U.S. 223 (1975).

The APA imposes a duty on the agencies to consider settlement offers. See 5 U.S.C.A. § 554(c)(1) (settlement offers from respondents in formal cases must be considered "when time, the nature of the proceeding, and the public interest permit"); cf. id. § 558(c) (licensee must usually be given an "opportunity to demonstrate or achieve compliance with all lawful requirements" before revocation proceedings commence). However, the APA imposes few limits on the agencies' discretion to accept or reject an offer. Thus, judicial review of a decision to settle a pending case will be very narrow or nonexistent. Compare NLRB v. United Food and Commercial Workers Local 23, 484 U.S. 112 (1987) (General Counsel of NLRB has unreviewable discretion to dismiss an unfair labor practice complaint pursuant to an informal settlement), with Arctic Slope Regional Corp. v. FERC, 832 F.2d

158 (D.C.Cir.1987) (reviewing termination of rate proceedings for abuse of discretion). Like decisions not to prosecute (see pp. 369–70 infra), settlements tend to be ill-suited to judicial supervision. Often they are based on factors that a court could not easily review, such as the history of negotiations between the agency staff and the respondent, the need to devote resources to other cases or investigations, the likelihood that the agency would prevail in litigation, or the precedential value of a favorable decision.

Recent years have seen growing interest in "alternative dispute resolution" processes in administrative law. Most of the attention has been devoted to "regulatory negotiation" in rulemaking, see pp. 342–44 infra, but agencies have also experimented with informal decisionmaking models in adjudicative settings. These models take a variety of forms. For example, *arbitration* generally entails voluntarily submitting a dispute to a neutral third person for a decision. The two sides present evidence and argument, but the procedures are more informal than those of the trial-type APA hearing. The arbitrator's decision is usually binding on both sides (although sometimes it is only advisory). *Mediation* involves enlisting a neutral figure to facilitate negotiation of a solution by the disputants themselves. Some mediators meet with the opposing sides jointly; others hold separate meetings using "shuttle diplomacy." Another approach used by some agencies is appointment of an *ombuds* (a term that is gradually displacing the traditional term "ombudsman"). The ombuds is an independent figure within an agency who hears complaints in confidence and assists in dispute resolution through advice, investigation, and persuasion, but not through actual decisionmaking power.

In 1990, in order to regularize and encourage agencies' use of these processes, Congress passed the Administrative Dispute Resolution Act, 5 U.S.C.A. § 571 et seq., also known as the ADR Act. Prior to this legislation, agencies generally doubted their power to enter into binding arbitration with a private party. The ADR Act now expressly authorizes administrative arbitration, but only where all parties to a dispute give their consent in writing. The Act also provides for streamlined selection of "neutrals" such as mediators and arbitrators, and for the confidentiality of documents they generate. Congress liberalized ADR procedures still further with amendments to the Act in 1996, and presidential executive orders have prodded agencies to make greater use of ADR techniques. Because of these external pressures, as well as the intrinsic appeal of efficiency in dispute resolution, these structured but informal methods of conducting administrative adjudications may become increasingly common and important in the future.

B. APPLICATIONS AND CLAIMS

One of the most common reasons for creating administrative agencies is to provide for the fast processing of large numbers of claims and applications. The agencies that are responsible for dispensing social welfare benefits, collecting taxes, and controlling immigration make millions of informal decisions each year, and these decisions significantly affect the lives of virtually all Americans. In a single year, for example, the Social Security Administration disburses about two hundred billion dollars and makes over four million determinations in administering the Old–Age, Survivors, Disability, and Health Insurance programs.

Some benefits programs, such as the veterans' benefits system, rely almost exclusively on informal, nonadversary procedures. In other programs, including most of the social welfare programs administered by SSA, an applicant whose claim is denied in an informally reached decision may then resort to a trial-type "fair hearing." Even when such an opportunity for a formal hearing is available, however, relatively few claimants take advantage of it; the remainder may be uninformed about their options, unable to secure legal services, or unable to represent their own interests adequately—or may simply be satisfied with the informal hearing they received.

Faced with the need to make an enormous number of decisions quickly, many of the agencies that process individual claims have developed sophisticated informal procedures in an effort to minimize the use of formal hearings. One of the most familiar examples is the Internal Revenue Service. Despite the formidable complexity of the tax laws, the IRS has developed forms that are relatively simple to complete, as well as a variety of informational pamphlets and simplified instructions for taxpayers. It also provides direct assistance and advice through regional offices located throughout the country. Computerized audit routines and cross-checks with state tax records "flag" suspicious returns for further analysis. When a question arises, a system of administrative reviews and a simplified "small claims" procedure serve to resolve most disputes. Thus, out of more than a hundred million individual tax returns filed annually, about one million may be examined; only about 100,000 cases are appealed administratively beyond the examination stage, and all but about 10,000 of these are settled by appeals officers.

An effective system for resolving disputes administratively, and for establishing some quality control over routine decisions, is essential if the claims processing agencies are to avoid paralysis. However, efforts to upgrade the system as a whole through management supervision can also threaten strongly felt commitments to the ideal of resolving individual cases fairly by giving the claimant a trial-type hearing. One example of this tension surfaced during the early 1980s, when the Social Security Administration implemented a statutory directive to improve the consistency of disability benefits decisions by "targeting" for appellate review Administrative Law Judges whose allowance rates exceeded the statistical average for all ALJs. This "Bellmon review" process resulted in a series of suits claiming that the focus on high allowance rates compromised the impartiality of the ALJs, and thereby denied the claimants a fair hearing. See pp. 271–72 infra. This experience illustrates the more general proposition that justice in a mass social welfare system is not a unitary value, but rather a balance among the frequently conflicting goals of carrying out the legislative mandate efficiently, providing assistance to individuals in distress, and evaluating the claimant's moral entitlement to public funds. Outside intervention, whether from courts or from legislatures, may disrupt the existing balance in unforeseen ways, and thereby undermine the quality of administrative justice. See generally Jerry L. Mashaw, *Bureaucratic Justice* (1983).

C. TESTS AND INSPECTIONS

A person seeking a driver's license must usually pass a written exam, an eyesight check, and a driving test. All of these are administered by trained inspectors who do not use formal judicialized procedures in making the decision to grant or deny the license. Routine use of trial-type hearings for these kinds of decisions would be not only slow and cumbersome, but also pointless: courtroom procedures such as sworn testimony and cross-examination would contribute relatively little to the straightforward processes of measurement and observation that are the basis of many administrative decisions.

Tests and inspections are used in a variety of regulatory programs where technical criteria or other objective standards are applied. Informal inspections determine whether planes and trains are in compliance with safety rules, agricultural products can meet quality standards, or periodicals can obtain second class mailing privileges. They may also form the basis of agency decisions as to whether foods and drugs are contaminated, pilots are physically fit to operate aircraft, or factories are in compliance with environmental standards. In addition, agencies may conduct tests and publish the results for the purpose of assisting consumer choice, as when the FTC releases statistics on the tar and nicotine content of cigarettes or the EPA measures the gas mileage of automobiles.

Although the savings in time and resources are great and the threat of inaccurate decision is generally small, the widespread use of administrative tests and inspections does give rise to some procedural concerns. Even when the test is simple and the results unambiguous, there is still a risk that the official conducting it will be careless or corrupt, or use defective measuring equipment. The inspector may be under pressure to make a certain number of inspections during the workday, or to maintain production at the inspected facility. Moreover, many decisions based on tests or inspections require a considerable amount of judgment or interpretation. The decision whether to certify a newly designed airplane as "airworthy" to carry passengers requires a series of engineering judgments about the problems that the plane is likely to encounter in operation, and about its ability to withstand a variety of predictable stresses and failures. Tests can provide the basis on which these decisions are made, but they will not necessarily furnish a clear answer. Decisions like the airworthiness certification may also involve an implicit value choice on matters such as whether the public interest is best served by allowing relatively easy certification, so that manufacturers and airlines can bring new airplanes into service quickly and cheaply, or whether the paramount interest in safety requires a high level of prior assurance, even though this may raise prices and stifle innovation. Ideally, basic policy choices of this nature should be made in visible, public proceedings with ample opportunities for interested persons to participate; yet, if the established criteria are vague or incomplete, the policy decisions may actually be made by the technicians who conduct the tests and inspections.

The D.C. Circuit was mindful of these concerns in a case interpreting the APA provision that excuses agencies from holding a trial-type hearing where "decisions rest solely on inspections, tests, or elections." 5 U.S.C.A. § 554(a)(3). In Union of Concerned Scientists v. U.S. NRC, 735 F.2d 1437 (D.C.Cir.1984), the Nuclear Regulatory Commission amended its rules to provide that the adequacy of emergency preparedness exercises conducted by communities near a new nuclear power reactor could no longer be litigated in licensing proceedings; instead, the agency would evaluate the required emergency drills as part of its pre-operation inspections of the plant. The court ruled that this was a misuse of the APA hearing exemption, because the agency's decision would not depend "solely" on facts observed by its inspectors. The NRC would also consider reports from other interested persons, and questions of credibility, conflict in testimony, and sufficiency of the evidence were likely to arise. Since the statutory formal hearing had been provided to resolve such conflicts, the court held, it was improper for the NRC to decide these issues outside of the hearing process.

Fairness to regulated parties may also be lacking if a decision is based on a test or inspection that they have no real opportunity to contest. When the environmental inspector takes an incriminating reading of the opacity of smoke rising from the company's stack, or draws a sample of the river water near its drain pipe, there may be no practical or effective way to contest the alleged violation unless there has been prior notice and an opportunity to conduct independent tests, or at least to observe the sampling procedure.

Several steps and strategies have been developed to minimize these risks. The skills and integrity of inspectors can be checked by setting minimum qualifications for these personnel, and by providing expert supervision (especially through unannounced spot checks). Apart from emergency situations— such as where contaminated perishable foods or livestock with contagious diseases have been discovered and must be destroyed immediately—it is usually possible to provide a check on the inspector's discretion by having a second official reinspect the goods, or even by providing the right to a trial-type hearing. Furthermore, although the Fourth Amendment warrant clause has only limited application to administrative searches, it ensures in many situations that the agency will have to submit to an independent review of the need for the inspection, or to other checks on administrative arbitrariness. See pp. 147–52 supra.

Whatever the legal checks on inspectors' behavior, agencies may find it prudent to display a healthy self-restraint in their use of tests and inspections. Experience in agencies like the Occupational Safety and Health Administration suggests that a rigid, penal style of enforcement can be counterproductive. If the inspector mechanically cites all violations without regard to the actual risks created or the reasons for noncompliance, the result may be only be resentment and resistance among the regulated. Eugene Bardach & Robert A. Kagan, *Going By the Book* (1983). On the other hand, an inspector who exercises sound discretion and responds intelligently to perceived problems can enhance the credibility of the regulatory program, and encourage voluntary compliance from regulated firms. See generally Philip K. Howard, *The Death of Common Sense* (1994).

D. SUSPENSIONS, SEIZURES, AND RECALLS

Many agencies have the authority to remove a product from the market, to seize property, or to suspend a license or a rate pending full adjudication of alleged violations. Federal agencies can summarily seize adulterated or misbranded foods and drugs, stop public trading in securities, and take control of banks that have become fiscally unsound. The licenses of doctors, lawyers, horse trainers, and innumerable others whose occupations are regulated at the state or federal level can usually be suspended when the responsible authorities have reason to believe that the licensee has failed to observe minimum professional standards. This power to issue orders that summarily terminate risks to the public health, safety, or economic welfare has historical antecedents in the common law power to abate public nuisances, but in the modern regulatory state the delegation of powers to take summary action has become widespread.

The justification for summary administrative powers is straightforward. When private conduct is arguably in violation of regulatory statutes and poses an immediate threat to the public, the responsible agency should not have to wait months or years until it can complete a formal trial-type proceeding before protecting the public from harm. But summary action can also have a devastating impact on those who are regulated, both in lost income and in damage to reputation. Recalls of defective or dangerous products or suspensions of occupational licenses for corruption or incompetence are often newsworthy events that carry a lasting stigma. Moreover, since summary action often must be taken on the basis of incomplete or untested information, there can be a high risk that the agency is wrong.

In recognition of these risks, some agencies are required to obtain court approval for summary actions, such as the Consumer Product Safety Commission's decision to remove appliances or other products from the market as imminent hazards. 15 U.S.C.A. § 2061. Another procedural protection against hasty or unauthorized summary action is the requirement that the agency hold a full hearing promptly after it has suspended a license or removed a product from the market. If the agency's rules or the relevant statutes do not provide a prompt post-deprivation hearing, procedural due process may require it. See Barry v. Barchi, 443 U.S. 55 (1979) (horse trainer's license could be suspended without prior hearing when horse trained by him had been drugged, but trainer had a constitutional right to a prompt postsuspension hearing), discussed pp. 225–26 infra.

In practice, most disputes over hazardous consumer products are resolved through voluntary recalls—although in many instances the manufacturer's "voluntary" participation results from considerable agency prodding and from its desire to avoid the adverse publicity that formal action could entail. From the agency's perspective, a voluntary recall is more attractive than a seizure action because it is usually quicker and requires fewer agency resources. See Teresa M. Schwartz & Robert S. Adler, *Product Recalls: A Remedy in Need of Repair,* 34 Case W.Res.L.Rev. 401 (1983–

84). The desire for expeditious results at low cost also helps to explain why product safety agencies tend to use voluntary recalls as a substitute for rulemaking. The rulemaking strategy requires the agency to commit substantial resources to generating the detailed explanatory statement and comprehensive factual record needed to satisfy a rigorous judicial "hard look." Jerry L. Mashaw & David L. Harfst, *The Struggle for Auto Safety* (1990).

Whatever its causes, the agencies' preference for recalls over rulemaking is troubling. Rules setting safety standards for new vehicles prevent injuries far more effectively than recall actions do. As often as not, car owners do not even respond to recall notices, and neither do the vast majority of owners of other consumer products. Moreover, extensive use of voluntary recalls can undercut agency accountability. When administrators fix the limits of acceptable risk in public rulemaking proceedings, all interested parties have an opportunity to participate in the formulation of policy. To the extent that regulatory action is instead accomplished through informal negotiation, this check on administrative discretion is bypassed.

E.   SUPERVISION

In many regulated industries, the agency's constant surveillance of business activities is similar to the physical inspection of regulated products. National bank regulation is one field where pervasive regulation takes place through informal supervision rather than through formal proceedings. Administrators determine who can open a bank, whether a branch bank can be established and where it can be located, what cash reserves must be maintained, what auditing procedures must be followed, whether the bank can enter other businesses, and the like. The administrator may even be empowered to take over a bank at his discretion, without a prior hearing, in order to protect its creditors. Fahey v. Mallonee, 332 U.S. 245 (1947); see also FDIC v. Mallen, 486 U.S. 230 (1988) (summary suspension of bank officer).

Compliance with this extensive regulatory framework is enforced by daily supervision and periodic (often unannounced) visits by bank examiners. When problems or potential violations are uncovered, they are usually resolved quietly by mutual consent. This system of intensive but informal regulation has worked in the banking field because banks are extremely concerned with maintaining public confidence in their fiscal soundness. A bank will surely lose business, and perhaps have to close its doors, if its financial stability is publicly questioned by a regulatory agency. Thus, the agency's decision simply to institute a formal proceeding may be a severe sanction.

The principal risk of continuing supervision is that the agency will have too much or too little "leverage" to enforce compliance with its policies. When the regulated industry is effectively precluded from challenging agency decisions in formal proceedings or on judicial review, as is often the case in bank regulation, the agency may be under little pressure to explain and rationalize its policies, or to apply them consistently. Here, as elsewhere, the development of "secret law" may result in inadequately considered policy choices and unfair or arbitrary treatment of the regulated. On the other hand, if the agency is unable to back up its supervisory efforts with a credible threat of formal proceedings or other sanctions, the regulatory program may be ineffective. Moreover, when an agency becomes too heavily dependent upon informal supervision, it will not develop the resources and staff expertise required to conduct formal proceedings effectively when the need arises.

F.   INFORMATION DISCLOSURE AND PUBLICITY

An administrator's decision to issue a press release, hold a news conference, grant an interview, or "leak" a story to the press is usually made informally, yet these publicity-generating activities can be as potent as a formal rule or order. Media coverage of agency activities serves several purposes. Agencies frequently use publicity to warn consumers about dangerous products or fraudulent sales practices. Consumers need to know if cans of a particular brand of soup may cause botulism, or if a new toy on store shelves has a defect that can harm their children. Reports by the press and the broadcast media can be an effective way to warn people of these risks. Indeed, information disclosure can serve as a regulatory strategy in its own right, a cheaper and less intrusive alternative to command-and-control approaches.

Modern information technology has vastly amplified the government's capacity to use information as a regulatory tool. All of the major federal agencies maintain websites, and many use these sites to publicize reports and data about conditions within their respective areas of responsibility. A prominent example is the Toxic Release Inventory (TRI) maintained by the Environmental Protection Agency. Established by the Emergency Planning and Community Right-to-Know Act of 1986, 42 U.S.C.A. § 11023, the TRI is an on-line compilation of annual reports that individual companies have filed about their releases of toxic chemicals. Similarly, the Department of Health and Human Services, as part of its National Toxicology Program, maintains a public database of substances that are "known or reasonably anticipated to be" human carcinogens. 42 U.S.C.A. § 241(b)(4).

Agencies' use of publicity and disclosure has troubling aspects, however. The effect of unfavorable publicity on a regulated industry can be devastating. Products and companies have been driven out of existence by it, and sometimes the warning turns out to have been a false alarm. A business can suffer competitive harm if its confidential commercial information is revealed to its rivals. Furthermore, the nation's growing awareness of terrorism and other national security risks has given rise to warnings that sensitive information about American facilities could fall into the wrong hands if thoughtlessly disseminated by government. In addition, agencies sometimes use the weapon of publicity to enhance, if not exceed, their delegated powers. When the regulated industry is very sensitive to adverse publicity, the agency can threaten disclosure to induce compliance, or use press coverage as a sanction to punish violators for past offenses.

The potential for misuse of agency disclosures has given rise to concerns about the fairness of this facet of the administrative process. In a few contexts, Congress has instituted safeguards. The Consumer Product Safety Commission, for example, cannot disclose information relating to manufacturers of consumer goods unless the agency has first provided the manufacturer with a summary of the information in question and an opportunity to comment on it. The CPSC also must take "reasonable steps" to assure the accuracy of the information that it releases, and publish a retraction if that information turns out to be wrong. However, these protections do not apply when the agency believes that a product is an imminent hazard to consumers. 15 U.S.C.A. § 2055; cf. CPSC v. GTE Sylvania, Inc., 447 U.S. 102 (1980) (same requirements apply when CPSC releases file information under the Freedom of Information Act). In addition, the Trade Secrets Act, 18 U.S.C.A. § 1905, prohibits agency disclosure of certain commercially sensitive information. The Supreme Court has allowed private persons to enforce the Act through so-called "reverse FOIA actions." See pp. 159–61 supra.

By and large, however, avenues of legal redress for companies that have suffered from unfavorable publicity have been quite limited, at least until very recently. The government's publication of an informational report has usually been held not to be judicially reviewable "agency action" under the APA. Flue–Cured Tobacco Coop. Stabilization Corp. v. U.S. EPA, 313 F.3d 852 (4th Cir.2002) (EPA report warning of dangers of secondhand tobacco smoke was unreviewable); Industrial Safety Equipment Ass'n v. EPA, 837 F.2d 1115 (D.C.Cir.1988) (agency booklet comparing petitioner's products unfavorably with others was unreviewable). Some older case law indicates that when adverse publicity is equivalent to a formal accusation of criminal wrongdoing, due process may compel the agency to allow the accused some opportunity to present evidence and cross-examine adverse witnesses. Compare Hannah v. Larche, 363 U.S. 420 (1960) (Civil Rights Commission not required to identify adverse witnesses or permit cross-examination in investigative hearings on racial discrimination), with Jenkins v. McKeithen, 395 U.S. 411 (1969) (state commission holding hearings on labor racketeering required to permit accused individuals to present live testimony and confront and cross-examine witnesses, because commission's investigative hearings were limited to alleged criminal violations). The authority of these precedents has been clouded, however, by recent indications in the case law that reputational loss, standing alone, does not trigger due process safeguards. See pp. 212–14 infra.

Recently, a government-wide approach to ensuring a degree of regularity in agency informational disclosures has begun to emerge. The so-called Information Quality Act (also known as the Data Quality Act) requires every agency, under OMB direction, to issue guidelines "ensuring and maximizing the quality, objectivity, utility, and integrity of information (including statistical information) disseminated by the agency." Moreover, the agency must "establish administrative mechanisms allowing affected persons to seek and obtain correction of information maintained and disseminated by the agency." Pub. L. No. 106–554, § 515 (2000), 44 U.S.C.A. § 3516 note. To date, petitions for correction filed under this Act have rarely been granted, but the Act is nevertheless having an influence on agency behavior, and that influence is likely to continue.

G. ADVICE AND DECLARATORY ORDERS

The most frequent contacts between private parties and administrators involve requests for advice about agency policies, procedures, or legal interpretations. Advice-giving can be beneficial to both the regulators and the regulated. In many situations an administrative statute and the agency's rules and precedents may convey no clear indication of how the agency would deal with a particular act or practice. Thus, even when a private party has access to good legal advice, she may be unsure about her duties and liabilities. By learning the agency's current interpretation of the law and perhaps also its enforcement intentions, she can make better decisions and avoid unexpected liabilities. In addition, when agency personnel have technical expertise in a particular field, they may be able to suggest efficient ways of complying with agency standards or regulations. A staff member of an environmental agency, for example, might be in a position to share his detailed knowledge of available pollution control technologies with persons working in the affected industries. Access to legal or technical advice from administrators can be particularly important to small businesses, both because they often lack the resources to master the requirements of all of the regulatory programs they encounter, and because they would be more severely damaged if an unwitting violation led to an enforcement action.

From the agency's perspective, advice to the public can be a useful way of inducing voluntary compliance at minimal cost. Giving advice is cheaper and faster than conducting a formal proceeding, or even a major investigation. Moreover, it is usually easier to prevent violations from occurring than to remedy them after the fact. For example, the agency has a definite interest in responding to an inquiry from a private party who is contemplating a major business project, because the requesting party is more likely to acquiesce in the agency's views before she has invested resources and effort in the proposed enterprise.

Agency advisory activities take many forms. At the simplest and most common level, an agency staff person provides information over the telephone or replies to a written inquiry. In some instances, however, the transaction or the point of law involved may be sufficiently important that either the agency or the private party will want a more formal expression of policy from a higher level of the bureaucracy. One of the most formal types of advice is the declaratory order. The APA states that an agency "may issue a declaratory order to terminate a controversy or remove uncertainty," and that these orders are to have "like effect as in the case of other orders." 5 U.S.C.A. § 554(e). Although the location of this provision in the "formal adjudication" section of the APA implies that it is applicable only if the ultimate agency decision would have to be based on a trial-type hearing, in practice the courts have regularly upheld declaratory orders issued in more informal settings. However, § 554(e) also provides that the issuance of declaratory orders is within the "sound discretion" of the agencies, and apparently few of them have exercised that discretion to make declaratory orders widely available. See generally Jeffrey S. Lubbers & Blake D. Morant, *A Reexamination of Federal Agency Use of Declaratory Orders*, 56 Admin. L. Rev. 1097 (2004).

Some agencies, however, have developed elaborate informal processes for rendering advisory opinions. The Internal Revenue Service's revenue ruling procedure is a sophisticated system that issues more than twenty thousand rulings annually. The Service distinguishes between two categories of written advice: unpublished "private letter rulings," which are issued by branch offices; and published rulings, which are approved in the Commissioner's office. The former outnumber the latter by about a hundred to one. Published revenue rulings are official statements of agency policy, and the public may rely on them. However, the Service takes the position that a private letter ruling applies only to the taxpayer to whom it was addressed; other taxpayers should not rely on it, even if their situations are identical, because such rulings have not received thorough consideration at the highest levels of the agency. By statute, they are not citable as precedent. 26 U.S.C.A. § 6110(k)(3).

The IRS revenue ruling system illustrates some of the dilemmas an agency faces in trying to develop a sound advisory opinion practice. The Service's refusal to be bound by private letter rulings has been criticized for allowing inconsistent treatment of similarly situated taxpayers and for discouraging reliance on administrative precedent. However, a policy of freely authorizing staff members to give binding advice to the public would create a risk that important policy issues would be decided by low level employees without adequate analysis, investigation, or review by supervisors. On the other hand, if the Service undertook to subject more of its advisory opinions to thorough exploration of relevant policy, factual, and legal issues, including high-level review, this administrative function could become so formal as to lose most of the advantages of speed and low cost previously mentioned. The agency would become less willing to give advice, and private parties would less often be able to obtain an answer quickly enough to serve their needs. Ideally, routine inquiries in areas of settled policy should be handled at the staff level, while unresolved issues of law or policy are referred to higher levels of the agency for more formal consideration. In practice, however, it is often difficult to apply this distinction to a particular request—or even to decide who should make the initial assignment.

A related question that arises when agencies give advice to the public is whether even the requesting party can confidently rely upon the advice she receives. In other words, is the agency estopped from changing its position if the regulated party relies on advice that is later discovered to be erroneous? The Supreme Court's answer to this question has been almost totally negative. Liberal rules on equitable estoppel, the Court has warned, would transfer control over the expenditure of public funds from the elected legislature to unelected civil servants who may disagree with Congress's decisions. Ultimately, the threat of liability for bad advice could induce the government to provide less advice in the first place. OPM v. Richmond, 496 U.S. 414 (1990). See also, e.g., Schweiker v. Hansen, 450 U.S. 785 (1981) (government not estopped from denying Social Security benefits even though government agent erroneously told applicant she was not eligible and prevented her from filing a claim); Federal Crop Ins. Corp. v. Merrill, 332 U.S. 380 (1947) (government not estopped when private party relied on misstatement regarding coverage of crop insurance policy, although a private insurer would have been estopped under the same circumstances). The Court has stopped short of saying that the government can never be estopped on the basis of officials' erroneous advice, see *Richmond*, supra, but it has clearly indicated that the essential elements of an estoppel—a definite misrepresentation of fact, resulting in reasonable detrimental reliance by the complaining party—will be strictly construed when the government has given bad advice. Heckler v. Community Health Services, 467 U.S. 51 (1984) (no estoppel where government's financial intermediary erroneously told health care provider that certain expenses were reimbursable; the incorrect advice was oral, and the only harm it caused was the provider's "inability to retain money that it should never have received in the first place").

The Court's strict rules on equitable estoppel have often been denounced as harsh. Fortunately, however, agencies generally do honor reasonable reliance interests as they make enforcement decisions, even where the law does not require them to do so. Moreover, in a few circumstances courts have indeed extended legal protection to individuals who relied on government advice, although the cases did not use the language of estoppel. Thus, one classic decision held that a Swiss national had not knowingly and intentionally waived his right to apply for

American citizenship, where official advice had assured him he could claim exemption from military service without penalty. Moser v. United States, 341 U.S. 41 (1951). More recent cases have pointed to incorrect advice by government agents as a factor that supported litigants' claims that they lacked "fair warning" of a regulatory prohibition and thus could not be penalized for violating it. United States v. Pennsylvania Ind. Chem. Corp., 411 U.S. 655 (1973) (criminal prosecution); General Electric Co. v. U.S. EPA, 53 F.3d 1324 (D.C.Cir.1995) (action for civil fine).

Another question that arises when agencies give advice to the public is whether their opinions are subject to judicial review. A declaratory order issued under § 554(e) of the APA is certainly reviewable. See Weinberger v. Hynson, Westcott & Dunning, Inc., 412 U.S. 609, 627 (1973). When a party seeks judicial review of a less formal opinion, however, the question is more difficult. Agencies generally are not required by statute to give advice to the public, and courts have been sensitive to the risk that an agency might write fewer advisory opinions if its pronouncements had to be thorough and polished enough to withstand judicial review. Review can also force the agency to litigate questionable interpretations of law or policy before the administrator's position has fully crystallized, and in a forum and a factual setting not of its choosing. On the other hand, denial of review can mean that the only way a private party can have her rights and liabilities finally determined is by ignoring the agency's advice and risking civil or criminal sanctions. The ripeness doctrine furnishes an apt framework for addressing these competing concerns, although the courts' application of the doctrine is highly discretionary. See pp. 397–401 infra.

H. CONTRACTS AND GRANTS

The federal government spends vast sums of money each year on grants, benefits, and the procurement of goods and services. Grant money pays for programs in fields ranging from education to medical research, and from crime control to pollution control. State and local governments receive most of the grant payments, but universities, hospitals, and community action groups may also be beneficiaries. The federal government is also the primary, or sole, customer for a host of business enterprises. Federal expenditures are largely made through informal action. Agencies are even exempted from the notice-and-comment rulemaking obligations of the APA when they issue rules relating to government "loans, grants, benefits, or contracts," 5 U.S.C.A. § 553(a)(2), although some agencies have adopted regulations declaring that they will not invoke this exemption.

A variety of disputes can arise between the federal government and its contractors or grantees. A disappointed applicant may contend that it was wrongly declared ineligible for funding; an agency may contend that a grant recipient kept inadequate records of its expenditures, or that the goods furnished by a contractor were of insufficient quality. Some agencies have well developed procedures for resolving issues of this kind. For example, the Department of Health and Human Services has long used a Grant Appeals Board, with elaborately defined rules of practice, to hear grievances involving its grantees. See 45 C.F.R. §§ 16.1 et seq. Other agencies have no systematic procedures for resolution of grant disputes, although the Administrative Conference has recommended a set of minimum procedures in this area. See ACUS Recommendation No. 82–2, 47 Fed.Reg. 30,704 (1982).

Procedures for resolving disputes regarding public contracts have become quite elaborate in recent years, in part because of scandals involving defense procurement. Congress passed the Competition in Contracting Act of 1984, 31 U.S.C.A. §§ 3551–56, to enhance the integrity of procurement activity through a regime of "full and open competition." Disappointed bidders on a contract now have broad discovery rights with which to acquire information that they can use in protesting an award to a competitor, and they can pursue their protests in a variety of forums. The resulting system maintains a high level of protection against fraud, discrimination, and arbitrariness in public contracting. It has been argued, however, that these safeguards have exacted a heavy price. Strict controls on official discretion may also impair the quality of agencies' decisionmaking, by limiting their ability to build up informal relationships with vendors and to obtain candid information from them, as private purchasers would normally be able to do. See Steven Kelman, *Procurement and Public Management: The Fear of Discretion and the Quality of Government Performance* (1990).

I. MANAGEMENT

The government also makes or implements policy in its role as manager, especially through its administration of the public lands. Approximately a third of the nation's land area is in government ownership, and agencies such as the Forest Service, the Bureau of Land Management, and the National Park Service often have considerable discretion in determining how the resources in these federal lands will be used. Issuance of grazing and timber harvesting permits and mineral leases, operation of recreational facilities, construction of public works ranging from backcountry hiking trails to massive dams and reservoirs, and provision of firefighting and rescue services are only a few of the activities that the land management agencies undertake. See Harold H. Bruff, *Executive Power and the Public Lands*, 76 U.Colo.L.Rev. 503 (2005).

Like the grant and contract functions, management activities are exempt from the APA rulemaking procedures (5 U.S.C.A. § 553(a)(2)) and have traditionally been conducted informally. Many of the statutes governing the management of the federal lands recite broad, conflicting objectives (e.g., wilderness preservation *and* economic development), and therefore provide few checks on agency discretion. However, some environmental statutes, particularly the National Environmental Policy Act, 42 U.S.C.A. §§ 4321–61, impose certain procedural requirements and provide opportunities for public participation. Under NEPA, major actions that will significantly affect the environment must be preceded by public release of an environmental impact statement assessing the costs and benefits of the proposal and reviewing alternatives. Interested groups and individuals may submit comments on the impact statement, so that major land use policy decisions are made in a process that resembles the APA's informal rulemaking procedures. However, NEPA does not confine the agencies' substantive discretion, and it does not reach the many decisions that do not constitute "major federal actions." Kleppe v. Sierra Club, 427 U.S. 390 (1976).

CHAPTER VI

PROCEDURAL DUE PROCESS

The Constitution is the source of many of the procedural principles that administrative agencies must observe. The Fifth Amendment, applicable to the federal agencies, provides that no person shall "be deprived of life, liberty, or property, without due process of law," and the Fourteenth Amendment contains a similar limitation on state action. The concept of procedural due process implies that official action must meet minimum standards of fairness to the individual, such as the right to adequate notice and a meaningful opportunity to be heard before a decision is made. This constitutional doctrine gives federal courts a potent tool with which to oversee the decisionmaking procedures of federal agencies when the applicable statutes and regulations permit the administrator to act informally. Equally important, the doctrine gives the federal judiciary a measure of control over the decisionmaking methods of state and local agencies, which otherwise are governed almost exclusively by state law.

Broadly speaking, judicial decisions applying the due process clauses to administrative action have developed a fairly well defined analytical framework. Since the constitutional language refers to denials of "life, liberty, or property," the threshold question is whether an adverse decision will deprive a person of one of these protected interests. Very few administrative decisions pose threats to life; thus, the usual starting point is to determine whether a protected property or liberty interest exists.

If these and certain other threshold issues are surmounted, the question becomes one of determining what process is "due" under the particular circumstances. This question is often difficult to answer, however, because modern administrative law tries to take account of the enormous diversity of situations in which due process claims can be advanced. Regulatory decisions affect a wide variety of private interests, and the government's justifications for summary action also differ from one setting to the next. In addition, a particular procedural right, such as the opportunity to confront and cross-examine adverse witnesses or the right to be heard by an impartial decisionmaker, may enhance the accuracy and fairness of the process more substantially in one setting than in another. Consequently, due process rights in administrative law can vary enormously, depending on the context in which they are asserted.

A. INTERESTS PROTECTED BY DUE PROCESS

Traditionally, the interests protected by the due process clauses were defined quite narrowly. Many government benefits and grants were considered mere gratuities or "privileges" rather than rights; like a private donor, the government could impose whatever conditions it wished on its gift, or even remove the benefit at will. This view was exemplified by Justice Holmes' famous dictum, in upholding the firing of a police officer for political activities, that "[t]he petitioner may have a constitutional right to talk politics, but he has no constitutional right to be a policeman." McAuliffe v. City of New Bedford, 155 Mass. 216, 29 N.E. 517 (1892). Reflecting this attitude, courts held for many years that government employment was not an interest protected by due process and thus could be terminated without any procedural protection. See Bailey v. Richardson, 182 F.2d 46 (D.C.Cir.1950), aff'd by equally divided Court, 341 U.S. 918 (1951).

During the 1960s, however, as the size of the bureaucracy grew and public concern about government's obligations to its citizens became more acute, the soundness of the right-privilege distinction was questioned. Commentators pointed out that a wide variety of forms of social wealth, ranging from TV station licenses to truck routes to occupational licenses to welfare benefits, were the results of government largess, and thus were "privileges." As government expanded, these new forms of wealth had become increasingly vital to the individual; often, the loss of a government job, or an occupational license, or a welfare payment, could deprive a person of her livelihood. Thus, to maintain the balance between government and individual, it was necessary to extend the protections of due process to this "new property." See generally Charles A. Reich, *The New Property*, 73 Yale L.J. 733 (1964).

Accordingly, the Supreme Court started to edge away from the right-privilege distinction. In Cafeteria & Restaurant Workers Union v. McElroy, 367 U.S. 886 (1961), the Court held that a government employee who was stripped of her security clearance, and thus her ability to work at a naval base, was not entitled to a specification of charges and an opportunity to know and refute adverse evidence. Nevertheless, the Court indicated that the right-privilege distinction was "perhaps [an] oversimplification"; the Court used a more flexible line of reasoning, arguing that the government's proprietary interest in unfettered management of a military base outweighed the employee's interest in keeping her job as a short-order cook at a specific site.

The Court finally abandoned the right-privilege distinction in Goldberg v. Kelly, 397 U.S. 254, 261–63 (1970). In that case, welfare beneficiaries in New York claimed that their payments had been terminated without due process of law. The Court said that these claims could not be defeated by a mere assertion that the benefits were gratuities or privileges. (Actually, the state defendants had made no such assertion, but the Court's dictum was quickly recognized as authoritative.) The welfare program in question was based on a system of statutory entitlements: all applicants who met the conditions defined by the legislature were entitled to receive public assistance. Consequently, the state had to afford due process safeguards—in this instance, an oral hearing—before it could terminate the benefits.

With the demise of the right-privilege distinction, the Court needed to develop a new method for deciding who was entitled to due process protection. The Court unveiled such an approach in Board of Regents of State Colleges v. Roth, 408 U.S. 564 (1972). There an untenured instructor at a state university was held to have no due process right to be heard when the university refused to renew his contract. Emphasizing the language of the Fourteenth Amendment, the Court noted that the requirements of procedural due process extend only to those who have been deprived of "liberty" or "property." The Court went on to explain that the loss of a governmental benefit is a deprivation of "property" only if the individual has a "legitimate claim of entitlement" to the benefit, rather than merely a "unilateral expectation" of it. Since neither state law nor university rules nor the contract itself had given Roth a legitimate basis for claiming that he was "entitled" to a renewal of the contract, he had possessed no "property" interest in continued employment beyond his contract year. Similarly, Roth had not been deprived of "liberty" in the constitutional sense, because, so far as the record showed, he "simply [was] not rehired in one job but remain[ed] as free as before to seek another."

The *Roth* approach of examining initially whether a plaintiff has been deprived of liberty or property has retained its vitality down to the present day. Both of these two pivotal concepts, however, have been refined by subsequent case law developments.

1. PROPERTY

In many administrative settings, it is easy to show that an agency decision has deprived someone of "property." For example, coercive regulation of business enterprises, almost by definition, invades their property interests, because it limits their freedom to engage in profitable activity. Thus, the difficult cases usually involve governmental benefits. In these so-called "new property" cases, *Roth* requires the court to consider whether the plaintiff had a "legitimate claim of entitlement" to the benefit of which she was deprived. The claim of entitlement does not arise from the Constitution itself; it must rest upon "existing rules or understandings that stem from an independent source such as state law." Thus, the plaintiff must demonstrate that some authoritative source of law "establishes a definite standard to guide the decision ..., rather than confiding the decision to the discretion of the administering authorities." Gilbert v. Frazier, 931 F.2d 1581 (7th Cir.1991). For example, the welfare claimants in *Goldberg* plainly had a property interest at stake, because the underlying federal legislation provided that everyone who satisfied certain criteria had a legal right to receive welfare payments. Similarly, the Court in *Roth* indicated that the teacher in that case would have been entitled to due process protections if he had been dismissed during the term of his contract, because the contract itself had secured his interest in employment during that period.

The companion case of Perry v. Sindermann, 408 U.S. 593 (1972), indicated, however, that an employee's claim of entitlement does not have to be based upon a written contract or a statutory grant of job tenure. There, a dismissed teacher claimed that the college had a de facto tenure system: policy guidelines issued by the state education system provided that teachers who had successfully completed a probationary period, as the respondent had, could expect continued employment. The Court analogized this informal tenure system to an implied contract term, and concluded that it was sufficient to give the dismissed teacher a constitutionally protected property interest.

The Court has extended the "entitlement" concept to many other kinds of cases in which a deprivation of "property" has been alleged. For example, when the state grants all children the right to attend public schools, and establishes rules specifying the grounds for suspension, it cannot suspend a given student for alleged misconduct without affording the student at least a limited prior hearing. Goss v. Lopez, 419 U.S. 565 (1975). Similarly, a horse trainer whose license was suspended had the right to due process (a prompt postsuspension hearing) because, according to the Court, New York law entitled him to keep the license unless it were shown "that his horse had been drugged and that he was at least negligent in failing to prevent the drugging." Barry v. Barchi, 443 U.S. 55 (1979). Even a cause of action can be a constitutionally protected property right. In Logan v. Zimmerman Brush Co., 455 U.S. 422 (1982), an Illinois commission was required by statute to redress all meritorious claims of employment discrimination against the handicapped. Therefore, when the agency denied relief to the plaintiff by invoking a blatantly unfair procedural rule (under state law, the complaint had to be dismissed if the commission did not schedule a hearing within 120 days, although plaintiff had no control over the agency's scheduling), it violated his due process rights.

On the other hand, the Court held in Town of Castle Rock v. Gonzales, ___ U.S. ___, 125 S.Ct. 2796 (2005), that a statute that appeared to guarantee strict enforcement of a domestic violence restraining order did not create a property interest. Reading the statute against the nation's longstanding tradition of police discretion, and taking account of feasibility limitations, the Court concluded that the state legislature could not really have meant to bestow upon individuals a categorical personal entitlement to enforcement. The tragic facts of *Castle Rock*, involving the police's failure to prevent an estranged husband from disobeying a restraining order and then murdering his children, make the holding unsympathetic, but the ruling may have been prompted by a concern that states would be less likely to adopt statutes that call for forceful enforcement of domestic violence protections if they would thereby expose themselves to substantial tort liability in a federal civil rights action if enforcement proves unsuccessful.

Of course, when Congress and the states create public benefits, they usually create procedures by which citizens can seek to protect those benefits. It took some time for the courts to work out the relationship between those procedures and the dictates of due process. One aspect of this problem came into focus in Arnett v. Kennedy, 416 U.S. 134 (1974). Kennedy, a federal civil service employee, was fired after accusing his superior of illegal activities. He filed suit, seeking a pretermination evidentiary hearing under the due process clause. The relevant statute, the Lloyd–LaFollette Act, provided that employees in Kennedy's job category could be dismissed "only for such cause as will promote the efficiency of the service"; therefore, he had a protected property interest. But the Act also provided that this right would be protected through a written protest procedure rather than a trial-type hearing. A plurality of three Justices, led by Justice Rehnquist, concluded that the legislatively created right not to be terminated except for cause could not be considered in the abstract, apart from the procedural mechanism that Congress had designed for its implementation. Rehnquist concluded that "where the grant of a substantive right is inextricably intertwined with the limitations on the procedures which are to be employed in determining that right, a litigant in the position of [plaintiff] must take the

bitter with the sweet." The other six Justices rejected Rehnquist's theory that the procedures provided
by the Act could define civil service employees' due
process rights. (Kennedy lost his case, however,
because only three of these Justices thought that
due process required an evidentiary hearing.)

Ultimately, the Court squarely rejected the *Arnett*
plurality's "bitter with the sweet" theory. In Cleveland Bd. of Education v. Loudermill, 470 U.S. 532
(1985), the Court insisted upon due process safeguards for a discharged city security guard who,
under Ohio statutes, could only have been fired for
cause. The Court emphasized that substance and
procedure are distinct in due process analysis. Once
a state creates entitlements through substantive
laws or standards, the adequacy of procedures used
to deprive individuals of those entitlements depends
on federal constitutional law, and state procedures
cannot foreclose the due process inquiry. On the
other hand, state-created procedures cannot *expand*
federal due process rights, either. Thus, a procedural guarantee in a state statute or regulation does
not create a property interest, *Town of Castle Rock
v. Gonzales,* 125 S.Ct. at 2811–13 (Souter, J., concurring); Bishop v. Wood, 426 U.S. 341 (1976), and
the breach of such a guarantee is not a due process
violation. Board of Curators v. Horowitz, 435 U.S.
78 (1978). A claimant in this situation must rely on
whatever remedy the state has provided. A federal
agency's breach of a federal statute or regulation, of
course, can be redressed under the APA. See pp.
104–05 supra.

Notice that cases like *Goldberg* arise out of government decisions that terminate benefits payments to persons who are already receiving them. Cases involving initial applications for benefits may require a different analysis. If the state has never decided that an applicant is entitled to benefits in the first place, it can defer making payments while it makes that decision, and this deferral does not require a prior due process hearing. American Mfrs. Mutual Ins. Co. v. Sullivan, 526 U.S. 40 (1999) (involving workers' compensation medical benefits). Assuming that the statutory scheme creates an entitlement, however, the state presumably could not make a *final* decision to deny the claimant's application without affording her a fair chance to be heard.

2. LIBERTY

The conceptual unity that the Court has reached in its definition of "property" is absent from its approach to the companion concept, "liberty." The *Roth* opinion itself showed the Court's ambivalence. On the one hand, the Court said that the definition of liberty must be "broad," encompassing " 'not merely freedom from bodily restraint but also the right of the individual to contract, to engage in any of the common occupations of life, to acquire useful knowledge, to marry, establish a home and bring up children, to worship God according to the dictates of ... conscience, and generally to enjoy those privileges long recognized ... as essential to the orderly

pursuit of happiness by free men' " (quoting Meyer
v. Nebraska, 262 U.S. 390, 399 (1923)). Yet the
holding in *Roth* belied this liberal spirit; at least,
the Court did not explain why the opportunity to
keep a teaching position at a state university, or
another government job, was not comparable to the
freedoms on the *Meyer* list. Indeed, the Court
seemed to be striving to keep its options open,
declaring that an interest would not qualify as
"liberty" merely because it was important to the
individual: "we must look not to the 'weight' but to
the *nature* of the interest at stake." This unconstrained approach plainly left room for odd dispari-
ties—as the Court demonstrated a few years later,
when it held, despite *Roth,* that a ten-day suspension from high school *did* implicate a liberty interest. Goss v. Lopez, 419 U.S. 565 (1975).

Despite the *Roth* opinion's reticence, one can
perceive various factors that may have made the
Court reluctant to extend due process guarantees to
all dismissed government employees. One such concern was expressed in Bishop v. Wood, 426 U.S. 341
(1976): a less restrictive approach could involve the
federal courts in the impossible task of supervising
"the multitude of personnel decisions that are made
daily by public agencies." Many of those decisions
are made by state or local agencies, so that federal-
ism concerns are also relevant. In addition, many
public employees enjoy nonconstitutional protections against arbitrary dismissal, by virtue of the
procedures of their civil service systems. With the
spread of collective bargaining in government, un-

ions and contractual grievance procedures often provide a further source of protection against improper dismissal or suspension. Yet another layer of protection stems from First Amendment case law: For example, government employees may not be dismissed for their political beliefs or affiliations unless "the hiring authority can demonstrate that party affiliation is an appropriate requirement for the effective performance of the public office involved." Branti v. Finkel, 445 U.S. 507 (1980).

The Court did say in *Roth* that the plaintiff would have had a stronger case if the employer, in declining to rehire him, had made a charge against him that might injure his reputation. The Court has adhered to this notion that reputational harm tends to show a deprivation of liberty, but has circumscribed it in a number of ways. First, the *Roth* opinion noted that the purpose of guaranteeing a hearing to a stigmatized employee is simply "to provide the person an opportunity to clear his name"; the employer is free to grant a name-clearing hearing and then to dismiss the employee for other reasons. Later decisions added further qualifications: stigmatizing reasons for a discharge are not actionable unless the employer discloses them to the public, *Bishop v. Wood,* supra, and unless the plaintiff raises a substantial issue about the accuracy of the charge. Codd v. Velger, 429 U.S. 624 (1977).

The most heavily criticized of the Court's opinions on the role of stigma is Paul v. Davis, 424 U.S. 693 (1976). In *Paul,* two local police departments included Davis' name and picture in a flyer listing "active shoplifters," which was distributed to hundreds of merchants in his home town. Despite Davis' claim that distribution of the leaflet impaired his future job opportunities and made him reluctant to enter stores for fear of being apprehended, the Court concluded that he had not suffered any injury to a constitutionally protected liberty interest. The Court said that injury to reputation does not entail a loss of liberty when it stands alone, but only when it is accompanied by some alteration in the plaintiff's legal status, such as the loss of employment in *Roth*. Few writers have thought that this analysis made sense, or that the Court was persuasive in its efforts to demonstrate that this restrictive concept of liberty was consistent with precedent.[1] The Court seemed to be motivated by a desire to keep the federal judiciary from absorbing too much of the business of state courts, which have historically protected reputation through defamation actions. Subsequently, however, the Court has come to understand that it can incorporate the adequacy of state remedies into its due process calculus more straightforwardly. See pp. 227–29 infra. Thus, it has become less inclined to use artificial limitations on

1. For example, in Wisconsin v. Constantineau, 400 U.S. 433 (1971), the Court condemned a state's practice of "posting"—causing lists of "excessive" drinkers to be posted in all city liquor stores. The Court found that the state had violated due process by publicly branding petitioner with this "degrading" label without giving her notice and an opportunity to defend herself. In *Paul,* however, the majority explained *Constantineau* as a case in which the stigma was accompanied by a change in legal status, because stores were forbidden to sell liquor to a person who had been "posted."

the scope of constitutionally protected interests as a means of preventing overlap between the Constitution and state tort law. Nevertheless, the precise holding of *Paul* has not been abandoned. Siegert v. Gilley, 500 U.S. 226 (1991) (derogatory evaluation letter from former supervisor did not deprive plaintiff of "liberty," despite harm to his future job prospects).

Another challenge has been to define the due process interests of prisoners. Prison bureaucracies and parole boards make decisions every day that in some sense affect the "liberty" of incarcerated persons, and the Court has felt a need to prevent the federal courts from being deluged with cases challenging these decisions on due process grounds. For a time the Court sought to identify those prisoners' cases qualifying for constitutional protection by relying on a *Roth*-like concept of entitlements, although that method now seems to have fallen out of favor. Under this reasoning, mandatory prison rules created a liberty interest, but discretionary ones did not. For example, a disciplinary proceeding to revoke a prisoner's "good time" credits (and thus to increase the time he would actually serve on his sentence) had to meet constitutional requirements of due process, because the statute made accrual of good time a right, subject to forfeiture only for serious misconduct. Wolff v. McDonnell, 418 U.S. 539 (1974). In contrast, a prisoner could be transferred from one prison to another without due process safeguards, because state officials had wide discretion to order the transfer, irrespective of any misconduct. Meachum v. Fano, 427 U.S. 215 (1976).

The Court has never explained why the entitlements concept, originally designed as an elaboration of the meaning of the term "property," was an appropriate tool for defining "liberty." At any rate, the Court largely abandoned this application of *Roth* in Sandin v. Conner, 515 U.S. 472 (1995). There the Court pointed out that its practice of giving dispositive significance to the presence or absence of mandatory language in prison regulations was forcing it to get bogged down in numerous minor details of prison administration. It also gave prison officials undesirable incentives to leave their procedures uncodified in order to avoid due process obligations. Accordingly, the Court held in *Conner* that state prison regulations will not create a liberty interest unless the deprivation "imposes atypical and significant hardship on the inmate in relation to the ordinary incidents of prison life." This test defeated the due process claim of the prisoner in *Conner*. He had been punished by being placed in solitary confinement because of prison misconduct, but this sanction scarcely differed from the sort of conditions the prison regularly imposed on other inmates for nonpunitive reasons, such as protective custody. However, assignment to a harsh "supermax" prison for an indefinite period, without parole, did constitute an "atypical and significant" hardship in Wilkinson v. Austin, 545 U.S. 209 (2005).

Prisoners who cannot point to an entitlement created by law or regulation remain free to rely on the Constitution as the source of an "inherent" liberty interest, but this line of argument has had mixed success. It has prevailed in cases in which a convicted criminal who has been conditionally released is sent back to prison because of some alleged misconduct. Obviously, such reincarceration entails a major loss of personal freedom, and due process protections have been accorded. See Gagnon v. Scarpelli, 411 U.S. 778 (1973) (probation revocation); Morrissey v. Brewer, 408 U.S. 471 (1972) (parole revocation). Yet the Court declined to find that a prisoner loses an inherent liberty interest by being refused parole in the first place. Greenholtz v. Inmates of Nebraska Penal & Correctional Complex, 442 U.S. 1 (1979) (noting the "human difference between losing what one has and not getting what one wants").

In some of these cases, the Court has argued that when an individual is validly convicted of a crime and sentenced to incarceration, he loses much of the inherent right to be free from bodily restraint that other citizens enjoy.[2] Thus, the transfer of a prisoner from one prison facility to another does not necessarily implicate due process, *Meachum v. Fano*, supra, even if the transfer takes him out of

2.   Outside the corrections area, the Court has had no hesitation about finding that direct governmental intrusions on physical freedom implicate the "liberty" element of due process. See Hamdi v. Rumsfeld, 542 U.S. 507 (2004) (detention of alleged enemy combatant); Parham v. J.R., 442 U.S. 584 (1979) (commitment of minors to mental institution).

state and far away from friends and relatives. Olim v. Wakinekona, 461 U.S. 238 (1983). Such a transfer is within the ambit of his sentence—that is, it is the sort of confinement that inmates should reasonably expect. On the other hand, an inmate's transfer from prison to a mental hospital for involuntary treatment and behavior modification is "qualitatively different" from what would be expected in his sentence, and therefore involves an inherent liberty interest. Vitek v. Jones, 445 U.S. 480 (1980).

B.　OTHER THRESHOLD ISSUES

Even where a plaintiff can show a "property" or "liberty" interest that has been infringed, she may face other threshold obstacles to her pursuit of a procedural due process claim. First, an injury to a protected interest does not qualify as a "deprivation" if it was inflicted through mere negligence rather than deliberately. Daniels v. Williams, 474 U.S. 327 (1986) (deputy who negligently left pillow on stairway, where prisoner tripped on it, did not "deprive" him of liberty). The Court observed in *Daniels* that "[h]istorically, [the] guarantee of due process has been applied to *deliberate* decisions of government officials to deprive a person of life, liberty, or property," and that to extend its scope to negligent actions would "trivialize" the Constitution. However, the Court declined to decide whether any kind of unintended conduct, such as reckless or grossly negligent behavior, might qualify as a "deprivation." (Normally, of course, when an agency imposes a penalty or withholds a benefit, it knows that it is causing the individual to suffer a loss; thus, the *Daniels* requirement of deliberate rather than negligent action is not an issue in the typical administrative law case.)

Second, only a person to whom the challenged order is directed is entitled to due process; a plaintiff who may be worse off because of government action toward a third party has no constitutional injury. Thus, in O'Bannon v. Town Court Nursing Center, 447 U.S. 773 (1980), the Court held that patients at a subsidized nursing home had no right to participate in proceedings to revoke the home's Medicaid certification and terminate its subsidy. The Court assumed that some of the elderly patients could suffer physical or psychological trauma from being forced to relocate; yet it concluded that this loss was only "an indirect and incidental result of the Government's enforcement action," and thus did not implicate their due process rights. The Court's reluctance to provide constitutional protection for this indirect benefit may have reflected its concern that a different result would greatly increase the number of persons entitled to participate in decisions, and thereby disrupt the functioning of welfare or regulatory programs. The Court also relied on the "indirectness" of the government benefit in Town of Castle Rock v. Gonzales, 545 U.S. ___, 125 S.Ct. 2796 (2005), as a reason not to afford due process protection to a woman who had obtained a domestic violence restraining order against her estranged husband. This extension of

O'Bannon seems debatable, however, because in the earlier case the interests that the patients sought to advance could be asserted more directly by the nursing home itself, whereas in *Castle Rock* the husband's interests were adverse to those of the plaintiff, who was the only person who was in a position to insist on enforcement.

A final limitation, which is of vital importance in administrative law, is that procedural due process guarantees are directed primarily at adjudicative action and are rarely applicable to agency rulemaking proceedings. The Court laid the foundations for this doctrine in two early property tax assessment cases. In Londoner v. Denver, 210 U.S. 373 (1908), the city of Denver sought to assess property owners for improvements to their street. Each owner's assessment was based on the amount of benefit accruing to her particular parcel. The Court held that the city had to afford each owner an evidentiary hearing. On the other hand, in Bi–Metallic Inv. Co. v. State Bd. of Equalization, 239 U.S. 441 (1915), the Court upheld an agency regulation increasing the valuation of all taxable property in Denver by 40 percent, even though the board had given no notice or hearing whatever to the affected property owners. "Where a rule of conduct applies to more than a few people," Justice Holmes wrote, "it is impracticable that every one should have a direct voice in its adoption." The *Bi–Metallic* doctrine—limiting due process rights in rulemaking—has been repeatedly reaffirmed in modern decisions. See, e.g., United States v. Florida East Coast Ry., 410 U.S.

224 (1973) (evidentiary hearing unnecessary in ICC proceeding to set uniform nationwide rail charges).

The *Bi–Metallic* principle has been explained on various grounds. One argument stresses the functional similarity between rulemaking and legislation. Since members of the public have no constitutional right to testify or submit evidence to Congress before a statute affecting them can be enacted, the argument runs, they also have no fundamental right to appear before agency officials who are exercising delegated legislative power. A second argument notes the impossibility of granting a hearing to everyone when a regulation applies to numerous individuals. Government "would likely grind to a halt were policymaking constrained by constitutional requirements on whose voices must be heard." Minnesota State Bd. for Community Colleges v. Knight, 465 U.S. 271 (1984). A third rationale is that rulemaking characteristically turns on "legislative facts" as opposed to "adjudicative facts." The terminology is that of Professor Davis, who famously defined adjudicative facts as those having to do with the parties to a dispute, while legislative facts are general propositions that a tribunal uses in formulating law or policy. 2 Kenneth Culp Davis, Administrative Law Treatise § 12:3 (2d ed.1979). Under this theory, the parties to an adjudication should be allowed broad participation rights, because they are normally in the best position to produce information about themselves and their activities. In contrast, the critical facts in a rulemaking proceeding are unlikely to be any more accessible to one member of the affected class than to another, and it would be wasteful to guarantee each member of the class a right to an individualized hearing.

The *Bi–Metallic* doctrine is certainly authoritative in situations that can be unambiguously characterized as rulemaking. However, it is less clear that the case applies with full force to proceedings that fall into the gray area between rulemaking and adjudication (see pp. 310–12 infra). The *Bi–Metallic* rationales tend to lose force as the number of persons affected by the rule shrinks. For example, when an agency proposes a regulation that would govern an industry in which there are only a few firms, granting a trial-type hearing to all of them might well be feasible. Moreover, the categories of adjudicative and legislative facts tend to merge in cases of this sort, because information about the companies that are to be regulated would probably be crucial to any decision about whether the proposed rule is sound policy. The Court has left the door open to due process protection in such cases. See Vermont Yankee Nuclear Power Corp. v. NRDC, 435 U.S. 519, 542 (1978). For the most part, however, the tradition represented by *Bi–Metallic* remains strong; courts that have insisted that the public be given some right to be heard in rulemaking proceedings have tended to avoid resting their holdings squarely on the due process clause. See pp. 328–35 infra.

C. THE PROCESS THAT IS DUE

Once it has been determined that a constitutionally protected liberty or property interest was infringed, the next stage of the due process analysis is to decide what procedures the Constitution requires. Much of the Supreme Court's case law on this topic can be understood as elaborating upon— or, more often, reacting against—the Court's expansive ruling in Goldberg v. Kelly, 397 U.S. 254 (1970). There the Court held that welfare recipients in New York had to be afforded an evidentiary hearing before they could be terminated from the program. At the hearing, they would be entitled to many of the procedural safeguards that had historically been available in court proceedings, such as the right to present a case orally, to confront adverse witnesses, to appear through an attorney, and to receive a decision based exclusively on the hearing record.

The *Goldberg* opinion gave rise to concern that the Court might soon impose trial-type procedures in many other programs, including ones in which courtroom methods would be ineffective or too expensive. In Mathews v. Eldridge, 424 U.S. 319 (1976), however, the Court demonstrated that it was determined to maintain flexibility in due process analysis. The Court declared that it would look at three factors in order to decide what due process requires in a given situation: "First, the private interest that will be affected by the official action;

second, the risk of an erroneous deprivation of such interest through the procedures used, and the probable value, if any, of additional or substitute safeguards; and finally, the Government's interest, including the function involved and the fiscal and administrative burdens that the additional or substitute procedural requirement would entail." Applying this balancing test, the Court held that an order terminating a person's Social Security disability benefits need not be preceded by an evidentiary hearing.

The *Mathews* test has been criticized as being so open-ended as to give courts little guidance: judges are put into the position of making policy choices much as a legislator would do. On the other hand, the test has also been criticized as too restrictive: it implies that procedures are to be evaluated solely on the basis of whether they promote or detract from accuracy, without regard to whether the process will likely be perceived as fair. But the Court has continued to invoke the three-factor test in a wide variety of factual settings. See, e.g., Hamdi v Rumsfeld, 542 U.S. 507 (2004) (applying *Mathews* to determine hearing rights of persons detained as suspected enemy combatants). Indeed, although at first the Court used the test primarily in "new property" cases, where government benefits were at issue, the Court has also applied the *Mathews* analysis in a more tradition-bound area of administrative law—coercive regulation of business. Brock v. Roadway Express, Inc., 481 U.S. 252 (1987) (using *Mathews* test to decide rights of employer who was ordered by government to reinstate an employee while the latter's allegations of retaliatory discharge were pending).

In applying the *Mathews* formula, a court is not limited to an either-or choice between a full trial-type hearing and the informal procedures the agency is already using. Rather, each procedural right must be analyzed separately, and alternatives or intermediate procedural models must be considered. For purposes of explanation, the procedural rights that have been examined most frequently in due process litigation can be grouped into several broad categories.

1. PRIOR NOTICE AND HEARING

"An elementary and fundamental requirement of due process in any proceeding which is to be accorded finality is notice reasonably calculated, under all the circumstances, to apprise interested parties of the pendency of the action and afford them an opportunity to present their objections." Mullane v. Central Hanover Bank & Trust Co., 339 U.S. 306, 314 (1950). Without proper prior notice to those who may be affected by a government decision, all other procedural rights may be nullified. The exact contents of the notice required by due process will, of course, vary with the circumstances. The *Goldberg* decision stated that welfare beneficiaries were entitled to a notice "detailing the reasons for the proposed termination." In another case, a municipal utility's notice threatening a customer with termination of service was held inadequate because it did not spell out the procedural avenues by which she could protest the proposed termination. Memphis Light, Gas & Water Div. v. Craft, 436 U.S. 1 (1978). On the other hand, the Court sustained the action of Massachusetts officials who sent a form letter to food stamp recipients advising them of a statutory change that could reduce or eliminate their benefits. Atkins v. Parker, 472 U.S. 115 (1985). Even though the notice did not inform recipients of their new benefit levels, it did give them a general awareness of the new law, so that they could make further inquiry and challenge the computations in their respective cases if they wished.

Although prior notice of threatened adverse action is generally required, there are some exceptions to this principle. Most involve a demonstrated need for immediate action to protect the public from serious harm. Thus, prehearing seizures of potentially dangerous or mislabeled consumer products have been upheld. Ewing v. Mytinger & Casselberry, Inc., 339 U.S. 594 (1950); North American Cold Storage Co. v. Chicago, 211 U.S. 306 (1908). Serious financial risks to the public or to the government's revenues may also justify summary action. See, e.g., FDIC v. Mallen, 486 U.S. 230 (1988) (upholding statute providing for summary suspension of bank officer who has been indicted for a felony involving dishonesty); Phillips v. Commissioner, 283 U.S. 589 (1931) (summary seizure of taxpayer's property to assure payment of taxes upheld against due process challenge). Even a threat to the integrity of state-sanctioned wagering on horse races has been held sufficient to justify summary suspension of the license of a trainer suspected of drugging horses. Barry v. Barchi, 443 U.S. 55 (1979). In *Barchi,* the Court added an important qualification: due process required a prompt postsuspension hearing, so that the horse trainer would have a reasonable opportunity to clear his name and the deprivation would not be unnecessarily prolonged. However, the state in that case had not attempted to justify its failure to grant a prompt hearing; and in subsequent cases, where government interests have been more clearly articulated, the Court has been reluctant to extend the *Barchi* caveat. For example, in *Mallen,* the Court held that a ninety-day wait between the bank officer's request for a hearing and the final decision would not necessarily violate due process, because of the public's strong interest in having the agency reach a well-considered decision about whether to reinstate him. Thus, the question of how quickly an agency must proceed with adjudication following a summary action depends on a careful weighing of competing interests. See City of Los Angeles v. David, 538 U.S. 715 (2003) (upholding, under balancing test, a 27–day wait before plaintiff could be heard on his claim for a refund of the state's fee for towing his illegally parked automobile). Even a nine-months' wait for adjudication to run its course is not necessarily too lengthy. Cleveland Bd. of Education v. Loudermill, 470 U.S. 532 (1985) (no unconstitutional delay in decision on whether to reinstate suspended public employee).

Another consideration that can militate against the right to predeprivation notice and hearing is the principle that "[p]laintiffs who assert a right to a hearing under the Due Process Clause must show that the facts they seek to establish in that hearing are relevant to the statutory scheme." Connecticut Bd. of Public Safety v. Doe, 538 U.S. 1 (2003). Because of this principle, the plaintiff in *Doe*, whom the state had listed on a public website as a convicted sex offender, had no procedural due process right to a hearing to establish that he was not currently dangerous. Under the applicable statute, the mere fact of the plaintiff's prior conviction was enough to subject him to being included on the registry, regardless of whether or not he actually was dangerous.

Still another limitation, in some cases, is the availability of statutory or common law remedies that can compensate the individual for her loss of liberty or property. Under the right circumstances, courts will hold that such a remedy itself provides the "process that is due." For example, in Ingraham v. Wright, 430 U.S. 651 (1977), the Court upheld a state statute and local school board regulations which authorized teachers to paddle students for misconduct, even though the students had no right to notice or a hearing before the punishment was inflicted. Under state law an injured student could bring a damage action if the teacher used excessive force, and this was considered adequate protection to satisfy the requirements of due process. Similarly, in Parratt v. Taylor, 451 U.S. 527

(1981), a prisoner claimed that state prison officials had negligently lost a hobby kit (worth $23.50) that had been mailed to him. The Court held that this "deprivation of property" had occurred *with* due process, because the state had made available a small-claims procedure by which he could seek compensation for his loss. The Court extended the *Parratt* holding to deliberate deprivations of property in Hudson v. Palmer, 468 U.S. 517 (1984). The plaintiff in *Hudson* was a prisoner whose personal effects had been intentionally destroyed by a prison guard. Again the Court found no due process violation, because the prisoner could have sought redress through a tort action.[3] More recently, the Court held that a state did not need to hold a due process hearing before it withheld payments to a subcontractor on a public works project during a labor dispute. The subcontractor's interests could be fully protected through an ordinary lawsuit for breach of contract. Lujan v. G & G Fire Sprinklers, Inc., 532 U.S. 189 (2001).

However, the principle that damage remedies can provide the "process that is due" has been largely confined to situations in which the state has strong reasons not to grant a predeprivation hearing. In *Ingraham,* the Court was concerned that a requirement of a prior hearing would deter teachers from paddling students and undermine their disciplinary

3. *Parratt* has since been overruled insofar as it assumed that due process constraints apply to deprivations that are merely negligent. See pp. 217–18 supra. However, this development does not impair the authority of *Hudson,* in which the deprivation was deliberate.

authority. In *Parratt* and *Hudson,* the Court saw no way in which the prison could have improved its procedures for preventing mistakes or unauthorized misconduct by its personnel; therefore, a compensation system was as good a solution as the state could provide. In contrast, where predeprivation process would be practicable, the Court has often insisted on it. For example, the municipal utility in *Memphis Light* could easily have given its customer an explanation of its protest procedure before shutting off her service. Accordingly, the Court found that the customer's due process rights had been violated, even though she theoretically could have retained an attorney and sued for an injunction or refund. The Court noted that it was unrealistic to expect a consumer to engage counsel in a case involving such small monetary stakes. Similarly, in Zinermon v. Burch, 494 U.S. 113 (1990), a mental patient sued hospital officials for institutionalizing him through "voluntary" commitment procedures at a time when he was incompetent to give valid consent. Despite the availability of state damage remedies, the Court allowed the plaintiff's due process challenge to proceed, because the state could practicably have devised additional safeguards to reduce the risk of erroneous commitment. See also Logan v. Zimmerman Brush Co., 455 U.S. 422 (1982) (state's use of unfair procedural rule to extinguish plaintiff's employment discrimination claim violated due process, although tort remedy was also available).

2. TRIAL–TYPE HEARINGS

Often a litigant claiming a denial of due process will ask the court to hold that the agency must afford her procedural rights similar to those used in judicial trials or formal administrative trial-type hearings—including the rights to present testimony orally and to confront and cross-examine adverse witnesses. In *Goldberg,* the Court held that welfare recipients facing termination of their benefits were entitled to nearly all of these rights. In subsequent cases, however, the Court has made clear that trial procedures are not essential for every government decision that might affect an individual. The suspended students in Goss v. Lopez, 419 U.S. 565 (1975), for example, were entitled only to an oral statement of the charges against them, and a chance to tell their side of the story. The discharged public employee in Cleveland Bd. of Education v. Loudermill, 470 U.S. 532 (1985), received a slightly more elaborate version of this informal oral hearing: he was entitled to "oral or written notice of the charges against him, an explanation of the employer's evidence, and an opportunity to present his side of the story." The employer subjected to a temporary reinstatement order in Brock v. Roadway Express, Inc., 481 U.S. 252 (1987), received similar rights, including the right to support its case with a written response and witness affidavits. As these examples make clear, the Supreme Court is reluctant to impose the full panoply of trial-type procedures when there is a reasonable likelihood that less burdensome oral proceedings will adequately protect the individual's interest.

In deciding what safeguards are required in a particular situation, courts are heavily influenced by the nature of the questions that are likely to arise. In *Goldberg,* the Court considered oral testimony and cross-examination essential in a welfare termination case, because "written submissions are a wholly unsatisfactory basis for decision" in proceedings where "credibility and veracity are at issue." On the other hand, an oral hearing may not be necessary when the usual questions to be resolved are relatively straightforward or objective. The Court relied on this proposition in *Mathews* as one basis for holding that the Social Security Administration complied with due process when it used written submissions as the basis for terminating an individual's disability benefits, with an evidentiary hearing available only after the cutoff.[4] The Court reasoned that the decision in such a proceeding was likely to turn on medical reports written by doctors, or on statistical evidence such as data concerning the availability of jobs in the national economy. These issues could be effectively aired through an exchange of documents. The *Mathews* opinion also noted that the opportunity to

4. The first factor in the *Mathews* calculus—the private interests at stake—also served to distinguish that case from *Goldberg.* The earlier case had observed that welfare claimants would be deprived of "the very means with which to live" if they were erroneously terminated. In contrast, *Mathews* pointed out that disability benefits recipients were not necessarily poor, and that those who were could fall back on other public assistance programs such as welfare and food stamps.

file written submissions had been characterized in *Goldberg* as an "unrealistic option" for most AFDC recipients, because they "lack the educational attainment to write effectively" and often "cannot obtain professional assistance." In *Mathews,* on the other hand, disability claimants could obtain assistance in completing the necessary forms from the local Social Security office, and most of the important medical evidence was provided directly by treating physicians, who presumably were competent to communicate clearly in written reports.[5]

Another line of cases deals with decisions that are regarded as so intrinsically nonlegal that trial processes would be incongruous. For example, the Court held that a medical school did not need to conduct a formal hearing before dismissing a student from school on account of her inadequate clinical ability. Board of Curators v. Horowitz, 435 U.S. 78 (1978). The decision involved essentially academic judgments and was thus unsuited to courtroom methods. The Court in *Horowitz* also suggested that relationships between faculty and students would suffer if decisionmaking on academic matters were to become too adversarial. Similarly, the Court declined to require trial-type hearings to test the wisdom of a parental decision to

5. Cf. Gray Panthers v. Schweiker, 652 F.2d 146 (D.C.Cir. 1980), appeal after remand, 716 F.2d 23 (D.C.Cir.1983) (to ensure personal attention as well as reliable decisions on credibility issues, HHS must provide some opportunity for oral contact with decisionmakers when it rules on Medicare claims for less than $100; but the contacts may be by toll-free telephone calls instead of face-to-face meetings).

place a child in a state mental hospital. Parham v. J.R., 442 U.S. 584 (1979). The Court thought that review by an independent medical professional would be sufficient, if not more reliable. In addition, a formal hearing might exacerbate tensions between parent and child. (However, in a closely related situation not involving potential danger to family relationships, the Court insisted on a formal hearing, with cross-examination rights afforded. Vitek v. Jones, 445 U.S. 480 (1980) (involuntary commitment of a prisoner to a mental institution).)

Even in administrative settings in which it is clear that trial-type hearings are generally available, such as those subject to the APA's formal adjudication procedures, agencies can decline to conduct a hearing on certain issues without violating due process. In some circumstances, for example, an agency may promulgate a legislative rule, and then refuse during subsequent adjudications to hold a hearing on issues that it has already decided in the rulemaking proceeding; or it may place a burden of going forward on private parties, and enter summary judgment against those who do not satisfy that burden. See pp. 294–300 infra. In addition, the doctrine of official notice allows agencies to rely on certain factual assumptions that have not been tested through the adversary process. See pp. 300–05 infra.

A broader position, long urged by Professor Davis, is that due process generally does not require a trial on issues of "legislative fact" arising during an adjudication. 2 Kenneth Culp Davis, Administrative Law Treatise § 12.5 (2d ed.1979). "Legislative" facts are general facts bearing upon issues of law or policy; they are contrasted with "adjudicative facts," which are facts about the specific parties to the case. The extent to which the Davis theory may be an overstatement has never been definitively resolved in the case law. The significance of this controversy has waned in recent years, however, as agencies have increasingly resolved legislative fact controversies through the rulemaking process, where the curtailment of due process rights is more firmly established. See pp. 219–21 supra.

3. RIGHT TO COUNSEL

Section 555(b) of the APA provides that "[a] person compelled to appear in person before an agency or representative thereof is entitled to be accompanied, represented, and advised by counsel." This guarantee, however, applies only to those compelled to appear, not those who appear voluntarily. Moreover, the APA does not apply to state and local bureaucracies, nor to federal agencies that are exempted by statute from APA coverage; and it says nothing about the person who is effectively denied representation because she cannot afford to retain a lawyer. Thus, there are a number of administrative settings in which an asserted due process right to appear through counsel could potentially become an issue.

The Supreme Court recognized such a right in *Goldberg,* holding that welfare beneficiaries facing termination of benefits must be allowed to retain counsel if they wish. Yet it is clear that due process does not guarantee a right to legal representation in every administrative proceeding. In Walters v. National Ass'n of Radiation Survivors, 473 U.S. 305 (1985), the Court rejected a due process challenge to a federal statute which limited the fees payable to lawyers representing veterans' benefit claimants to a maximum of $10. Despite the fact that this fee limit virtually precluded claimants from retaining private attorneys, the Court found no basis for overturning the presumption of constitutionality that should be accorded to a federal statute. Congress's paternalistic objectives of keeping the process nonadversarial and informal and keeping the veteran from having to share his award with an attorney were found to be valid and important government interests that would be frustrated if attorneys routinely became involved. Moreover, it was not clear that lawyers' participation would materially increase the accuracy of decisionmaking: the key issues were medical rather than legal, and the claimants could obtain representation from lay service representatives whose success rates were high. Given these protections and the existence of a regulation requiring the agency to resolve all doubts in favor of the claimant, the Court concluded that no constitutional right to legal representation was necessary.

Practically speaking, the *Walters* ruling may not be very important. The fee limitation in veterans' cases was relaxed in 1988, and there are few if any

other administrative schemes in which Congress
has expressly taken a position against attorney involvement. Indeed, most state and federal agencies
routinely allow any party to be represented by
counsel, although statutes occasionally authorize
them to review attorney fees for reasonableness.
See U.S. Dep't of Labor v. Triplett, 494 U.S. 715
(1990) (rejecting due process attack on such a statute for want of proof that representation was impaired).

Appointment of counsel for those who cannot
afford to retain their own is a different story. Although such appointments are common in criminal
proceedings, they are rare in administrative law.
Indeed, the Supreme Court has yet to identify even
one administrative setting in which indigent parties
must routinely be provided with attorneys. In Gagnon v. Scarpelli, 411 U.S. 778 (1973), the Court
gave several reasons for rejecting such a right in the
context of parole and probation revocation hearings.
Providing counsel in all cases would not only be
expensive, but would also make the parole board's
role "more akin to that of a judge at a trial, and less
attuned to the rehabilitative needs of the individual
probationer or parolee." Indeed, the presence of
counsel and the resulting increase in procedural
formality might make the agency "less tolerant of
marginal deviant behavior." Thus, although the
Court could see a need for appointed counsel in
some cases, it held that these determinations "must
be made on a case-by-case basis in the exercise of a
sound discretion by the state authority," taking

into account factors such as the complexity of the case and the individual's ability to speak for himself.

At times, the concerns mentioned in *Gagnon* have led the Court to mandate "assistance" for inmates who need it, while leaving the state free to designate a nonlawyer to serve that function. For example, at a hearing to determine whether to transfer a prisoner to a mental institution, the prisoner has a due process right to qualified and independent assistance, but the advisor may be a mental health professional or a competent lay person rather than an attorney. Vitek v. Jones, 445 U.S. 480 (1980). See also Wolff v. McDonnell, 418 U.S. 539 (1974) (in prison disciplinary proceedings, inmates have no constitutional right to retained or appointed counsel, but should be provided with assistance in certain cases).

4. AN IMPARTIAL DECISIONMAKER

"[O]f course, an impartial decision maker is essential" to an adjudication that comports with due process. Goldberg v. Kelly, supra. There are several kinds of disqualifying bias. For example, an agency official should be disqualified from sitting in an adjudicatory proceeding if his service as an advocate at an earlier stage of the controversy, or his overt comments, suggest that he may have prejudged facts that will be at issue in the case. See pp. 286–91 infra. But even in the absence of direct evidence about a particular officeholder's experiences or views, courts will sometimes discern an unacceptable risk of bias when an adjudicator has strong incentives to decide the case on grounds other than the merits.

For example, one well established ground for disqualification is the administrator's personal financial stake in the outcome. Thus, in Tumey v. Ohio, 273 U.S. 510 (1927), the Court held that a mayor who received a share of the fines levied on persons convicted in the town court could not constitutionally preside over their trials. The same conclusion has been reached when financial benefit accrues to some agency or unit of government and the person making the decision is closely identified with the operation of that agency. See, e.g., Ward v. Village of Monroeville, 409 U.S. 57 (1972) (violation of due process when fines levied in traffic court by the mayor increased village revenues). However, a prosecutorial agency that keeps a portion of the fines collected in the cases it brings is not necessarily disqualified, if those cases will be adjudicated by independent officers who have no stake in the outcome. Marshall v. Jerrico, Inc., 446 U.S. 238 (1980). Nor is it a violation of due process for private insurance carriers to participate (under contract with the government) in making determinations of Medicare benefits, because the carriers pay benefits from federal funds, not their own pockets. Schweiker v. McClure, 456 U.S. 188 (1982).

Another type of indirect financial stake which may require disqualification of the decisionmaker arises when the administrator is affiliated with a business and has the power to eliminate or restrict competition through his official acts. This situation frequently arises in state occupational licensing systems, where the licensing boards are customarily made up of individuals who practice in the regulated industry. In Gibson v. Berryhill, 411 U.S. 564 (1973), a state board composed solely of optometrists who were in practice for themselves had brought a disciplinary action against optometrists who were in practice as employees of a corporation, charging that the corporate business connection was an unethical practice. The Court held that the board members' possible pecuniary interest in excluding competitors was sufficient to render the impartiality of the board constitutionally suspect. In Friedman v. Rogers, 440 U.S. 1 (1979), however, a similar claim was rejected, because no disciplinary proceeding had been brought against the complaining party. The *Friedman* holding is difficult to explain, but it may rest on a belief that states would be unable to find knowledgeable regulators for the professions if they could not look to practitioners in the relevant occupational groups. Thus, the Court is willing to accept some risk of occupational bias in the day-to-day administration of a licensing scheme. At the same time, the Court finds this risk intolerable in a case like *Gibson,* where an individual stands accused of wrongdoing—perhaps because the private interest in procedural fairness is at its zenith in accusatory proceedings.

In many agencies which adjudicate violations of regulatory statutes and regulations, the agency heads who will make the final decision also make the preliminary determination to initiate the proceeding by voting to issue a complaint. In doing so, they may examine evidence gathered by the staff for the purpose of determining whether they have "reason to believe" a violation has occurred. This practice has long been considered constitutional. See, e.g., FTC v. Cement Inst., 333 U.S. 683 (1948). Due process does not require a strict "separation of functions" between prosecuting and decisionmaking officials, and "mere exposure to evidence presented in nonadversary investigative procedures is insufficient in itself" to overcome the presumption that the official will decide impartially. Withrow v. Larkin, 421 U.S. 35 (1975) (permitting members of state board of medical examiners to exercise multiple functions). However, this due process doctrine has its critics. See pp. 280–85 infra.

5.   FINDINGS AND CONCLUSIONS

Administrative law sets great store by reasoned findings accompanying agency decisions, and this attitude is reflected in due process doctrine. In a formal adjudication governed by the APA, the agency's decision must include a statement of "findings and conclusions, and the reasons or basis therefor, on all the material issues of fact, law, or discretion presented on the record." 5 U.S.C.A. § 557(c)(A). Even when the agency is engaged in informal rulemaking under the APA, it is required to "incorporate in the rules adopted a concise general state-

ment of their basis and purpose." 5 U.S.C.A.
§ 553(c). A statement of reasons may be important
not only to the perceived fairness of the process, but
also to the quality of the decision. The need to
prepare a written explanation may impose some
discipline on the agency, by pressuring decisionmakers to consider the evidence more carefully and
to examine the legal and policy justification for the
action more closely. When the grounds for the decision are committed to writing, it is easier for a
higher level administrator to review it, and thereby
provide a check on the discretion of the lower-level
officials. Finally, a reasonably detailed statement of
reasons makes it possible for a reviewing court to
examine the actual basis of the agency's decision,
rather than rationalizations it has produced after
the fact. See pp. 107–11 supra.

The Supreme Court acknowledged the importance of an agency statement of reasons in
Goldberg, holding that due process required the
welfare agency to give some explanation of its action to affected individuals. The Court added, however, that the statement "need not amount to a full
opinion or even formal findings of fact and conclusions of law." Comparable requirements that the
administrators inform the accused of the information and evidence relied upon have been imposed in
prison disciplinary hearings, Wolff v. McDonnell,
supra, and parole revocation proceedings, Morrissey
v. Brewer, 408 U.S. 471 (1972). But no written
statement of reasons is required when the prescribed due process hearing is extremely informal,

as in the presuspension discussion between an accused student and his teacher, Goss v. Lopez, supra, or when the substantive decision has been left to the "unfettered discretion" of the agency: "A state cannot be required to explain its reasons for a decision when it is not required to act on prescribed grounds." Connecticut Board of Pardons v. Dumschat, 452 U.S. 458 (1981) (denial of petition for commutation of sentence).

Related to the reasons requirement is the notion that a constitutionally adequate decision must be supported by some minimum quantity of evidence. For example, in Superintendent, Mass. Correctional Inst. v. Hill, 472 U.S. 445 (1985), the Court ruled that it would violate due process to revoke an inmate's good time credits without any evidentiary support in the record. However, the opinion emphasized that only a very limited fact review was required. Instead of examining the whole record (as it would do in reviewing an adjudicative decision under the Administrative Procedure Act), the reviewing court was merely to see whether there was "any evidence in the record that could support the conclusion reached."

D.   THE FUTURE OF THE "DUE PROCESS REVOLUTION"

No doubt the Supreme Court's due process decisions have their share of seeming inconsistencies. It is hard to understand, for example, why the right to prior notice and hearing applies to some relatively minimal injuries, such as a ten-day suspension from high school *Goss* but not to such relatively serious deprivations as a severe beating by one's teacher *Ingraham* or the decertification of one's nursing home *O'Bannon*. Nevertheless, the overall trend is clear: after the initial expansion of procedural rights ushered in by *Goldberg* the Court has become markedly more reluctant to find that agency action has infringed a constitutionally protected interest, and also more skeptical about the value of trial-type procedures.

As the Court has struggled with a growing workload of procedural due process cases, it has attracted criticism for both the methods and the goals of its analyses. The utilitarian interest-balancing of the *Goldberg* and *Mathews* decisions, which remains the dominant approach to due process today, has the advantage of being flexible in application and functional in approach. It asks important questions about what improvements in accuracy and fairness will result from the use of particular procedural devices, and how much it will cost the agency and the public to provide the requested rights. However, the Court's due process analysis has some significant shortcomings as well. By looking to positive law—primarily statutes and administrative regulations—as the principal source of the entitlements protected by due process, the Court's approach not only makes it easy for legislators and administrators to deprive claimants of procedural protections, but also creates a positive incentive for them to do so. By keeping their decisionmaking standards vague and discretionary, administrators can avoid the due process obligation to use minimally fair procedures—and also minimize their accountability.

Moreover, even when the claimant can establish a substantive entitlement, the interest-balancing analysis makes it possible—and perhaps too easy—for government to override the individual's interests. Unless the utilitarian calculus is applied with appropriate sensitivity to the worth and dignity of the individual, government's efficiency claims can become a cloak for petty oppression and harassment.

Perhaps the most fundamental argument against the interest-balancing analysis, however, is that the courts may lack the competence and the data to make it work properly. Thorough information about the real-world effects of a given procedure and the implications of eliminating it is not available in most litigation records—indeed, much of it may not be available anywhere—and if it were, it is not clear that generalist judges would be able to interpret it properly. As a result, the procedural cost-benefit calculus often becomes an exercise in poorly informed guesswork.

Because the Supreme Court speaks with finality in matters of constitutional interpretation, the codes of administrative procedure that it promulgates when it holds that an agency has violated due process are highly resistant to change. Premature constitutionalization of the administrative process can cut short promising improvements and forestall experimentation. Moreover, it is not clear that court-imposed procedures improve the quality of justice dispensed by the agencies, even in the short run. Studies have found, for example, that the procedural rights won in *Goldberg* were a rather hollow victory for the welfare recipients, because the vast majority of claimants are not able to make effective use of the trial-type hearing opportunities. Until we have developed a much fuller understanding of the practical operations of informal administrative decisionmaking, it may be wise to focus attention on statutory, administrative, and managerial attempts to improve the basic fairness of informal adjudications, while reserving the due process clause for truly severe deprivations of individual rights.

CHAPTER VII

FORMAL ADJUDICATIONS

The procedures used by administrative agencies to adjudicate individual claims or cases are extremely diverse. Hearing procedures are shaped by the subject matter of the controversy, the agency's traditions and policies, the applicable statutes and regulations, and the requirements imposed by reviewing courts. Thus, any general description of administrative adjudications must be subject to numerous exceptions and qualifications.

Within the federal system, sections 554, 556, and 557 of the APA establish some minimum procedures for administrative adjudications. Proceedings held according to this set of standards are generally known as "formal adjudications." Formal adjudications are also called "evidentiary hearings," "full hearings," "on-the-record hearings," or "trial-type hearings." The last of these terms is probably the most accurate and descriptive. Typically, such cases involve proceedings conducted by an administrative law judge (ALJ) in a manner that resembles the trial phase of civil litigation, followed by an appeal to the agency head or another reviewing authority. At the same time, as will be seen below, there are also significant differences between agency trial-type hearings and court trials.

However, it is important to remember that the APA's procedural requirements apply to only a small proportion of agency adjudications—only those which are "required by statute to be determined on the record after opportunity for an agency hearing." 5 U.S.C.A. § 554(a). (See accompanying chart.)[1] This means that the APA's adjudication procedures are implicated only when some statute *outside the APA itself*—usually the agency's authorizing statute—directs the agency to hold an evidentiary hearing and decide the case on the basis of the record that results from that hearing.[2] Often, regulatory legislation is unclear as to whether it means to call for APA adjudication. In that situation, early cases sometimes presumed that any statute that prescribes a "hearing" prior to issuance of an adjudicative order is intended to trigger the APA formal adjudication procedures. Seacoast Anti–Pollution

1. Section 554(a) of the APA contains a number of specific exemptions to the Act's formal hearing requirements. Trial-type hearings are not required, for example, in "proceedings in which decisions rest solely on inspections, tests, or elections," or in "the conduct of military or foreign affairs functions." 5 U.S.C.A. §§ 554(a)(3), (4).

2. In addition, by virtue of a judicially devised gloss on § 554(a), the APA adjudication procedures come into play when an evidentiary hearing is required by the Constitution rather than by a statute. Wong Yang Sung v. McGrath, 339 U.S. 33 (1950). The consequence of this holding in *Wong Yang Sung* was that officers who presided over deportation hearings could not also be involved in the investigation of deportation cases. However, Congress soon amended the Immigration and Nationality Act to exempt immigration officers from this separation-of-functions requirement. 8 U.S.C.A. § 1252(b); see Marcello v. Bonds, 349 U.S. 302 (1955) (upholding statute).

League v. Costle, 572 F.2d 872 (1st Cir.1978); Marathon Oil Co. v. EPA, 564 F.2d 1253 (9th Cir.1977). Increasingly, however, this presumption has been rejected, because it is at odds with the usual policy of deferring to agencies' interpretations of their own enabling legislation. Dominion Energy Brayton Point, LLC v. Johnson, 443 F.3d 12 (1st Cir.2006) (overruling *Seacoast*); Chemical Waste Mgmt., Inc. v. U.S. EPA, 873 F.2d 1477 (D.C.Cir.1989).

An Overview of the APA Procedural Models

	Adjudication	Rulemaking
Informal	—	§ 553 [notice and comment]
Formal	**Triggered by § 554(a):**	**Triggered by § 553(c):**
	§ 554 [notice to parties, separation of functions]	
	§ 556 [trial-type hearing with ALJ, exclusive record]	§ 556 [trial-type hearing with ALJ, exclusive record]
	§ 557 [formal findings, ban on ex parte contacts]	§ 557 [formal findings, ban on ex parte contacts]

Agency adjudications that are conducted outside the APA framework are commonly called "informal." They may be governed by special statutory procedures or the agency's own regulations, and of course must always comply with the requirements of procedural due process. See Chapters 5 and 6 supra. Within those boundaries, however, the procedures used in informal agency adjudication are essentially discretionary and not subject to second-guessing by a court. See Pension Benefit Guaranty Corp. v. LTV Corp., 496 U.S. 633 (1990), discussed at pp. 168–69 supra. While their procedures tend to be similar to those followed in formal adjudications, they generally are conducted by presiding officers or "administrative judges" (i.e., not independent ALJs).

Although still important as a procedural standard, the relative significance of formal adjudication in administrative law has declined in recent decades. At one time, agencies usually made their most important policy decisions in formally adjudicated cases. Today, they tend to use rulemaking for this purpose instead. Furthermore, an increasing number of agencies have obtained statutory authority to decide individual cases through informal adjudication systems that resemble but do not fully conform to the APA model. Despite these trends, however, formal adjudication remains the preeminent model by which agencies make their most momentous decisions on an individualized level. It also provides a benchmark by which simpler adjudication systems are often evaluated. It thus merits detailed attention here.

A. PARTIES
1. NOTICE

A formal adjudication, like a civil trial, is an adversary decisionmaking process. It depends upon the litigating parties to gather and present relevant evidence, and to challenge the evidence introduced by other parties. Thus, adequate notice of the other side's contentions is an essential prerequisite to fair and effective adjudication. See also pp. 224–25 supra. The APA provides that "persons entitled to notice of an agency hearing shall be timely informed" of the time and place of the hearing, the legal authority that the agency is relying on, and "the matters of fact and law asserted." 5 U.S.C.A. § 554(b). Thus, if the agency changes or conceals its theory so that the respondent is deprived of a reasonable opportunity to challenge it, a reviewing court may set aside an order because of inadequate notice. See, e.g., Morgan v. United States, 304 U.S. 1, 18–19 (1938) *(Morgan II)*; NLRB v. I.W.G., Inc., 144 F.3d 685 (10th Cir.1998).

Nevertheless, the APA is generally interpreted as adopting the philosophy of "notice pleading": actual notice of the relevant facts and issues is sufficient, so long as the respondent has a fair opportunity to know and challenge the positions taken by adverse parties. Thus, proof may vary from the pleadings, and pleadings may be amended to conform to the proof. Tasty Baking Co. v. NLRB, 254 F.3d 114 (D.C.Cir.2001). If anything, technical defects in pleadings are less significant in administrative practice than in civil litigation. Many regulated industries have continuous dealings with the staffs of the agencies that oversee their operations, and in the process they often learn informally what facts and issues the agency considers crucial in a pending adjudication. In addition, agencies do not necessarily follow the "continuous hearing" practice of the courts. Instead, they may adopt an "interval hearing" system in which, for example, the government presents its case and the hearing is then recessed for a period of weeks or months so that the respondent can prepare a defense. See, e.g., NLRB v. Remington Rand, Inc., 94 F.2d 862 (2d Cir.1938).

2.   INTERVENTION

When an agency adjudication affects individuals or organizations who are not named parties, they will often seek to participate in the hearing. The methods by which an interested person may participate are generally similar to those available in civil litigation. They include testifying at the request of the agency staff or one of the named parties; supplying documentary evidence to them; requesting permission to file an amicus curiae brief and perhaps to present oral argument; and seeking to intervene as a party. In recent years, as environmental, consumer, and other "public interest" groups have become more actively involved in the administrative process, requests to intervene in agency adjudications have increased. Intervenor status generally has several advantages over more limited forms of participation, including the right to control the presentation of evidence supporting the intervenor's position, to cross-examine other parties' witnesses, and to appeal an adverse initial decision. However, intervention is also more costly to the agency in hearing time and other resources, and named parties in the case may fear that the intervenor's participation will be harmful to their interests. As a result, disputes often arise as to whether an interested person or group should be allowed to intervene in an agency adjudication.

The APA does not directly deal with the right to intervene in formal adjudication, and the standards for intervention set forth in pertinent agency statutes and rules of practice are usually vague. For example, a provision of the Federal Trade Commission Act simply states that intervention shall be allowed in formal adjudications "upon good cause shown." 15 U.S.C.A. § 45(b); see Firestone Tire & Rubber Co., 77 F.T.C. 1666 (1970). For many years, in the absence of statutory guidance, reviewing courts typically resolved intervention disputes by drawing analogies to the law of standing to seek judicial review of administrative action, discussed at pp. 371–87 infra. They often argued that in administrative fora, as in judicial ones, participation by "public interest" groups is an especially helpful means of furthering the mission of an agency that is itself charged with promoting the public interest. See, e.g., National Welfare Rights Org. v. Finch, 429 F.2d 725 (D.C.Cir.1970); Office of Communication of United Church of Christ v. FCC, 359 F.2d 994 (D.C.Cir.1966). Today, however, a court is likely to accord an agency at least some discretion to decide whether or not to allow intervention. Thus, in Envirocare of Utah, Inc. v. NRC, 194 F.3d 72 (D.C.Cir. 1999), the Nuclear Regulatory Commission refused to allow a licensed nuclear waste disposal company to intervene in a proceeding in which the Commission was considering granting licenses to two competitors. The court upheld this refusal, relying on the general principle of judicial deference to agencies' interpretations of the statutes they administer, as well as the Commission's legitimate desire to avoid disruptions of its proceedings.

Whatever their legal obligations, however, agencies today tend to be receptive to intervention. They have become more aware of the positive contributions that intervenors can make to their decisions, and more sensitized to the practical costs (such as judicial reversals and congressional criticism) that may result from a refusal to permit public participation. The Administrative Conference of the United States has endorsed this spirit of liberality and recommended that administrators and reviewing courts should consider several functional factors in determining whether a person will be allowed to intervene in an agency adjudication. According to ACUS, the decisionmaker should take into account not only the intervenor's interest in the subject matter and the outcome of the proceeding, but also the extent to which other parties will adequately represent the intervenor's interest, the ability of the prospective intervenor to present relevant evidence and argument, and the effect of intervention on the agency's implementation of its statutory mandate. ACUS Recommendation 71–6, 38 Fed.Reg. 19782 (1973).

As the right to participate has become widely accepted, attention has shifted to finding ways to assure that participation will be effective. For many public interest groups, the principal barriers to effective participation are costs and attorneys' fees. During the 1970s some agencies experimented with direct subsidies to groups and individuals who lacked the resources to present their views in particular proceedings, but this device generated political opposition and has been essentially defunct since the early 1980s. A more viable alternative today is a claim for attorney fees and costs under the Equal Access to Justice Act, 5 U.S.C.A. § 504. However, EAJA fees are available only to prevailing parties, i.e., parties who have won relief on the merits of their claims through a judgment or consent decree. If the suit merely serves as a "catalyst" for the defendant's decision to cease the challenged conduct voluntarily, the plaintiff is not deemed to have "prevailed." Buckhannon Board & Care Home, Inc. v. West Va. Dep't of Health & Human Resources, 532 U.S. 598 (2001). Moreover, EAJA fees are available only if the government's litigating position was not "substantially justified," i.e., "justified to a degree that could satisfy a reasonable person." Pierce v. Underwood, 487 U.S. 552 (1988).[3] Another limitation in the EAJA is that fees are reimbursable only if they were incurred in adversary adjudication under the APA. Ardestani v. INS, 502 U.S. 129 (1991) (no recovery for fees incurred

3. The Act uses the same standard as the basis for reimbursing litigants for the expense of challenging the government's actions in court. 28 U.S.C.A. § 2412(d)(1)(A).

during deportation case conducted solely under Immigration and Nationality Act). For the most part, therefore, organizations that wish to participate in the administrative process are still dependent on the contributions of their members and occasional support from private foundations to finance their advocacy.

3.   CONSOLIDATION AND THE COMPARATIVE HEARING

When an agency conducts adjudications in licensing proceedings, and there are multiple applicants for a single license, the agency's discretion to determine which parties will be heard may be limited by the "*Ashbacker* doctrine." The principle was first articulated in Ashbacker Radio Corp. v. FCC, 326 U.S. 327 (1945), where the FCC had received applications from two companies seeking licenses to provide radio broadcast services on the same frequency in adjoining communities. The applications were mutually exclusive, because if both were granted, each station's signal would cause electrical interference with the other's, making it impossible for most listeners to hear the programs. The statute provided that the agency could grant a license without a formal hearing, but it required an opportunity for trial-type hearing before a license application was denied. The FCC granted the first license application without hearing, then set the other down for evidentiary hearing. The Supreme Court concluded that this procedure violated the second broadcaster's statutory right to a "full hearing," because the prior grant to the first applicant made the subsequent hearing a sham. To preserve the hearing rights of both parties, the Commission was required to consolidate the mutually exclusive applications and hold a single "comparative hearing" in which each licensee would have an opportunity to show that he was best qualified to serve the public interest.

In the Telecommunications Act of 1996, 110 Stat. 56, Congress limited the significance of the *Ashbacker* principle in the broadcasting context, by authorizing the FCC to renew an incumbent's license on the basis of good performance, regardless of whether another applicant might do a better job. 47 U.S.C. § 309(k)(4). However, this development has not put an end to comparative hearings in cases in which there is no incumbent (as in *Ashbacker* itself). Bachow Communications, Inc. v. FCC, 237 F.3d 683 (D.C.Cir.2001). Moreover, the *Ashbacker* principle has been applied in other fields of regulation in which multiple applicants compete for valuable operating rights. Although the physical impossibility of granting two licenses, as in broadcasting, may present the most obvious case for a comparative hearing, courts have also invoked the doctrine in cases of "economic mutual exclusivity"—where one or both of the applicants may be driven out of business if two licenses are granted, because there is not enough business in the relevant market area to support both of them. See, e.g., Midwestern Gas

Transmission Co. v. FPC, 258 F.2d 660 (D.C.Cir. 1958) (applicants for gas pipeline certification).

B. DISCOVERY

In most civil cases brought in federal and state courts, the litigants are routinely permitted to conduct extensive discovery through a variety of devices such as oral depositions, written interrogatories, bills of particulars, and requests for admissions and stipulations. The advantages of liberal pretrial discovery are widely acknowledged: it assures fairness to the litigants and prevents "trial by surprise"; it encourages settlements; and it can improve the efficiency of the trial and the quality of the decision. Despite its general acceptance in the courts, however, pretrial discovery is not always available in administrative adjudications. Apart from the Freedom of Information Act, the APA contains no provisions relating to discovery against the agency (although it does give parties a limited right to obtain subpoenas against third parties, 5 U.S.C.A. § 555(d)). Nor do many agency enabling acts deal explicitly with the subject of discovery. Agency practice appears to be highly varied. A few agencies, such as the Federal Trade Commission, have adopted broad discovery provisions modeled on those used in the federal courts. 16 C.F.R. § 3.31 et seq. Other agencies, such as the NLRB, provide only limited opportunities for a respondent to discover the evidence against her before the hearing. The latter agencies' reluctance to expand discovery rights may be traceable in part to apprehension that such procedures lead to costly and time-consuming "discovery wars," such as those which have often been fought in complex court litigation. In 2004, for example, the Nuclear Regulatory Commission revamped its procedures for licensing nuclear reactors, replacing its court-like discovery procedures with a limited system of mandatory disclosures. A court held that the revision was consistent with the APA and was a reasonable response to the NRC's unfavorable experience under the former system. Citizens Awareness Network v. United States, 391 F.3d 338 (1st Cir.2004).

An additional, major reason why many agencies limit discovery rights is the availability of alternative methods for disclosing information necessary to assure a fair hearing and a decision based on the best available evidence. Most formal agency adjudications are preceded by a staff investigation, which is usually backed by the subpoena power. In contrast to a private litigant, who is primarily concerned with gathering and presenting information to support her own "theory of the case," the agency staff typically has a broader obligation to collect all relevant information that might be of use to the decisionmakers. If the staff is diligent in performing its duties, it may cover much of the ground that would be relegated to discovery in civil litigation. Moreover, the Freedom of Information Act, 5 U.S.C.A. § 552, is a powerful "discovery" tool which private parties can use to learn what information is available in the agency's files. See generally pp. 153–61 supra. Since bureaucracies typically commit most significant information to writing, a carefully drafted FOIA request can often give a comprehensive picture of the agency's "case." Another source of discovery is the "*Jencks* rule." First developed in criminal prosecutions, see Jencks v. United States, 353 U.S. 657 (1957), and later codified in the Jencks Act, 18 U.S.C.A. § 3500, the rule requires government attorneys who are acting in a prosecutorial capacity to disclose prior statements made by prosecution witnesses after the witness has testified. See, e.g., Blackfoot Livestock Comm'n Co. v. Dep't of Agriculture, 810 F.2d 916 (9th Cir.1987). Under these circumstances, respondents in agency adjudications will frequently have the functional equivalent of the protections afforded by a formal discovery system.

C. EVIDENCE

1. PRESENTATION OF CASE

In broad outline, the form of many agency adjudications resembles that of a court trial. After the prehearing stage of pleadings, motions, and prehearing conferences is completed, an oral hearing is held before an official who is called a judge. The agency and the respondent are represented by counsel who introduce testimony and exhibits. Witnesses may be cross-examined, objections may be raised, and rulings issued. At the conclusion of the testimony, the parties submit proposed findings and conclusions and legal briefs to the presiding officer. The administrative law judge then renders his initial decision, which may be appealed to the agency heads. Beneath these surface similarities, however, there are significant differences between judicial and administrative adjudications.

The APA adopts the common law rule that "the proponent of a rule or order has the burden of proof." 5 U.S.C.A. § 556(d). According to the Supreme Court, this means that the moving party bears the burden of persuasion. Thus, the APA prevented the Department of Labor from enforcing a rule under which a miner could recover black lung benefits from his employer if there was equally probative evidence for and against his disability claim. Director, OWCP v. Greenwich Collieries, 512 U.S. 267 (1994). However, the Court in that case distinguished NLRB v. Transportation Mgmt. Corp., 462 U.S. 393 (1983), which held that when a discharged employee establishes that antiunion animus contributed to her employer's firing decision, the Board *may* shift to the employer the burden of proving that it would have fired the employee even if her union activities had not been a motivating factor. Thus, § 556(d) does not prevent an agency from using its substantive authority to define an issue as an affirmative defense; it only means that the proponent must carry the burden of persuasion with respect to whatever elements remain part of the prima facie case. Another provision in § 556(d) establishes that the burden of persuasion in APA adjudications is met by the "preponderance of the evidence" standard. Steadman v. SEC, 450 U.S. 91 (1981). Where, however, the APA does not apply and Congress has not otherwise prescribed the degree of proof, courts have felt at liberty to impose stricter standards in order to protect important private interests. Thus, in a deportation proceeding, which was exempted from the APA, the Court applied the "clear and convincing evidence" standard, because of the impact of such a proceeding on personal liberty and security. Woodby v. INS, 385 U.S. 276 (1966). But see Vance v. Terrazas, 444 U.S. 252 (1980) (upholding Congress's substitution of the preponderance of evidence standard for the *Woodby* standard in denaturalization cases, and distinguishing *Woodby* as being based on administrative common law).

Perhaps the most distinctive feature of many administrative adjudications is the substitution of written evidence for direct oral testimony. The APA explicitly authorizes this practice in formal rulemaking proceedings and in adjudications "determining claims for money or benefits or applications for initial licenses," by providing that "an agency may, when a party will not be prejudiced thereby, adopt procedures for the submission of all or part of the evidence in written form." 5 U.S.C.A. § 556(d). Use of written direct testimony can take several forms. One of the simplest and least productive is the use of "canned dialogue"—previously written questions and answers that are read into the record in place of live testimony. More effective and efficient is the practice originally developed by the ICC, in which verified written statements are prepared by witnesses and submitted to adverse parties for rebuttal. There are also some intermediate methods, such as the practice developed by the FTC in rulemaking hearings. Witnesses in those proceedings are required to submit advance texts of their testimony; then, at the hearings, they are requested to provide a brief oral summary of the principal points in their statements, much as witnesses in congressional hearings are encouraged to do. The bulk of hearing time can then be devoted to questioning and cross-examination designed to clarify and test the witnesses' conclusions.

One reason why written evidence plays such a significant role in administrative practice is the nature of the issues involved in many agency adjudications. In court proceedings, the crucial evidence is frequently eyewitness testimony relating to a particular transaction or event. In administrative adjudications, however, the crucial evidence may well be expert opinion testimony on matters such as the medical diagnosis of the injuries suffered by a claimant for disability benefits, the economic justification for a proposed merger of two regulated companies, the impact of a proposed utility power line on wildlife habitat, or the perceptions of a random sample of consumers who responded to a survey questionnaire regarding their understanding of certain sales representations. The demeanor of the witness usually contributes little to the assessment of such evidence; more important are the qualifications and background of the expert, the adequacy of his data base and methodology, and the soundness of the inferences he has drawn from available information. Cross-examination may occasionally be useful in illuminating these matters, but direct oral testimony using the courtroom question-and-answer format is of little value, particularly when the administrator has some expertise in the subject matter of the expert's testimony.

2.   CROSS–EXAMINATION

Few issues in administrative law have proven as controversial as the proper role of cross-examination in formal proceedings. The APA is deceptively simple; it merely provides that a party to an evidentiary hearing is entitled "to conduct such cross-examination as may be required for a full and true disclosure of the facts." 5 U.S.C.A. § 556(d). The Act's legislative history indicates that Congress was seeking to draw a line between an unlimited right of cross-examination, with all the cost, delay, and waste that unrestricted questioning can produce, and a reasonable opportunity to test opposing evidence.

One reason for the APA's guarded approach to cross-examination is that the utility of that device can vary according to the purpose for which it is used, the nature and importance of the testimony that is being attacked, and the skills and backgrounds of the hearing participants. When the direct testimony is based upon eyewitness observations, cross-examination that is directed at witness credibility, veracity, and perception may be a useful means of testing the truth of the specific factual assertions. However, most observers seem to agree that credibility attacks are rarely successful when the witness is an expert. Questioning that is designed to clarify expert testimony or expose its substantive limitations may sometimes be useful, particularly when the decisionmaker is unfamiliar with the subject matter of the testimony. More frequently, however, it is a waste of time. Few cross-examiners have sufficient technical sophistication to meet an expert on her own ground and challenge her methodology or analysis convincingly.

The Nuclear Regulatory Commission recently tested the limits of the APA's flexible approach to cross-examination when it revised its hearing procedures for licensing nuclear reactors. Its rules created a presumption that questioning of witnesses should be conducted by presiding officers, not parties. Parties would need to seek special permission to engage in cross-examination, which would have to be conducted according to a specific plan submitted to the presiding officer in advance. In Citizens Awareness Network, Inc. v. United States, 391 F.3d 338 (1st Cir.2004), the court upheld these rules, relying on the NRC's assurance that it would administer them in conformity with § 556(d). The success of this experiment remains to be seen.

Few agencies have sought to curb cross-examination as forcefully as the NRC has. As a general rule, a party who wants to conduct cross-examination in a formal adjudicative hearing bears the burden of showing why she needs it. Cellular Mobile Systems of Pa., Inc. v. FCC, 782 F.2d 182 (D.C.Cir.1985). In practice, however, the lack of clear standards puts considerable pressure on an ALJ to allow relatively unconstrained questioning. Any attempt to cut off a line of inquiry might invite a reversal and remand by the higher levels of the agency or by the courts, and the hearing time spent in disputes over the permissible scope of cross-examination might well be greater than the time the examination itself would consume. Thus, the practical situation in the agencies often seems to approach the unrestricted cross-examination that the drafters of the APA sought to avoid.

3.   ADMISSIBILITY AND EVALUATION OF EVIDENCE

In comparison with court trials, administrative adjudications generally are governed by liberal evidentiary rules that create a strong presumption in favor of admitting questionable or challenged evidence. This difference between courts and agencies is reflected in the ways in which the two tribunals deal with the problem of hearsay evidence—that is, statements that were made outside the hearing and are subsequently offered in evidence to prove the truth of the matter asserted. The Federal Rules of Evidence, which govern hearings before federal courts and magistrates, adopt the rule that hearsay is inadmissible, and then proceed to carve out more than twenty technical exceptions to that general standard. Rules 802–03. A few agencies are required by statute to follow the Federal Rules (as in the case of the NLRB, 29 U.S.C.A. § 160(b)) or have voluntarily adopted the Rules for use in their own proceedings. Most agencies, however, rely on the APA, which establishes a much simpler standard for administrative trial-type hearings. Section 556(d) provides that "[a]ny oral or documentary evidence may be received, but the agency as a matter of policy shall provide for the exclusion of irrelevant, immaterial, or unduly repetitious evidence." This provision opens the door to any evidence that the presiding officer admits and only *suggests* that insignificant or redundant evidence should be rejected. Moreover, the APA pointedly omits "incompetent" evidence, such as hearsay, from the list of evidence that should not be received. As a result, much material that would be inadmissible in court is routinely accepted in a formal administrative adjudication. Its exclusion may even be reversible error.

The reason for the APA's liberal rules of admissibility can be traced to basic differences in the nature of courts and administrative agencies. Judicial rules of evidence are formulated with the understanding that a significant proportion of cases will be tried to a jury. It is generally assumed that lay jurors tend to overestimate the probative value of hearsay testimony, particularly when the litigants are deprived of the opportunity to cross-examine a declarant who is not a witness in the proceeding. Thus, admitting such evidence in the absence of reliable circumstantial guarantees that it is trustworthy could be prejudicial to the party against whom it is offered. However, there is much less risk of unfairness or error when the factfinding is performed by expert administrators. In the administrative context, it makes sense to save the time and effort that would be spent ruling on questions of admissibility, and let the decisionmakers take account of the lesser probative value of hearsay or other questionable evidence in making their findings. In other words, the fact that a particular bit of evidence is hearsay should go to its weight, but not to its admissibility, in a formal agency adjudication.

Thus, in administrative hearings, the crucial question often is whether, after hearsay or other "tainted" evidence has been received, the ALJ or agency heads should *rely* on this evidence in reaching their decisions. An administrative decision that rests on hearsay evidence is not impermissible as such. See p. 100 supra. It has long been recognized, however, that hearsay can vary greatly in its reliability, ranging from "mere rumor" to "the kind of evidence on which responsible persons are accustomed to rely in serious affairs." NLRB v. Remington Rand, Inc., 94 F.2d 862, 873 (2d Cir.1938). When an agency determines whether a particular item of hearsay is sufficiently trustworthy to support a finding of fact, much depends upon the quantity and quality of the evidence that each side has placed on the record, the kinds of issues being decided, the impact of an adverse decision on the litigants, and other circumstances surrounding the case.

D. THE INSTITUTIONAL DECISION

In court litigation, decisions are essentially personal: the trial judge who issues findings and conclusions has heard the presentation of evidence and has also reviewed the relevant points of law personally, perhaps with the aid of one or two clerks. Even on appeal, the judges who make the decision and the clerks who assist them listen to arguments and review records and briefs themselves. Administrative agencies are not designed to function like courts, however, and even in formal adjudications the process of decision may be much different from the judicial model. The administrative decisionmaking process is often described as an "institutional decision," in recognition of the fact that it is the product of a bureaucracy rather than of a single person or a small group of identifiable people.

Most regulatory agencies are hierarchies, headed by political appointees who have the responsibility for establishing general policies. Technical expertise is found primarily at the lower levels, among the protected civil service employees, and the expertise needed to decide a particular case may be spread among several bureaus or divisions within the agency. Thus, a central problem of the institutional decision is when and how the officials responsible for making the decision can take advantage of this reservoir of expertise without violating the requirements of fairness to the litigating parties.

The Supreme Court leaned strongly in the direction of "fairness" concerns in the first *Morgan* case, where it held that a statute that gave a private party the right to a "full hearing" required a personal decision by the agency head. Chief Justice Hughes, writing for the majority, reasoned that the duty to decide "cannot be performed by one who has not considered evidence or argument.... The one who decides must hear." Morgan v. United States, 298 U.S. 468, 481 (1936). However, this principle was too broad to be taken literally, and the Court soon began to cut back on the *Morgan I* decision. The case returned for a second round of Supreme Court review after a trial had been held on the details of the agency's decisionmaking process, and the Court made clear that the administrator was not required to be physically present at the taking of testimony. Rather, it was sufficient that he "dipped into [the record] from time to time to get its drift," read the parties' briefs, and discussed the case with his assistants. Morgan v. United States, 304 U.S. 1, 18 (1938) *(Morgan II)*. The Court further declared that reviewing courts should rarely, if ever, probe beneath the record of an agency decision to uncover flaws in the process by which the agency reached its decision. See pp. 110–11 supra. The practical effect of this presumption of regularity is to make it virtually impossible for a challenging party to show that an administrator has failed to give sufficient personal attention to a decision.

A related challenge has been to define the circumstances in which an agency head can properly delegate the power to decide a particular controversy or class of cases to subordinate officials instead of personally hearing and deciding. This latter question (which is technically known as the "subdelegation" problem, because it involves a redelegation by the agency heads of powers originally delegated to them by the legislature) has generally been resolved by recognizing a broad power in top administrators to assign responsibilities to their subordinates. This was not always the prevailing view. In a few early cases, courts strictly construed statutory delegations and concluded that powers had to be exercised personally by the agency heads. See, e.g., Cudahy Packing Co. v. Holland, 315 U.S. 357 (1942) (agency head must sign subpoenas). Today these early constraints on subdelegation have become obsolete. Contemporary statutes and reorganization plans usually contain broad grants of authority to subdelegate decisions. The price control statute that was upheld against a nondelegation attack in Amalgamated Meat Cutters v. Connally, 337 F.Supp. 737 (D.D.C.1971), discussed pp. 23–24 supra, was typical: it provided that "[t]he President may delegate the performance of any function under this title to such officers, departments, and agencies of the United States as he may deem appropriate." 84 Stat. 800, § 203 (1970). And court decisions no longer tend to read subdelegations in an artificially narrow manner. See, e.g., Touby v. United States, 500 U.S. 160 (1991).

The effective abandonment of both the *Morgan I* and subdelegation limitations on the institutional decision is understandable. The number of formal adjudications heard in many agencies, and the size of the records compiled in major contested proceedings, make it physically impossible for agency heads to conduct more than a selective policy review of staff recommendations. In any event, it is not clear that they should do more than that. Agency heads and top program administrators are typically political appointees who are selected primarily on the basis of their ability to make policy consistent with the goals of the Administration. They are not normally skilled at presiding over trial-type hearings or sifting through volumes of detailed evidence. In the contemporary administrative agency, those functions have been largely taken over by the administrative law judge.

1. THE PRESIDING OFFICER

One of the significant changes that accompanied the passage of the Administrative Procedure Act in 1946 was the enhancement of the status and independence of the hearing officer. These officials, who were formerly known as "trial examiners" or "hearing examiners" and are now called "administrative law judges" or ALJs, have several statutory protections. They are appointed through a professional merit selection system, which requires both high performance on a competitive examination and, in many instances, experience in the particular regulatory program; they may not be assigned to perform duties inconsistent with their judicial functions; and they are tenured employees who may be removed or disciplined only for good cause. 5 U.S.C.A. §§ 3105, 5372, 7521.

The limits of the ALJs' independence were tested by the "Bellmon review program" conducted by the Social Security Administration during the 1980s. The agency, concerned about widespread inconsistency and inaccuracy in ALJs' decisions in disability benefits cases, began making active use of its authority to conduct internal review of decisions by ALJs. Rulings by those ALJs who had been rendering the highest percentage of decisions favorable to claimants were singled out for special attention in this program. The judicial response to the program was mixed. One court concluded that the "targeting" of individual ALJs had compromised their statutorily guaranteed independence by exerting subtle pressure on them to rule against claimants more often. Association of Administrative Law Judges v. Heckler, 594 F.Supp. 1132 (D.D.C.1984). Another court, finding no direct coercion to maintain a fixed percentage of reversals, upheld the program as a legitimate management tool. Nash v. Bowen, 869 F.2d 675 (2d Cir.1989). Within a few years the most intrusive features of the program were abandoned, but the scars that it had created in the relationship between the agency and its ALJs were more enduring.

In a formal trial-type hearing, the ALJ has two primary functions: to conduct the hearing, and to render an initial or recommended decision. Both responsibilities are governed by detailed provisions of the APA. Section 556(b) requires that an ALJ preside at the taking of evidence in a formal adjudication, unless one or more of the agency heads personally conduct the hearing. Another section of the Act delegates broad power to the ALJ to control the proceeding. When authorized by statute and agency rules of practice, the ALJ may issue subpoenas and administer oaths, rule on offers of proof, dispose of procedural requests, and otherwise "regulate the course of the hearing." 5 U.S.C.A. § 556(c). As a practical matter, the ALJ may have greater affirmative responsibility than a trial judge to assure that a full and accurate record is developed at the hearing. Most agencies have been given a statutory mission to accomplish, and they have the duty to develop the facts needed to carry out that mandate. Thus, the hearings need not be structured as pure adversary contests in which the presiding officer serves as a passive referee. In some programs, particularly those involving welfare or disability benefit claims, the hearings may be largely "inquisitorial," with the ALJ taking an active part in questioning witnesses and eliciting relevant facts.

After the hearing has concluded, the parties normally submit proposed findings of fact and conclusions of law, see 5 U.S.C.A. § 557(c), and then the ALJ prepares a decision.[4] Under § 557(b), this may be either an initial or a recommended decision. The

4. In both formal and informal adjudication, it is standard practice to disclose the presiding officer's decision to the parties, so that they may comment on it. § 557(c); Ballard v. Commissioner, 544 U.S. 40 (2005) (finding a requirement of such disclosure implicit in the practice rules of the Tax Court).

distinction lies in the effect of the ALJ's determination: an initial decision becomes the final agency action unless it is reviewed by an appeal board or the agency heads, while a recommended decision *must* be considered and acted upon by the agency leadership before it takes effect. The existence of these two forms of ALJ decisions may be viewed as a recognition of the fact that agency adjudications have a widely varying policy content. If the proceeding involves routine application of settled principles to a particular fact situation, then it may be efficient to let the ALJ's initial decision become final without review by the agency heads. On the other hand, when a proceeding has been brought as a "test case" to develop policy in an area that is currently unsettled, the use of a recommended decision assures that the top leadership will consider the policy implications of the case. Finally, the APA acknowledges that some agency actions are virtually pure policy choices, even though they may have been preceded by a trial-type hearing. In these situations, a tenured ALJ may have much less to contribute to the ultimate determination than the political appointees who head the agency. Thus, § 557(b) provides that in initial licensing cases and formal rulemaking proceedings, the presiding officer may simply certify the record to the agency heads, and they in turn may issue a tentative decision for comment by the parties.

Regardless of whether it takes the form of an initial or a recommended decision, the ALJ's determination in a formal adjudication is likely to carry considerable weight with the ultimate agency decisionmakers. The ALJ has seen and heard the witnesses personally, and he has usually devoted more time and effort to mastering the issues than the higher level officials who will review his determination. However, the APA makes clear that the agency heads are not required to defer to the ALJ's factfinding in the same way that an appellate court must defer to the trial judge's factual determinations. Section 557(b) states that "[o]n appeal from or review of the initial decision, the agency has all the powers which it would have in making the initial decision, except as it may limit the issues on notice or by rule." One reason for this difference between judicial and administrative practice may be the importance of factual matters in the formulation of agency policy. When the agency makes policy through adjudicative decisions, the key policy issues may have a substantial factual component. In this situation the agency heads who have the primary responsibility for formulating policy should not be bound by the factual conclusions of a tenured ALJ, particularly on debatable issues of general or "legislative" fact. Policymakers should have some accountability to the political process, and the statutory provision giving them plenary authority to find facts bolsters this allocation of responsibility. However, the power of the agency to find facts *de novo* can cause conceptual problems for a reviewing court when the agency heads and the examiner have reached different conclusions. See pp. 100–01 supra.

2. EX PARTE CONTACTS

Like a court case, a formal agency adjudication is supposed to be decided solely on the basis of the record evidence. This principle is embodied in § 556(e) of the APA, which provides that "[t]he transcript of testimony and exhibits, together with all papers and requests filed in the proceeding, constitutes the exclusive record for decision." The primary reason for requiring this "exclusiveness of the record," as it is sometimes called, is fairness to the litigating parties. If the right to a trial-type hearing is to be meaningful, a participant must be able to know what evidence may be used against her, and to contest it through cross-examination and rebuttal evidence. These rights could easily be nullified if the decisionmakers were free to consider facts outside the record, without notice or opportunity to respond.

The most common problem of extra-record evidence occurs when there are ex parte contacts— communications from an interested party to a decisionmaking official that take place outside the hearing and off the record. There are several reasons why ex parte contact issues arise more frequently in agency proceedings than in court trials. Judicial decisions are almost always made on the record, after an adversary proceeding; the few exceptions, such as applications for a temporary restraining order, are clearly defined and relatively well understood. In this setting, litigants and their attorneys generally assume that it is improper to discuss the merits of pending cases with the judge outside of the formal proceedings. However, on-the-record proceedings comprise only a small part of the workload in most administrative agencies.

The great bulk of agency decisions are made through informal action, or through public proceedings like notice-and-comment rulemaking where ex parte contacts may be not just permissible but affirmatively desirable. Frequently, regulated companies or interest group representatives will be involved in several pending proceedings before an agency, perhaps involving related issues. In this continuing course of dealing, it is easy for even the most careful person to slip and touch upon issues that are under consideration in a formal adjudication. This is not to suggest that all improper ex parte contacts between regulators and regulated are inadvertent; but it does seem clear that regulatory officials function in a complex environment where the line between "responsive government" and "backroom dealing" is often indistinct.

The APA as originally enacted did not deal explicitly with ex parte contacts, and as a result claims of improper ex parte influence were generally evaluated under the due process clause of the Constitution See, e.g. WKAT v. FCC, 296 F.2d 375, 383 (D.C.Cir. 1961). In 1976, however, the APA was amended and now contains detailed provisions governing ex parte contacts in formal adjudications. Section 557(d)(1) prohibits any "interested person outside the agency" from making, or knowingly causing, "any ex parte communication relevant to the merits of the proceeding" to any decisionmaking official. It also imposes similar restraints on the agency decisionmakers, who are defined to include any "member of the body comprising the agency, administrative law judge, or other employee who is or may reasonably be expected to be involved in the decisional process." The prohibitions on ex parte contacts come into play when a proceeding has been noticed for hearing, unless the agency has designated some earlier time. 5 U.S.C.A. § 557(d)(1)(E).

When an improper ex parte contact does take place, the APA requires that it be placed on the public record; if it was an oral communication, a memorandum summarizing the contact must be filed. Id. § 557(d)(1)(C). An outside party who made or caused an improper contact can also be required to show cause "why his claim or interest in the proceeding should not be dismissed, denied, disregarded, or otherwise adversely affected on account of such violation." Id. § 557(d)(1)(D). Ultimately, however, the decision whether to impose such a sanction is a matter for judicial discretion. Professional Air Traffic Controllers Org. v. FLRA, 685 F.2d 547 (D.C.Cir.1982). *PATCO* arose out of a Federal Labor Relations Authority proceeding to decertify a union of air traffic controllers that had led its members in an illegal strike against the government. The evidence showed that a prominent labor leader had met privately with a member of the FLRA, urging him not to revoke the union's certification. Although the court was convinced that this contact was illegal, it did not overturn the FLRA's order, because the discussion of PATCO's situation had been brief, the labor leader had made no threats or promises, and the conversation had not affected the outcome of the case.

A case that arose before the APA amendments illustrates how concerns about ex parte contacts can lead to constraints on political oversight of agency decisionmaking. In Pillsbury Co. v. FTC, 354 F.2d 952 (5th Cir.1966), the FTC rendered an interlocutory decision on a question of antitrust law in a merger case and remanded the case to the ALJ for further hearings. Shortly afterwards, at a congressional oversight hearing, several senators were extremely critical of the Commission's ruling. They subjected the FTC chairman and some agency staff members to detailed, hostile questioning. Despite the fact that the chairman disqualified himself from participating in the case when it returned to the Commission for review, the court held that the entire agency was disqualified. In the court's view, the congressional pressure had so interfered with the agency's process of decision that the respondent could not get a fair hearing. However, the passage of time and the consequent changes in agency personnel had diluted the risk of future prejudgment, and so the court remanded the case for further proceedings.

Analytically, the court's decision is somewhat questionable, because the FTC adhered in its final opinion to the same legal position that it had taken originally, a fact indicating that it had not been influenced by congressional pressure. Moreover, the colloquy at the hearing had concerned purely legal issues, not factual ones, and members of Congress surely have a legitimate interest in urging an agency head to follow legislative intent as they interpret it. Nevertheless, the *Pillsbury* doctrine, as codified in § 557(d), has become well established and serves as a significant constraint on political intervention into formal adjudications—not only by the legislative branch, but also by the executive branch. See Portland Audubon Soc'y v. Endangered Species Comm., 984 F.2d 1534 (9th Cir.1993) (remanding case in which ex parte contacts by White House aides had allegedly induced agency to allow logging by timber companies in Oregon forests, despite risks to a species of spotted owl).

The scope of the *Pillsbury* principle is limited, however. It does not apply in the early stages of an administrative investigation, when formal adjudication may be on the horizon but is not imminent. DCP Farms v. Yeutter, 957 F.2d 1183 (5th Cir. 1992). Nor does it apply to informal adjudications; in those proceedings, the legal constraints on ex parte contacts derive from substantive law, not due process. D.C. Fed'n of Civic Ass'ns v. Volpe, 459 F.2d 1231 (D.C.Cir.1971), discussed supra pp. 49–50.

3. SEPARATION OF FUNCTIONS

When an agency is conducting a formal adjudication, a variant of the ex parte contacts problem often arises within the agency. Usually, agency staff members are assigned to act as advocates in trial-type hearings. For example, staff attorneys may be designated "counsel supporting the complaint" in a disciplinary proceeding and instructed to act as prosecutors presenting the case against the respondent. When the proceeding is structured in this fashion, a question may arise as to whether the staff attorneys may consult with the decisionmakers outside the record of the proceeding.

From the perspective of the accused respondent, this sort of consultation is likely to seem just as unfair as any other ex parte communication by an adverse party. On the other hand, there are valid policy reasons for permitting free communications within the agency. Many administrative decisions, including those made in formal adjudications, involve highly technical issues. The expertise necessary to understand those issues is usually found at the staff levels of the agency rather than among the ALJs and the agency heads; thus, insulating the decisionmakers from expert staff could undermine the quality of the decision.

The APA seeks to resolve this tension by defining a limited class of agency staff members who are specifically prohibited from consulting with decisionmakers in a formal adjudication. This ban on internal communications is generally referred to as "separation of functions." Section 554(d) provides that any employee who is "engaged in the performance of investigative or prosecuting functions" may not participate in the decision or advise the decisionmakers in that case or any factually related case. Any input from the prosecuting staff must come "as a witness or counsel in public proceedings." Id. Thus, the APA acknowledges that a staff member who acts as an advocate is likely to have strong views on the merits, and that it would be unfair to the respondent to give such persons preferential access to the decisionmakers. However, agency employees who have not taken on an adversary role in the particular hearing will be more objective, and the agency heads should be free to call upon them when they need assistance in interpreting the record evidence. Finally, the APA recognizes that the risk of unfairness is likely to be small when the proceedings do not have an accusatory or adversary tenor. Section 554(d) provides that the separation of functions requirements do not apply to initial licensing or rate cases—proceedings that are designed to decide technical or policy questions rather than to impose sanctions for past conduct.

Although the agency decisionmakers may consult with nonprosecuting staff members when they are evaluating the record of a formal proceeding, this does not mean that they are free to obtain additional, nonrecord evidence from these agency employees. The principle of § 556(e) that the transcript, exhibits, and other formal filings constitute the "exclusive record for decision" still applies, and consideration of nonrecord evidence may be reversible error. A decision by the Administrator of the EPA authorizing the construction of a nuclear power plant was reversed on this ground in Seacoast

Anti–Pollution League v. Costle, 572 F.2d 872 (1st Cir.1978) (a case that has since been overruled on other grounds, see p. 248 supra). The Administrator had established a "technical review panel" of agency scientists to assist him in reviewing an initial decision involving the thermal pollution that would result from the proposed reactor. The court held that this review panel had not merely analyzed the record, but rather had supplemented it with additional scientific material that should have been introduced as evidence. Because the Administrator had relied on their assessments, reversal was required.

In addition to the limits on internal consultation imposed by § 554(d) of the APA, it has sometimes been argued that agencies should have a structural separation of functions. That is, some commentators have contended that a system of administrative adjudication is inherently unfair when a single individual or group of individuals investigates, decides to issue a complaint, conducts the hearing, reviews the initial decision, imposes the sanctions, and checks compliance with the orders. In its most robust form, this line of criticism concludes that an independent system of "administrative courts" should be established solely for the purpose of hearing and deciding cases brought by the agencies.

However, the notion that the mixture of prosecuting and deciding powers in a single agency is inherently so unfair as to constitute a denial of due process of law was unanimously rejected by the Supreme Court in Withrow v. Larkin, 421 U.S. 35 (1975). The Court pointed out that, even in criminal trials, judges make a variety of preliminary determinations that are analogous to the agency's decision to issue a complaint: arrest and search warrants are issued by judges who may later preside at the trial, and "[j]udges also preside at preliminary hearings where they must decide whether the evidence is sufficient to hold a defendant for trial." Moreover, trial judges who are reversed in civil appeals, and administrators who have had their decisions remanded by the courts for further deliberations, are not considered incapable of giving fair and impartial consideration to the merits of the case. Thus, the due process claim fails unless the protesting party can demonstrate some particular bias which goes beyond the mere combination of prosecuting and adjudicating functions in a single agency.

The APA tacitly adopts the same view as *Withrow*. It provides that "the agency or a member or members of the body comprising the agency"—that is, the agency heads—are exempted from separation of function requirements. 5 U.S.C.A. § 554(d)(C). Because of this exemption, the top leaders in most agencies can coordinate, and be accountable for, the entire range of activities that occur within their domain. Nevertheless, Congress has occasionally responded to concerns about combined functions by enacting statutes that require strict separation of prosecuting and deciding functions in specific agencies. The National Labor Relations Board is a good example. In 1947, Congress separated the responsibility for investigating violations and issuing complaints from the Board, and conferred it on an independent General Counsel. The Board members who ultimately hear and decide these cases have no control over the General Counsel or the decision to prosecute. Similarly, when Congress enacted the Occupational Safety and Health Act in 1970, it assigned the adjudicative function to a review commission that has no responsibility for deciding which cases will be brought initially.

Concerns about the potential unfairness of combining multiple powers in a single agency are not wholly insubstantial. It is probably true, at least in some instances, that an agency head who has reviewed an investigative file and concluded that there was enough evidence to issue a complaint will be more likely to find the respondent guilty when he later reviews the initial decision. Moreover, an administrator who has himself been responsible for committing substantial staff resources to an enforcement proceeding may be reluctant to rule, in the end, that it was all for naught. Nevertheless, the price of total insulation of the adjudicators could often be high, especially where issues are technically complex or there is a need for a coherent national regulatory policy in a particular field. The cost of creating equal expertise in two separate institutions could be high or even prohibitive. Just as troublesome is the likelihood that separate bureaucracies would work at cross purposes; the possibilities for policy stalemate or confusion could increase markedly.

E. BIAS AND PREJUDGMENT

The right to an administrative trial-type hearing would have little meaning if the decisionmaker held a personal grudge against one of the litigants, or had already made up his mind about the facts of the case before any evidence was taken. Thus, in agency adjudications as in court trials, due process combines with statutory provisions to require that the decisionmaker be impartial. See pp. 237–40 supra; 5 U.S.C.A. § 556(b) (procedures for ruling on claims that decisionmakers are biased or otherwise disqualified from participating in formal adjudications).

However, a decision as to whether an administrator has violated the requirement of impartiality is in some ways more complex than a decision as to whether a judge should recuse herself from hearing a case. Courts generally perform only one function, the resolution of disputes in adversary proceedings, while agencies typically have been delegated a variety of managerial and policymaking responsibilities in addition to the power to adjudicate particular cases. The actions taken and the statements made by administrators in the course of these nonadjudicative duties may create the appearance that a particular case has been prejudged, if not the reality. Yet stringent prohibitions on the appearance of prejudgment in formal adjudications could make it difficult for administrators to perform their nonjudicial functions adequately. In addition, most agencies have a statutory mandate to fulfill; rather than simply resolving disputes that are presented to them, agencies are supposed to implement important social policies such as protecting consumers from dangerous foods and drugs or preventing unscrupulous practices in the sale of securities. To this extent, at least, most agencies have what might be considered a "built–in bias."

In responding to these conflicting pressures, the law has generally demonstrated a keen awareness that an agency decisionmaker should be open minded, but not empty headed. The political appointees who head the agencies are chosen in large measure because of the policy positions they have publicly taken, and it would be absurd to require that the Secretary of Transportation have no ideas on the subject of auto safety or that the Administrator of the Environmental Protection Agency be indifferent to the problems of pollution. Thus, an administrator who has taken public positions on controversial matters of law or policy is generally not disqualified from deciding cases that raise those issues. United States v. Morgan, 313 U.S. 409, 421 (1941) (*Morgan IV*). The same rule generally applies to judges who have spoken out on matters that are at issue in pending cases. In Laird v. Tatum, 409 U.S. 824 (1972), Justice Rehnquist refused to disqualify himself from participating in a case concerning the constitutionality of government surveillance of political activity, even though he had testified on behalf of the Administration in congressional hearings dealing with the same activities and had made other public statements in support of the government's position before being appointed to the Court. Since virtually all of the Justices have expressed public opinions on constitutional issues before their appointment to the Court, and have written opinions on these questions as part of their judicial duties, a rule that required disqualification for prior statements on issues of law and policy would prevent the Court from functioning. See Republican Party v. White, 536 U.S. 765 (2002) (endorsing Rehnquist's view).

Similar reasoning was applied to administrative adjudicators in FTC v. Cement Institute, 333 U.S. 683 (1948). There, the Federal Trade Commission had issued public reports and given testimony in Congress concluding that a particular system of pricing that was widely used in the cement industry violated the antitrust laws. When the agency later issued a complaint against one of the companies using the pricing system, the respondent claimed that the agency's prior reports showed impermissible prejudgment of the issues. The Court disagreed, noting that Congress' very purpose had been to establish an expert agency which could engage in both reporting and adjudicative functions; adoption of the respondent's theory would have made the congressional plan unworkable. The Court was also concerned that a rigid approach to disqualification would mean that no administrative tribunal would be able to adjudicate the case. This latter consideration is sometimes called the "rule of necessity": an adjudicator should not be disqualified if the case could not be heard otherwise. This principle has enabled the courts to sit in cases involving judicial salaries. United States v. Will, 449 U.S. 200 (1980). Similarly, in *Cement Institute,* there was no provision for substituting commissioners, and no other agency could bring a cease and desist proceeding against the respondents if the FTC were held unable to act.

Courts have taken a stricter position in cases in which a regulatory commissioner has used a speech or interview to discuss facts that are at issue in a pending case. The test applied in this situation emphasizes both actual and apparent fairness: the reviewing court will inquire whether a disinterested observer would conclude that the administrator has in some measure prejudged the facts of the case. In two well-known cases involving a single FTC chairman, the D.C. Circuit ordered disqualification because of speeches in which the chairman had mentioned companies by name and suggested that he already considered them lawbreakers. Texaco, Inc. v. FTC, 336 F.2d 754 (D.C.Cir.1964), vacated and remanded on other grounds, 381 U.S. 739 (1965); Cinderella Career & Finishing Schools, Inc. v. FTC, 425 F.2d 583 (D.C.Cir.1970) *(Cinderella II).* The court's apparent assumption that the chairman had not needed to comment on the pending cases in the first place could be questioned, because speeches, articles, and interviews are helpful tools that enable administrators to inform the public about agency policy and activities. However, an administrator can avoid the appearance of partiality by simply discussing the issues in the case more guardedly. See Kennecott Copper Corp. v. FTC, 467 F.2d 67 (10th Cir.1972) (neutral description of complaint's allegations was permissible). By the same token, the issuance of a factual press release that merely describes the filing of a complaint does not violate the respondent's right to an impartial decisionmaker. FTC v. Cinderella Career & Finishing Schools, Inc., 404 F.2d 1308 (D.C.Cir.1968) *(Cinderella I).*

In some situations, disqualifying bias can be shown by circumstantial evidence rather than by an overt statement by the official. For example, an adjudicator who has become personally familiar with the evidence by serving in an adversary capacity as an investigator or advocate is disqualified from participating in the decision. Thus, in American Cyanamid Co. v. FTC, 363 F.2d 757 (6th Cir.1966), a commissioner who had investigated the respondent's practices in his prior job as staff counsel to a congressional committee was held ineligible to participate in an adjudication where the same practices were alleged to be violations of the antitrust laws.

Finally, although ideological commitments are usually not sufficient to disqualify adjudicators, the opposite is true when administrators have a financial or other personal stake in the decision. In this situation disqualification is required not only by due process, see pp. 238–39 supra, but also by statutes, executive orders, and agency regulations prohibiting conflicts of interest. Most of these provisions follow the general approach taken in the federal judicial disqualification statute: a judge must recuse herself in any case in which she "has a financial interest in the subject matter ... or any other interest that could be substantially affected by the outcome of the proceeding." 28 U.S.C.A. § 455(b)(4). Troublesome questions regarding the applicability of these standards may arise, particularly when an agency adjudicator comes to government service from private practice and his law firm has been active in representing clients before the agency. However, the general principle is well established: a personal stake in the outcome, however small, constitutes grounds for disqualification.

F. FINDINGS, CONCLUSIONS, AND REASONS

A formal adjudication concludes with the issuance of a written decision, and the APA has detailed provisions governing the contents of the agency's final product. Section 557(c) requires that the parties be given an opportunity to submit proposed findings and conclusions, or "exceptions" to the proposed decision (usually in the form of briefs), before the agency renders a recommended, initial, or final decision. The APA then directs that "[a]ll decisions" in formal adjudications, whether preliminary or final, "shall include ... findings and conclusions, and the reasons or basis therefor, on all the material issues of fact, law, or discretion presented on the record." Id.

There are several reasons for requiring agencies to state in detail the factual, legal, and policy bases of important decisions. Exposure of the agency's reasoning helps to assure that administrators will be publicly accountable for their decisions, and that interested persons will have better guidance on the agency's current policy. The need to prepare a detailed analysis of the evidence and arguments can also exert some discipline on the decisionmaking process, by forcing the responsible officials to deal with each party's points carefully and systematically. Finally, statements of findings, conclusions, and reasons make meaningful judicial review possible: without them, a reviewing court will likely find it very difficult to determine whether the agency has exceeded the bounds of the power conferred by the legislature, or has abused its discretion by taking account of factors not properly relevant to its decision, or has found facts without a sufficient evidentiary basis.

Unfortunately, much of the value of the APA requirements governing findings and statements of reasons is lost when the opinions are not prepared, or at least carefully considered, by the responsible decisionmakers. Traditionally, top administrators in some agencies that have a large volume of adjudications have delegated most of the responsibility for documenting their decisions to specialized opinion writing staffs. The opinions prepared by these staffs may rely heavily on standard "boilerplate" passages, and they may be written with a view towards minimizing the discussion of points that might cause problems on judicial review. In these circumstances, the opinion-writing process does not really impose any discipline on the decision, and a reviewing court cannot be sure that it is considering the actual bases for the agency action: the opinion becomes more of a rationalization for the decision than an explanation.

CHAPTER VIII

PROCEDURAL SHORTCUTS

Many administrative statutes contain clauses conferring broad rights to trial-type hearings. Administrative hearings, however, can be costly in time, manpower, and other resources, and they sometimes make only a marginal contribution to the quality of information available or to the acceptability of the final decision. Thus, agencies often have an incentive to develop procedural techniques for avoiding unnecessary hearings or for narrowing the issues that will be considered in a formal setting. Several such techniques are examined in this chapter.

A. LEGISLATIVE RULEMAKING

Most agencies now operate under statutory schemes that permit them to issue legislative rules. Once such a rule has been promulgated, private parties have no further right to be heard at the agency level on the issues addressed in the rule; those issues will remain settled until the rule is revoked, or invalidated by a court. (The term "substantive rules" is sometimes used as a synonym for "legislative rules," but it is slightly misleading, because a *procedural* rule can also be "legislative," settling the issues it addresses.) Sometimes it is unclear whether an agency's rulemaking authority applies to a given administrative function; private parties may contend that this authority cannot be used to defeat their own statutory right to a trial-type administrative hearing. In general, however, the Supreme Court has rejected these contentions, preferring to construe agencies' rulemaking powers expansively.

Early experiments in using rulemaking to streamline adjudications were initiated by licensing agencies. The Federal Communications Commission, for example, was required to hold a "full hearing"—a formal adjudication under the APA—before refusing an application for a broadcast license. In United States v. Storer Broadcasting Co., 351 U.S. 192 (1956), the Commission had issued multiple ownership rules reducing the number of television outlets that could be controlled by one licensee. Storer, which exceeded the new maximum limit, had applied for an additional license before the rule became final, but the FCC nonetheless dismissed the application as not conforming to the new rule. Storer claimed that this procedure was a denial of its statutory right to a full hearing, but the Supreme Court held that the rule was valid and therefore the denial of a trial-type hearing was proper. Subsequent decisions made clear that the *Storer* principle was not limited to the communications field. See Mobil Oil Exploration & Prod. Southeast Inc. v. United Distrib. Cos., 498 U.S. 211 (1991) (upholding FERC rule that established a pre-authorization procedure for abandoning supply contract obligations); FPC v. Texaco, Inc., 377 U.S. 33 (1964) (upholding FPC rule that imposed conditions on the grant of gas pipeline certificates); American Airlines, Inc. v. CAB, 359 F.2d 624 (D.C.Cir.1966) (en banc) (upholding CAB rule that effectively modified some air carriers' certificates by prohibiting the companies from transporting cargo through "blocked space" arrangements). In short, even where a statute calls for individualized determinations, an agency may use rulemaking to resolve some of the relevant issues "unless Congress clearly expresses an intent to withhold that authority." American Hosp. Ass'n v. NLRB, 499 U.S. 606 (1991) (upholding rule defining appropriate bargaining units in hospitals).

The rules challenged in *Storer* and *Texaco* had actually been relatively flexible, for they had provided that companies could ask for a waiver on the basis of individual circumstances. However, a rule that lacks a waiver provision can still be valid. For example, the Court allowed the FCC to adopt a flat rule that radio stations' changes of format would never be considered during license renewal proceedings. FCC v. WNCN Listeners Guild, 450 U.S. 582 (1981).

The Court followed similar principles when it upheld the "medical-vocational guidelines" used by the Secretary of Health and Human Services in the Social Security disability program. Heckler v. Campbell, 461 U.S. 458 (1983). Under the Social Security Act, benefits are to be paid to persons who are so severely disabled that they cannot engage in any work available in the national economy. The claimant's job qualifications are to be judged in light of four variables: age, education, work experience, and physical ability. The guidelines, also known as "grid regulations," listed numerous combinations of the four threshold variables and stated, for each combination, whether a worker with those qualifications was employable. Thus, administrative law judges (ALJs) hearing disability benefits claims would no longer rely on expert testimony in deciding whether a claimant was employable; instead, they would simply make findings concerning the four variables, and reference to the guidelines would then automatically determine whether the claimant was entitled to benefits. The Court concluded that, although the Act states that the disability determination is to be made on the basis of evidence adduced at a hearing, this provision "does not bar the Secretary from relying on rulemaking to resolve certain classes of issues."

The rules upheld in *Campbell* were controversial, for they tended to curb ALJs' ability to respond to individual circumstances that might come to light at an evidentiary hearing. As the Court noted, however, use of the guidelines enhanced the efficiency of the program and helped bring about uniform results nationwide. Moreover, the process was not entirely impersonal, because an ALJ still had to use individualized judgment in assessing a claimant's particular abilities.

In any event, *Campbell* endorsed rulemaking only with respect to "issues that do not require case-by-case consideration," and subsequent cases have demonstrated that the Secretary's rulemaking authority has limits. In Bowen v. Yuckert, 482 U.S. 137 (1987), another HHS rule provided that a claimant would automatically be deemed ineligible for benefits if her impairments were not "severe" enough to significantly limit her ability to do most jobs. The Court upheld the rule, but two concurring Justices cautioned the Secretary to use the rule with restraint, because aggressive applications of the rule could (and in the initial months of the rule actually did) deny benefits to claimants who had a statutory right to receive them. Later, in Sullivan v. Zebley, 493 U.S. 521 (1990), the Court struck down a third rule, under which a child would be deemed ineligible for benefits unless she had one of 182 medical conditions listed in the rule. The statute extended benefits to all children suffering from impairments of "comparable severity" to those which would entitle an adult to benefits, and the Court believed that the HHS rule would inevitably deny benefits to some children who met that statutory standard. Thus, although the Court has strongly supported the use of rulemaking, it also acknowledges that an agency's rulemaking power is circumscribed by whatever substantive provisions define the agency's regulatory authority.

B. SUMMARY JUDGMENT

Another way in which an agency can avoid unnecessary hearings is to adopt a summary judgment procedure. For the most part, administrative summary judgment rules are similar to Rule 56 of the Federal Rules of Civil Procedure: a judgment on the merits may be rendered without hearing when there is no genuine issue of material fact to be tried. An agency, however, typically has much wider substantive policymaking authority than a court. It can sometimes use this authority to redefine the underlying legal standards, and then enter summary judgment against parties who fail to show a triable issue under the new standards.

The Supreme Court addressed one example of this technique in Weinberger v. Hynson, Westcott & Dunning, Inc., 412 U.S. 609 (1973). In 1962, Congress directed the Food and Drug Administration to withdraw from the market any therapeutic drug that could not be proved by its manufacturer to be effective. More than 16,000 claims of effectiveness had to be reviewed, yet the statute required the agency to give a manufacturer "due notice and opportunity for hearing" before withdrawing approval of any drug. To cope with its massive assignment, the FDA promulgated rules stating that it would evaluate the effectiveness of a given drug only on the basis of adequate and well-controlled clinical studies, not anecdotal reports from sources such as practicing physicians. The agency also adopted a summary judgment procedure, under which a manufacturer facing disapproval of a drug would be denied a hearing unless it could demonstrate in advance that it could present a "genuine and substantial issue of fact" under the new rules. In *Hynson,* a company that had been subjected to summary judgment sought judicial review, claiming that the FDA's procedure violated its statutory right to a full hearing. The Court generally upheld the FDA's summary judgment practice. A primary factor in the Court's reasoning was the common sense notion that it would be pointless to hold a hearing if the challenging party had no chance of succeeding on the merits. It was also clear that the FDA could not accomplish its statutory mission of getting ineffective drugs off the market if it were obliged to grant a trial-type hearing on every claim, however insubstantial.

The Supreme Court's support for summary judgment has continued since *Hynson*, see Costle v. Pacific Legal Found., 445 U.S. 198 (1980), and its use in the agencies seems to be growing. Nevertheless, judges have drawn upon their experience in civil litigation to prevent agencies from abusing the device. Thus, when courts have found that the parties to a case have each submitted evidence on a disputed proposition, so as to create a genuine issue of material fact, they have invalidated administrative summary judgments and required the agency to allow full evidentiary proceedings, just as they would do in a civil case. See, e.g., Crestview Parke Care Center v. Thompson, 373 F.3d 743 (6th Cir. 2004); Rogers Corp. v. EPA, 275 F.3d 1096 (D.C.Cir. 2002).

C. OFFICIAL NOTICE

In the same manner that courts can bypass the normal process of proof by taking judicial notice of facts, administrative agencies sometimes overcome deficiencies in the record of a formal proceeding by taking "official notice" of material facts. Indeed, agencies enjoy considerably wider power than courts to dispense with formal proof. In federal courts, for example, the rules of evidence limit judicial notice of adjudicative facts to propositions that are "beyond reasonable dispute, in that [they are] either (1) generally known within the territorial jurisdiction of the trial court, or (2) capable of accurate and ready determination by resort to sources whose accuracy cannot reasonably be questioned." Fed.R.Evid. 201(b). These strict limits are unsuitable for administrative agencies, which often are created precisely so that they can become repositories of knowledge and expertise. Because they are continuously active in the fields of their specialties, agency officials are frequently aware of extra-record facts that bear on cases pending before them. A liberal system of official notice can contribute to the convenience and efficiency of the decisional process, by avoiding the need for repetitive, time consuming proof of matters that have already been thoroughly investigated.

It is sometimes argued that an agency should have especially broad freedom to take official notice of "legislative" facts (general facts bearing on law or policy) as opposed to "adjudicative" facts (facts concerning the immediate parties to a case). This proposition is implicit in the above-mentioned evidence rule, which applies only to adjudicative facts and thus imposes no curbs at all on judicial notice of legislative facts. Fed.R.Evid. 201(a). The distinction rests on the widely held belief that trial-type processes are relatively unhelpful in the development of legislative facts (see pp. 233–34 supra), and thus may be foregone more readily when an agency wants to rely on such facts. Indeed, the procedures for taking official notice in an adjudication, described later in this section, closely resemble the procedures that agencies typically use in the rule-making process, which is expressly designed for resolution of legislative fact issues.

One should not assume, however, that an agency may never take official notice of an adjudicative fact except in the circumstances specified in Rule 201(b). For example, in Market Street Ry. v. Railroad Comm'n, 324 U.S. 548 (1945), the agency was setting rates for a streetcar company and needed to know the company's operating revenues for 1943. It took notice of figures in the company's monthly operating reports, which had been filed with it after the record closed. The Supreme Court upheld this procedure, noting that the company had never contended that the figures in its own reports were erroneous or had been cited misleadingly. The modern trend, then, is to apply a "rule of convenience" under which a wide range of facts, both legislative and adjudicative, are potentially susceptible of official notice. Castillo–Villagra v. INS, 972 F.2d 1017 (9th Cir.1992).

However, official notice is often confused with the application of expertise in the *evaluation of evidence*. In drawing conclusions from a record, administrative law judges and agencies may rely on their special skills in engineering, economics, medicine, etc., just as judges may freely use their legal skills in reading statutes and applying decided cases in the preparation of their opinions. They also resort to theories, predictions, and intuitions that are inherently incapable of exact proof. See pp. 119–21 supra. Properly speaking, however, these evaluations and insights are not within the concept of official notice. Rather, official notice comes into play when an agency that *could* have documented one of its factual premises on the record chooses to avoid that process for efficiency reasons.

Because of its breadth, official notice has the potential to interfere with the due process right to a fair administrative hearing. The main way in which the law addresses this concern is by imposing procedural safeguards. First, the noticed material must be specifically identified. The agency cannot rest on a vague claim that it is an expert; it must explain with particularity the sources of its information. Ohio Bell Tel. Co. v. Public Util. Comm'n, 301 U.S. 292 (1937); Air Prods. & Chems., Inc. v. FERC, 650 F.2d 687 (5th Cir.1981). Second, it must give the opposing party a meaningful chance to rebut the information or to present additional arguments that would put the noticed facts into a more favorable light. United States v. Abilene & Southern Ry., 265 U.S. 274 (1924). This latter requirement is codified in the APA: "When an agency decision rests on official notice of a material fact ... a party is entitled, on timely request, to an opportunity to show the contrary." 5 U.S.C.A. § 556(e). In practice, the APA obligation need not be burdensome. Most courts hold that an agency may even cite officially noticed facts for the first time in its final opinion, so long as it allows the opposing party to rebut these facts by filing a petition for rehearing. *Market Street Ry.*, supra. But see *Castillo-Villagra*, supra (requiring pre-decision warning that official notice will be taken; court thought petition for rehearing was inadequate protection because alien might be deported while waiting for agency to act on it).

The right of rebuttal has also been held to encompass a right to have one's effort to "show the contrary" either accepted or appropriately refuted. Thus, in Union Electric Co. v. FERC, 890 F.2d 1193 (D.C.Cir.1989), the commission took official notice of recent changes in the rates of return on Treasury bonds, using this data as a rough measure of a utility's reduced cost of equity capital. Although the agency allowed the company to contest this inference in a petition for rehearing, it gave no persuasive reason for rejecting the company's argument. The court held that this cursory response violated § 556(e). This aspect of official notice procedure seems to overlap with the agency's overall duty of reasoned decisionmaking, and the scope of that duty is somewhat indeterminate. Indeed, on similar facts, another court upheld the agency because it found that the agency's inference *had* been reasonable. Boston Edison Co. v. FERC, 885 F.2d 962 (1st Cir.1989).

Judging from the small number of reported cases, the doctrine of official notice has apparently not been used extensively or creatively by many agencies. This reluctance may be partly a result of uncertainties in the applicable legal standards; without clear tests indicating when official notice is proper, agencies may be unwilling to risk reversal by taking notice of nonrecord facts. It remains a potentially useful device for simplifying and expediting hearings.

CHAPTER IX

RULES AND RULEMAKING

One of the most important developments in administrative law during the late twentieth century was the agencies' growing reliance on rulemaking as a means of formulating policy. Administrative rulemaking is not a recent invention; the federal executive departments have issued legally binding rules since the beginning of our national government, and the Administrative Procedure Act as originally passed in 1946 had several provisions dealing with rulemaking procedure. In the 1970s and 1980s, however, the number and significance of decisions being made in agency rulemaking proceedings increased dramatically.

Much can be said in favor of this trend. As commentators have argued, the rulemaking process can be more efficient than case-by-case adjudication, because it can resolve a multiplicity of issues in a single proceeding. A clear general rule can produce rapid and uniform compliance among the affected firms or individuals; the scope of an adjudicative precedent may well be harder to define, because its reach will usually depend to some degree on the facts of a particular case. At the same time, rulemaking can provide individuals with important protection. "When a governmental official is given the power to make discretionary decisions under a broad statutory standard, case-by-case decisionmaking may not be the best way to assure fairness.... [The use of rulemaking] provides [regulated persons] with more precise notice of what conduct will be sanctioned and promotes equality of treatment among similarly situated [persons]." Dixon v. Love, 431 U.S. 105 (1977). Furthermore, rulemaking proceedings can put all affected parties on notice of impending changes in regulatory policy, and give them an opportunity to be heard before the agency's position has crystallized.

Despite these advantages of rules over individual adjudications, the agencies probably would not have made such a marked shift toward rulemaking without some external pressures. From the agency's perspective, writing a general rule is often more difficult than deciding a particular case, and the likelihood of producing an undesirable or unintended result is correspondingly greater. Moreover, general rules are more likely to inspire concerted opposition from those who will be covered by them. An individual case isolates one respondent, generally selected because of questionable actions, for possible sanction, but a general rule can inspire the whole industry (whose members may or may not have engaged in similar actions) to fight—not only before the agency but in the courts, the Congress, and the media as well. In short, promulgating a rule can be more costly to the agency in time, effort, and good will than deciding a series of cases.

The major impetus for agencies to make greater use of their rulemaking authority came from Congress. Regulatory statutes enacted during the 1970s often contained express grants of rulemaking authority, and some of them specifically instructed agencies to proceed by general rule. Moreover, agencies' procedural choices were influenced by the changing nature of the tasks they were being asked to perform. In the wave of health, safety, environmental, and consumer-protection legislation that burgeoned during the 1970s, Congress created programs under which administrative officials would be responsible for regulating hundreds of thousands of workplaces or pollution sources, or millions of consumer transactions. The agencies could not hope to accomplish these missions unless they were prepared to make liberal use of rulemaking authority.

The courts, too, encouraged broader use of rulemaking. Where an agency's authority to proceed by rulemaking was in doubt, they tended to find that the agency did have such authority. For example, in National Petroleum Refiners Ass'n v. FTC, 482 F.2d 672 (D.C.Cir.1973), the FTC proposed a regulation that would have required service stations to post octane ratings on gasoline pumps. Industry groups brought suit, pointing out that the Commission was attempting to make use of a half-century-old statutory provision that it had never before regarded as a source of authority to issue substantive rules. The court turned this challenge aside, declaring that the agency's power to make rules should be "interpret[ed] liberally" in light of the numerous benefits of administrative rulemaking. Similarly, the courts were unsympathetic to arguments that an agency's rulemaking authority should be construed narrowly in order to preserve regulated parties' right to a full hearing in adjudicative proceedings in which the rule might be applied. See pp. 294–98 supra. Some courts even attempted to *force* agencies to use rulemaking, although the weight of authority strongly disfavors such efforts. See pp. 344–50 infra.

The growth of rulemaking gave rise to a searching reexamination of the adequacy of the procedures that agencies followed in adopting rules. Courts and legislatures became more willing to experiment with new variations on the APA's procedural models, as they sought to accommodate traditional rulemaking practices to the new kinds of decisions that agencies were making. Eventually this wave of procedural reform ebbed in significance, at least within the courts. Meanwhile, other innovations emerged, such as electronic docketing, negotiated rulemaking, and intensified executive oversight. To this day, the rulemaking process remains one of the most dynamic areas of administrative law.

A. THE TYPES OF ADMINISTRATIVE RULES

The APA divides agency action into the broad categories of adjudication and rulemaking, and creates different procedural models within each category. Thus, to find out what procedures the APA requires an agency to use in promulgating a particular rule or standard, one must first make sure that the decision in question is a rule, and then determine what type of rule it is.

1. *Rules Defined.* According to the APA, a rule is "the whole or a part of an agency statement of general or particular applicability and future effect designed to implement, interpret, or prescribe law or policy" or to establish rules of practice. 5 U.S.C.A. § 551(4). Any other agency action is an adjudicative "order." Id. § 551(6). These definitions, however, are often taken less seriously than one might expect, because they differ significantly from the usual understanding of the two terms.

The APA's reference to rules of "particular applicability," which seems contrary to the very idea of a rule, is something of an historical anomaly. It is designed to preserve the traditional understanding that ratemaking proceedings (that is, those concerned with the approval of "tariffs" or rate schedules filed by public utilities and common carriers) should be regarded as rulemaking proceedings rather than adjudications. In most instances, however, rules can be identified by the fact that they apply to a general *class* of persons or situations. Indeed, the premise that rules tend to be general in their applicability is at the heart of the policy justifications for the distinction between rulemaking and adjudication in administrative procedure. See pp. 219–21 supra.

Another source of difficulty is the language in § 551(4) indicating that rules must be of "future effect." Although the vast majority of administrative rules do concern future standards of conduct, agencies occasionally issue rules that are intended to operate retroactively. In Bowen v. Georgetown Univ. Hosp., 488 U.S. 204 (1988), the Court held that a statute will not be construed to authorize an agency to issue retroactive legislative rules "unless that power is conveyed in express terms." This holding rests on the potential for unfairness that exists when officials impose liability for an act that was legal when it was done. The Court did not suggest, however, that when Congress *has* authorized retroactive regulations (see, e.g., 26 U.S.C.A. § 7805(b) (tax rulings)), the agency's pronouncement is not a "rule" for APA purposes. To be sure, a concurring opinion in *Georgetown* did assert that § 551(4) bars retroactive rules. That reasoning is flawed, however, because the APA language is merely a definition, not an enabling provision. Thus, a holding that a retroactive rule is not a "rule" for APA purposes would not prevent the agency from issuing such rules, but rather would permit the agency to issue them *without the safeguards of APA rulemaking procedures*—surely an anomalous result, in light of the distinctive potential for abuse that inheres in retroactive lawmaking.

In practice, therefore, the primary factor distinguishing a rule from an adjudicative order is the "general applicability" of the former. This distinction corresponds to the usage that administrative lawyers commonly employ: An agency action that is addressed to *named parties* is an adjudication (except in ratemaking cases); an action that is addressed to a *category* of persons or situations is a rule.[1]

2. *Binding and nonbinding rules.* The most important and familiar type of rule is the *legislative* rule (sometimes called a substantive rule). It has several distinctive characteristics. It has "the force and effect of law" and is always "rooted in a grant of [quasi-legislative] power by the Congress." Chrysler Corp. v. Brown, 441 U.S. 281, 302 (1979). A valid legislative rule conclusively settles the matters it addresses, at least at the administrative level. Of course, to say that such a rule has "the force and effect of law" does not mean that it is immune from judicial review; courts can entertain challenges to the rule on various grounds. See pp. 115–24 supra. It does mean, however, that unless the rule is overturned by a court (or rescinded by the agency), it is binding on both private parties and the government itself. This *binding effect* is the chief identifying feature of a legislative rule: its nature and purpose is to alter citizens' legal rights in a decisive fashion.

1. However, when it is apparent that a rule will affect only a few identifiable persons, due process may require the agency to afford procedural safeguards resembling those available in adjudication. Vermont Yankee Nuclear Power Corp. v. NRDC, 435 U.S. 519, 542 (1978); see also Sangamon Valley Television Corp. v. United States, 269 F.2d 221 (D.C.Cir.1959), discussed at pp. 335–36 infra.

Of course, not all agency pronouncements that fit within the APA's broad definition of "rule" are legislative rules. The courts have explored the boundaries of the narrower term in the course of applying the APA's rulemaking provisions. The APA generally requires that the issuance of rules be preceded by a public procedure, usually a notice-and-comment process, but it exempts "interpretative rules, general statements of policy, [and] rules of agency organization, procedure, and practice" from this command. 5 U.S.C.A. § 553(b)(A). Congress excluded interpretive rules and policy statements (which are sometimes collectively known as "guidance documents") from the APA's procedural obligations because they are *not* legislative rules. Thus, in order to determine whether a given rule was issued in compliance with the APA, courts must regularly distinguish legislative rules from those more informal pronouncements. This has never been an easy task. During the 1970s some courts maintained that an agency is obliged to allow notice and comment before issuing any rule that has a "substantial impact" on the public. See, e.g., Pickus v. U.S. Bd. of Parole, 507 F.2d 1107, 1112 (D.C.Cir. 1974). This test subsequently fell out of favor, because it was too much at odds with the language of the APA: virtually any significant rule can have a substantial impact. Friedrich v. Secretary of HHS, 894 F.2d 829 (6th Cir.1990). Even in today's more restrained legal environment, however, the exemptions for guidance documents continue to generate confusion and extensive litigation.

A *general statement of policy* states how the agency intends to use its lawmaking power in the future but does not attempt to bind anyone immediately. The APA exempts these pronouncements from public procedure because they do not, in themselves, alter anyone's legal rights. In a subsequent proceeding, however, the agency cannot cite the policy statement as settling any issues; opposing parties have a right to be heard as though the statement had never been issued. The court found this exemption applicable in Pacific Gas & Elec. Co. v. FPC, 506 F.2d 33 (D.C.Cir.1974), in which the Commission had tentatively endorsed a particular set of priorities for allocating natural gas in the event of a shortage, but had indicated that in later proceedings it would give further consideration to its suggested approach, in light of any counterarguments presented by companies that favored alternative approaches.[2] Thus, the exemption applies to a pronouncement that merely provides a starting point for the exercise of discretion. Interstate Natural Gas Ass'n of Am. v. FERC, 285 F.3d 18, 58–60 (D.C.Cir.2002); American Hosp. Ass'n v. Bowen, 834 F.2d 1037 (D.C.Cir.1987).

2. In Lincoln v. Vigil, 508 U.S. 182 (1993), the Court stated, without much explanation, that the policy statement exemption applied to a decision by the Indian Health Service to shut down a program through which it had dispensed health care services to Indian children. *Vigil* has so far had little impact, perhaps because the Court's reliance on the exemption seems questionable: Although the agency's action did not formally curb any Indians' right to request services, the termination of the program eliminated any practical possibility that their requests would be granted, and in that sense was definitive rather than tentative.

However, courts do not always take an agency's representations as to its intentions at face value. If the language of the statement, or the way in which the agency implements it, suggests that the agency will not give opposing parties a genuine opportunity to reopen the issues, the court may conclude that the agency is trying to give the statement the force of law, making notice and comment essential. Courts often ask whether the document is being used in a manner that makes it binding "as a practical matter." Appalachian Power Co. v. EPA, 208 F.3d 1015 (D.C.Cir.2000). For example, in Community Nutrition Inst. v. Young, 818 F.2d 943 (D.C.Cir.1987), the FDA issued "action levels" assuring corn producers that they would not face prosecution if they did not exceed certain maximum levels of contamination in their products. On the surface, these statements were merely informational and nonbinding. In practice, the agency appeared to regard them as binding; it had even established a procedure for "exempting" producers from the prescribed levels in special circumstances. Accordingly, the court held that the action levels were not general statements of policy and could not stand in the absence of APA procedures. Although cases like *Community Nutrition*, which apply the policy statement exemption narrowly, serve a useful purpose insofar as they promote public input in agency decisionmaking, they also have a worrisome side. The public has a vital interest in knowing what an agency's discretionary policies are. If statements disclosing those policies are too readily held to trigger notice-and-comment obligations, agencies may simply decide to issue fewer advisory statements.

An *interpretive rule* differs from a legislative rule in that it is not intended to alter legal rights, but to state the agency's view of what existing law already requires. In some situations, the exemption for interpretive rules is relatively easy to apply. For example, if an agency has no delegated lawmaking authority, its rules are necessarily interpretive. See General Electric Co. v. Gilbert, 429 U.S. 125, 141 (1976) (discussing EEOC guidelines). On the other hand, where a statute is drafted in such a way that it cannot come into play until the administering agency issues implementing rules, those rules cannot be interpretive and must be issued through APA procedure. American Mining Cong. v. MSHA, 995 F.2d 1106 (D.C.Cir.1993).

Many cases applying the interpretive rules exemption, however, cannot be resolved on so categorical a basis. They plunge the courts into difficult case-by-case judgments. Sometimes those judgments turn on the extent to which the agency intends to apply the statement in a binding fashion, or actually does so. New York City Employees' Retirement Sys. v. SEC, 45 F.3d 7 (2d Cir.1995) (SEC no-action letters were nonbinding and thus interpretive); Alaska v. U.S. Dep't of Transp., 868 F.2d 441 (D.C.Cir.1989) (regulation was evidently intended to have binding effect and thus was not an interpretive rule). In this respect, their approach is similar to the test for general statements of policy. In addition, however, courts often examine the substance of an agency's interpretation in relation to the provision that it purports to interpret (which may be a statute or a prior legislative rule). In general, statements that largely track the language of the underlying provision, or appear to be "fairly encompassed" within that language, stand a good chance of being found to satisfy the exemption. Air Transport Ass'n of America, Inc. v. FAA, 291 F.3d 49 (D.C.Cir.2002). Conversely, if the statement expresses a position that does not seem to follow directly from the language or purposes of the provision, a court is more likely to infer that the agency is trying to establish a new legal obligation, making compliance with APA procedure essential. Sprint Corp. v. FCC, 315 F.3d 369 (D.C.Cir.2003); Hoctor v. USDA, 82 F.3d 165 (7th Cir.1996). However, not all courts apply the reasoning of *Sprint* and *Hoctor* with much vigor, if at all; in some cases, agency statements that extrapolate from highly ambiguous or open-ended language in a statute or regulation have been found to fall within the interpretive rules exemption. Shalala v. Guernsey Memorial Hosp., 514 U.S. 87 (1995); *American Mining*, supra. At present, none of these varying approaches predominates, and the case law remains in disarray.

Changes over time in an agency's interpretation can also be important in applying the exemption. The Supreme Court noted in *Guernsey* that a statement would lose its exemptive status if it were inconsistent with an existing legislative rule. In other words, a pronouncement that effectively amends a legislative rule must itself be legislative. See, e.g., Hemp Industries Ass'n v. DEA, 333 F.3d 1082 (9th Cir.2003); National Family Planning & Reprod. Health Ass'n v. Sullivan, 979 F.2d 227 (D.C.Cir.1992). The logic behind these cases is straightforward. Because the prior legislative rule has the force of law, it is binding on the agency until the agency revokes or revises it, a task that of course requires rulemaking procedure. Some courts of appeals, however, have extended the principle of these cases further. According to Alaska Prof. Hunters Ass'n v. FAA, 177 F.3d 1030 (D.C.Cir.1999), an agency is required to use notice and comment if it wishes to adopt an interpretation that is inconsistent with a prior *interpretation of a legislative rule* (see also Shell Offshore, Inc. v. Babbitt, 238 F.3d 622 (5th Cir.2001)). The soundness of *Alaska Hunters* is widely questioned. Agencies frequently revise their readings of their own regulations, as a result of changes in agency leadership or the lessons of experience. It is difficult to see why a second reading cannot be considered an "interpretation" merely because it differs from the first. *Alaska Hunters* is also in serious tension with the acknowledged principle that an agency may use an interpretive rule to revise its reading of a regulatory *statute*, provided it explains its reasons for the change. See, e.g., Erringer v. Thompson, 371 F.3d 625 (9th Cir. 2004); National Org. of Veterans' Advocates v. Secretary of Veterans Affairs, 260 F.3d 1365 (Fed.Cir. 2001); Warder v. Shalala, 149 F.3d 73 (1st Cir. 1998). This controversy provides further evidence of the widespread uncertainty about the scope of the exemption.

B. RULEMAKING PROCEDURES

Agency rulemaking proceedings can take on three different procedural forms under the APA: they may be formal, informal, or exempted completely from the Act's procedural requirements. In addition, the basic APA procedural models have sometimes been supplemented or modified by Congress in particular grants of rulemaking authority, and reviewing courts have, at least in the past, occasionally required agencies to use procedures other than those specified in the APA. Before discussing these latter "hybrid" rulemaking approaches, however, it is necessary to examine the three kinds of rulemaking proceedings contemplated by the APA.

1. THE APA PROCEDURAL MODELS

a. *Exempted Rulemaking.* The general rulemaking provision of the APA, § 553, contains several exemptions that authorize agencies to issue final rules without any public participation. The exemptions for interpretive rules and policy statements have just been discussed. In addition, § 553(a) completely exempts from public notice and opportunity to comment all rulemaking proceedings relating to "a military or foreign affairs function" or "agency management or personnel or to public property, loans, grants, benefits, or contracts." Commentators have strongly criticized these sweeping exemptions, and the Administrative Conference of the United States has recommended that they be repealed or narrowed. ACUS Recommendation No. 73–5, 39 Fed.Reg. 4847 (1974) (military or foreign affairs); ACUS Recommendation No. 69–8, 38 Fed. Reg. 19,782 (1973) (grants or benefits). The exemption for proprietary matters, such as grants and benefits, seems particularly difficult to justify. When it was originally enacted, there was a general assumption that private parties had few procedural rights when the government action affected a "privilege" or a "mere gratuity" rather than private property. That distinction has now been rejected as unsound and unworkable in contemporary due process analysis; see pp. 201–04 supra. The government uses the spending power to pursue a wide variety of social objectives, and the effect of the § 553 exemption is to immunize many important policy decisions from public participation—although some agencies have softened this impact by passing regulations that waive any reliance on the exemption.

The APA also permits agencies to issue *procedural rules* without prior notice. § 553(b)(A). This exemption reflects "the congressional judgment that such rules, because they do not directly guide public conduct, do not merit the administrative burdens of public input proceedings." U.S. Dep't of Labor v. Kast Metals Corp., 744 F.2d 1145 (5th Cir.1984). For example, an agency's decision about where it will concentrate its enforcement resources does not alter anyone's substantive rights and thus is within the exemption. Id.; American Hosp. Ass'n v. Bowen, 834 F.2d 1037 (D.C.Cir.1987). Unlike the interpretive rule and policy statement exemptions, however, the procedural rules exemption does not rest on an implied contrast with legislative rules, for procedural rules are often "legislative" in character: if written in a way that draws upon the agency's delegated lawmaking power, they are binding on both citizens and the agency. See Service v. Dulles, 354 U.S. 363 (1957).

The final APA rulemaking exemption applies when "notice and public procedure ... are impracticable, unnecessary, or contrary to the public interest." 5 U.S.C.A. § 553(b)(3)(B). The "impracticable" and "contrary to public interest" branches of this exemption apply when the rule is urgent, or a delay in its issuance would frustrate the rule's purpose. See, e.g., Jifry v. FAA, 370 F.3d 1174 (D.C.Cir.2004) (upholding FAA's summary adoption of post–9/11 rule authorizing immediate revocation of alien pilot's flight privileges if Transportation Security Administration determines that pilot is a security threat). The "unnecessary" branch applies when the subject matter is so routine or trivial that the value of public participation would be negligible. When an agency invokes either branch of this exemption, the APA requires it to make a "good cause" finding and incorporate in the final rule a brief statement of its reasons for avoiding public participation. The finding is subject to judicial review, and frequently encounters a skeptical reception in the courts. See, e.g., New Jersey v. U.S. EPA, 626 F.2d 1038, 1049–50 (D.C.Cir.1980) (EPA's approval of state plans for compliance with Clean Air Act required public comment, despite time pressure created by statutory deadline).

While these exemptions from public participation are quite broad, an agency is generally free to give affected persons more opportunities to participate than the Act requires. Thus it can use notice-and-comment procedures, or confer informally with affected interest groups, or hold public hearings on important rules that are technically exempt from the APA. The Administrative Conference recommended that agencies provide such opportunities for public participation when an interpretive rule or general policy statement "is likely to have a substantial impact on the public." ACUS Recommendation No. 76–5, 41 Fed.Reg. 56,769 (1976). ACUS also recommended that agencies should provide an opportunity for post-promulgation comment after they have issued rules as impracticable or contrary to public interest under the "good cause" exception. ACUS Recommendation 95–4, 60 Fed.Reg. 43,108 (1995). Rules issued on this basis are often called *interim final rules*, because they are both interim (they will be reconsidered and perhaps replaced in light of comments received) and final (they go into effect immediately). For rules issued under the "unnecessary" branch of the "good cause" exemption, ACUS recommended that the agency use *direct final rulemaking. Id.* This is a technique by which the agency adopts a rule without prior notice and comment but announces that it will withdraw the rule if anyone files an adverse comment within a short stated period thereafter. Such a commitment effectively provides a "reality check" for the agency's assumption that the rule will prove noncontroversial, but the agency remains free to propose it again using the normal notice-and-comment process.

b. *Informal Rulemaking.* The basic rulemaking procedure prescribed by § 553 of the APA is generally called "informal" or "notice-and-comment" rulemaking. In the absence of directives to the contrary in an agency's enabling legislation, the APA's informal rulemaking procedures will apply whenever the agency issues substantive rules. Thus, if the statute merely authorizes the agency to issue regulations and those regulations affect the legal rights of private parties, the agency will be required to follow the notice-and-comment procedure of § 553.

The APA's informal rulemaking process is simple and flexible, consisting of only three procedural requirements. First, the agency must give prior *notice,* which is usually accomplished by publication of an item in the Federal Register. The notice must contain "either the terms or substance of the proposed rule or a description of the subjects and issues involved," as well as a reference to the legal authority for issuing the rule and information about the opportunities for public participation. 5 U.S.C.A. § 553(b). After publication of the notice of rulemaking, the agency must "give interested persons an opportunity to participate" through *submission of written comments* containing data, views, or arguments. 5 U.S.C.A. § 553(c). The agency is not required to hold any oral hearings under this section; it has discretion to decide whether interested persons will be allowed to submit testimony or to present oral argument to the decisionmakers. Finally, after the agency has considered the public comments, it must issue with its final rules "a concise general *statement of ... basis and purpose.*" Id. Reviewing courts expect the agency to spell out in detail its reasons for issuing a rule; thus, statements of basis and purpose have become increasingly lengthy in modern practice. See Automotive Parts & Accessories Ass'n v. Boyd, 407 F.2d 330, 338 (D.C.Cir.1968) (statement must be complete enough to enable the reviewing court "to see what major issues of policy were ventilated by the informal proceedings and why the agency reacted to them as it did").

Recently, advances in electronic technology have led a number of agencies to incorporate use of the Internet into their notice and comment process. At some agency websites, members of the public can find notices of pending rulemaking proceedings, access background materials, submit on-line comments, and read and respond to comments filed by others. Congress has encouraged this sort of "electronic docketing" in § 206 of the E–Government Act of 2002, Pub.L.No. 107–347, 44 U.S.C.A. § 3501 note. A project that may culminate in access to similar services at a single portal for all the major regulatory agencies is under development by the Office of Management and Budget at *www.regulations.gov*.

Whether conducted on-line or off-line, the notice-and-comment rulemaking procedures spelled out in the APA provide an efficient means by which administrators can acquire information and reach a prompt decision. From the point of view of a party who opposes a particular rule, however, the procedures may seem much less fair than trial-type hearings, where parties enjoy extensive rights to know and challenge opposing evidence. The APA informal rulemaking provisions do not expressly require the agency to expose its factual, legal, and policy support to public criticism. Unless a challenging party is able to obtain internal agency documents under the Freedom of Information Act, see pp. 153–61 supra, she may not be able to discover the agency's supporting evidence and analysis until the rule has been issued and an action has been brought in court to challenge its validity. Consequently, informal rulemaking may produce inaccurate or misguided decisions if the agency is not sufficiently rigorous or self-disciplined in gathering and analyzing information. For these reasons, regulated industries and other constituency groups have often sought additional procedural safeguards in administrative rulemaking. One strategy they have used is to attempt to invoke the APA's formal rulemaking procedures.

c. *Formal Rulemaking.* Section 553(c) of the APA contains an exception to the general principle that administrative rulemaking requires, at most, a notice-and-comment process. It states that "[w]hen rules are required by statute to be made on the record after opportunity for an agency hearing," the agency must follow sections 556 and 557 of the APA—that is, it must afford most of the procedures required in formal adjudication. Thus, when some other statute (usually the one that delegates rule-making authority) directs the agency to do so, it must conduct a trial-type hearing and provide interested persons with an opportunity to testify and cross-examine adverse witnesses before issuing a rule. (See chart on p. 248.) This process is traditionally called "rulemaking on a record" or "formal rulemaking."

Since legislative drafters are often not attuned to the nuances of the APA, the relevant statutes may be ambiguous with respect to whether Congress intended the agency to use formal or informal rule-making. This was the situation that the Supreme Court encountered in United States v. Florida East Coast Ry., 410 U.S. 224 (1973). The statute merely provided that the Interstate Commerce Commission "may, after hearing," issue rules establishing incentive per diem charges for the use of freight cars. The protesting railroad argued that this language required the ICC to follow the APA's formal rule-making procedures, and the legislative history did tend to support this conclusion. But the Supreme Court held that notice and comment rulemaking would suffice; although a statute did not have to track verbatim the APA phrase "on the record after opportunity for an agency hearing" in order to trigger the formal rulemaking requirements, a clear expression of congressional intent was necessary. In effect, the *Florida East Coast* decision created a strong presumption in favor of informal rulemaking.

Although the point was not openly discussed in the opinion, the *Florida East Coast* decision may be based upon a belief that trial-type hearings are generally not desirable in rulemaking. Commentators have criticized formal rulemaking as a costly, cumbersome process that contributes little to the quality of decision. The experience of the FDA, which was required to use formal rulemaking in some of its regulatory programs, is often cited as illustrative. In the notorious Peanut Butter rulemaking, for example, the parties consumed weeks of hearing time and hundreds of pages of transcript so that experts could be cross-examined on such issues as whether peanut butter should contain 87 or 90 percent peanuts. See Corn Products Co. v. FDA, 427 F.2d 511 (3d Cir.1970). Another FDA formal rulemaking dealing with vitamin supplements was an even longer exercise in futility. After it had held 18 months of hearings, the agency lost on appeal because it had unduly restricted cross-examination of a government expert. National Nutritional Foods Ass'n v. FDA, 504 F.2d 761, 792–99 (2d Cir.1974). In other agencies, the costs and delays associated with formal rulemaking led to the virtual abandonment of regulatory programs. Robert W. Hamilton, *Procedures for the Adoption of Rules of General Applicability: The Need for Procedural Innovation in Administrative Rulemaking,* 60 Cal.L.Rev. 1276, 1283–1313 (1972). Against the background of this experience, the Supreme Court's reluctance to conclude that an ambiguous statute required formal rulemaking is understandable. Today, formal rulemaking has been nearly abandoned in federal agency proceedings.

Even when a statute does plainly require formal rulemaking, the APA permits some departures from the procedures used in formal adjudications (described in Chapter 7). The most notable difference is that the strict separation of functions requirements of § 554(d) do not apply. Decisionmakers in a formal rulemaking are free to consult with staff experts throughout the agency, including those who were responsible for presenting the agency's position at the hearing. Unlike adjudications, rulemaking proceedings are generally not accusatory; consequently, there is less need to isolate the decisionmakers from a potentially adversary staff in order to assure fairness to the accused. Also, in formal rulemaking the agency may substitute written submissions for oral direct testimony and may forego the ALJ's initial or recommended decision. Id. §§ 556(d), 557(b). However, the § 557(d) ban on ex parte contacts with outsiders does apply.

2. JUDICIALLY IMPOSED PARTICIPATION RIGHTS

In the late 1960s, as rulemaking became an increasingly important form of administrative decisionmaking, dissatisfaction with the rulemaking procedures provided by the APA began to spread. Informal rulemaking was simple and efficient, but it gave interested persons few rights to know and contest the basis of a proposed rule. Formal rulemaking, on the other hand, provided abundant opportunities to participate and to challenge the agency's proposal, but at the cost of near paralysis. As these shortcomings became more apparent, courts, commentators, and legislators attempted to develop intermediate procedural models that would permit effective public participation in rulemaking while avoiding the excesses of trial procedure. These compromise procedures were generally described as "hybrid rulemaking."

Reviewing courts were among the most active proponents of hybrid rulemaking procedures. Although constitutionally based notions of fundamental fairness seemed to underlie this development, the courts generally did not rest their holdings squarely on the Constitution, doubtless because of the traditional understanding that the due process clause has little application in rulemaking cases. Nevertheless, they readily found a variety of other legal bases for imposing hybrid rulemaking procedures. Inartful or ambiguous legislative drafting sometimes provided an opportunity for creative judicial interpretation. For example, in Mobil Oil Corp. v. FPC, 483 F.2d 1238 (D.C.Cir.1973), the court held that the FPC had to employ hybrid procedures, including evidentiary hearings on some contested issues, in setting rates to be charged by pipelines transporting certain kinds of hydrocarbon products. The holding was based on a statute providing that courts should review these rules using the substantial evidence test (a standard of review normally associated with formal proceedings).

In other instances, the courts reinterpreted the APA provisions governing informal rulemaking to enhance the opportunities for meaningful public participation. This approach is illustrated by United States v. Nova Scotia Food Prods. Corp., 568 F.2d 240 (2d Cir.1977), where the court found an APA violation in the FDA's failure to make a key scientific study available to potential commenters. "To suppress meaningful comment by failure to disclose the basic data relied upon," the court reasoned, "is akin to rejecting comment altogether." Finally, some of the hybrid rulemaking opinions had little direct basis in the texts of statutes or constitutional provisions. In essence, the courts created a judicial common law of rulemaking procedure.

Whatever their legal bases, the hybrid rulemaking requirements generally fell into two broad categories. First, as in *Nova Scotia,* the courts pressed agencies to disclose the data on which a proposed rule rested, so that opposing parties could offer responses. As a well-known case remarked, "It is not consonant with the purpose of a rule-making proceeding to promulgate rules on the basis of inadequate data, or on data that, [to a] critical degree, is known only to the agency." Portland Cement Ass'n v. Ruckelshaus, 486 F.2d 375, 393–94 (D.C.Cir. 1973). Second, as in *Mobil Oil,* reviewing courts sometimes remanded rules with instructions that the agency allow cross-examination on particular issues, even though the proceeding was generally governed by the APA's informal rulemaking provisions. It was in a case of the latter variety that the Supreme Court ultimately intervened, writing an unusually strong opinion that effectively halted the judicial development of hybrid rulemaking procedures.

Vermont Yankee Nuclear Power Corp. v. Natural Resources Defense Council, Inc., 435 U.S. 519 (1978), arose out of a rulemaking proceeding in which the Atomic Energy Commission (the predecessor of the Nuclear Regulatory Commission) sought to determine the weight that it should assign to the environmental effects of radioactive waste when it conducted individual licensing proceedings for nuclear power plants. The agency was authorized to use informal rulemaking in issuing this kind of rule, but it had voluntarily held an oral hearing at which witnesses were questioned by agency representatives. On judicial review, the District of Columbia Circuit held that the agency had not permitted sufficient exploration of key testimony concerning its plans for disposal of nuclear waste: on remand, environmentalist intervenors would be entitled to fuller procedural opportunities, such as discovery or cross-examination.

The Supreme Court unanimously reversed, denouncing the D.C. Circuit's opinion as "Monday morning quarterbacking." The Court said that, except in "extremely rare" circumstances, courts may not force agencies to utilize rulemaking procedures beyond those prescribed in the APA or other statutory or constitutional provisions. In the Court's view, the APA enacted " 'a formula upon which opposing social and political forces have come to rest' " (quoting Wong Yang Sung v. McGrath, 339 U.S. 33, 40 (1950)), and it is not the province of the judiciary to alter that legislative judgment. The Court also rejected the argument that additional procedures such as cross-examination would provide a more adequate record for agency decision and judicial review. On the other hand, the Court was convinced that judicially imposed hybrid rulemaking requirements would impose real costs. If the courts were free to devise procedural requirements on an ad hoc basis, "judicial review would be totally unpredictable"; the agencies, seeking to avoid reversals, would inevitably gravitate towards using highly adversarial procedures in every case.

In general, courts have faithfully adhered to *Vermont Yankee*'s admonition against imposing rulemaking procedures beyond those mandated by statute. This does not mean, however, that judicial supervision of the rulemaking process has become insignificant. In the first place, courts can still enforce the APA's requirements, and they often do so aggressively. Not infrequently, for example, an agency is held to have violated its notice obligations under 5 U.S.C.A. § 553(b) because it promulgated a final rule that is not a "logical outgrowth" of the proposed rule on which it solicited comments. See, e.g., Chocolate Mfrs. Ass'n v. Block, 755 F.2d 1098

(4th Cir.1985). And courts have had little difficulty adhering to the *Nova Scotia* principle that basic factual assumptions underlying a proposed rule must be made available for comment by interested parties; this principle is now regarded as implied by § 553(b) or § 553(c). See, e.g., Chamber of Commerce v. SEC, 443 F.3d 890 (D.C.Cir.2006); Mortgage Investors Corp. v. Gober, 220 F.3d 1375 (Fed. Cir.2000).

Moreover, *Vermont Yankee* has not been read as detracting from the courts' ability to engage in rigorous review of the *substance* of agency rulemaking activities.[3] Modern "hard look" review, as exemplified by decisions like *State Farm,* demands that an agency build a record in support of a rule and respond to significant comments made by participants in the rulemaking proceeding. See pp. 116–19 supra. Indeed, the *Vermont Yankee* opinion expressly reaffirmed the principle that the rationality of an agency rule must be judged on the basis of the record that was before the agency when it issued the rule. In a sense, this principle contradicts the Court's emphasis on deference to Congress, because the notion of a rulemaking record is itself a judicial creation that was never envisioned by the framers of the APA. See pp. 111–15 supra. Be that as it may,

---

3. On remand in the *Vermont Yankee* case itself, the D.C. Circuit set aside the AEC rule on the merits as an abuse of discretion. The Supreme Court again reversed, but did so in a narrowly written opinion that displayed no overall displeasure with the D.C. Circuit's policy of subjecting administrative rules to a "hard look." Baltimore Gas & Electric Co. v. NRDC, 462 U.S. 87 (1983).

the Court's stance is understandable in pragmatic terms: the agency has a duty to build a record that demonstrates that it has exercised its discretion seriously and responsibly, but it has wide latitude to determine the best way to assemble that record.

Some agencies, however, still follow hybrid rule-making procedures because of legislative mandates that obligate them to do so. In several regulatory statutes adopted in the 1970s, Congress showed considerable willingness to experiment with variations on the APA rulemaking models, often borrowing devices that had first been developed in the hybrid rulemaking cases. See, e.g., 42 U.S.C.A. § 7607(d) (EPA rulemaking under Clean Air Act); 15 U.S.C.A. § 57a (FTC consumer protection rule-making). By the 1980s this legislative trend had faded away: Congress, too, seems to have recognized the large differences between writing a rule and trying a case. Indeed, experience with the legislatively imposed hybrid procedures has not been encouraging. The Administrative Conference of the U.S. concluded that its detailed study of hybrid rulemaking procedures used by the FTC provided "compelling evidence" that trial-type hearing procedure "is not an effective means of controlling an agency's discretion in its exercise of a broad delegation of legislative power which has not acquired, in law, specific meaning." ACUS Recommendation No. 80–1, 45 Fed.Reg. 46,772 (1980). Nevertheless, Congress has not repealed many of the 1970s mandates;

they remain on the books, as a continuing legacy of the hybrid rulemaking era.

3. EX PARTE CONTACTS
AND PREJUDGMENT

The rise and fall of faith in procedural formality, which was so prominent in the debate over participation rights, has been replicated in other controversies concerning the rulemaking process. For example, § 553 of the APA says nothing about the problems of ex parte contacts and administrative bias. As rulemaking grew in importance during the 1970s, however, it was often argued that courts should devise safeguards in those areas, borrowing from the principles enforced in formal adjudications. See generally pp. 276–91 supra. The debate was a vigorous one, for important procedural values were at stake on both sides of the issues. Ultimately, however, the balance seems to have been struck decisively on the side of administrative flexibility in the rulemaking setting.

Even before the era of the hybrid rulemaking decisions, there had been one occasion on which a court overturned a rule issued in notice-and-comment proceedings because the decisionmakers had engaged in off-the-record discussions with an interested party. In Sangamon Valley Television Corp. v. United States, 269 F.2d 221 (D.C.Cir.1959), the court set aside a rule reallocating a television channel from one city to another, because a corporate official of an interested license applicant had met informally with the FCC commissioners to discuss the merits of the proceeding. The court noted that the proceeding involved "conflicting private claims to a valuable privilege": although the rule on its face made only a general determination as to the number of stations that would be available in the two cities, in effect it determined which of several competing applicants would get a license. In this respect, the proceeding was functionally similar to a comparative licensing adjudication. Because of this unusual circumstance, *Sangamon* was viewed for many years as having no application to most rulemaking proceedings.

The situation was less closely analogous to adjudication when the D.C. Circuit set aside another FCC rule on ex parte contact grounds in Home Box Office, Inc. v. FCC, 567 F.2d 9 (D.C.Cir.1977). In the course of developing a rule regulating pay cable television, the commissioners had held a number of private meetings with interested participants. The court felt that it would be "intolerable" if there were one rulemaking record for insiders, and another for the general public. In addition to this concern for the fairness of the process, the court reasoned that nonrecord communications would undermine the effectiveness of judicial review, because the reviewing judges would not have access through the rulemaking record to all of the material considered by the agency.

By the time it decided Sierra Club v. Costle, 657 F.2d 298 (1981), the D.C. Circuit seemed to have come full circle from *HBO* to the belief that ex parte contacts during informal rulemaking are not only permissible, but affirmatively desirable. In rejecting environmentalists' claims that EPA rules governing air pollution from coal-fired power plants should be set aside because of ex parte contacts with industry representatives and others, the court noted: "Under our system of government, the very legitimacy of general policymaking performed by unelected administrators depends in no small part upon the openness, accessibility, and amenability of these officials to the needs and ideas of the public from whom their ultimate authority derives, and upon whom their commands must fall." The court discounted the risk that the agency might be influenced by undisclosed information, because the underlying statute required EPA to justify its rule on the basis of a publicly available administrative record. (The court's reasoning seems equally applicable to other rulemaking situations, because it is now standard practice for courts to review a rule on the basis of the administrative record. See pp. 111–15 supra.) However, the statute did require the agency to put any written communication having "central relevance" to the rule on the public record so that other participants would have an opportunity to respond, and the court reasoned that *oral* communications of equal relevance should be treated in the same way.

The courts have been equally lenient, if not more so, in permitting agency heads to consult freely with their own staffs. In United Steelworkers of America v. Marshall, 647 F.2d 1189 (D.C.Cir.1980),

the challenged contacts were between the Occupational Safety and Health Administration and some
consultants hired by the agency to analyze the
record of a rulemaking proceeding establishing permissible levels of worker exposure to airborne lead.
The court recognized that "nothing in the Administrative Procedure Act bars a staff advocate from
advising the decisionmaker in setting a final rule,"
and that *Vermont Yankee* militated against any
judicial effort to impose additional procedural requirements in rulemaking. The court then held
that, although the consultants had earlier appeared
as witnesses in the proceeding, they were "the
functional equivalent of agency staff." Inasmuch as
there was no strong evidence that the agency had
relied on otherwise undisclosed facts or legal arguments supplied by the consultants, their work in
summarizing and analyzing the record had been a
legitimate part of the agency's deliberative process.

Reluctance to force rulemaking into the mold of
adjudicative procedure is also evident in the law's
response to the issue of prejudgment in rulemaking.
In Association of Nat'l Advertisers, Inc. v. FTC, 627
F.2d 1151 (D.C.Cir.1979), the court concluded that
the FTC chairman should not be disqualified from
participating in a rulemaking proceeding to ban
advertisements directed at young children, even
though he had made statements and written letters
indicating that he strongly favored some regulatory
action against the advertisers. The court reasoned
that administrators should be encouraged to speak
their minds on the issues involved in pending rule-

making proceedings, so that they can engage in direct, candid dialogue with affected interest groups, and thereby assess the political acceptability of different policy choices. In rulemaking, therefore, the test for disqualification should not be whether the decisionmaker appears to have prejudged any fact issue (the test applied in adjudicative proceedings), but whether "clear and convincing evidence" shows that he has an "unalterably closed mind" on the pending matters.[4] One might suspect that the court's test will, as a practical matter, virtually immunize agency officials from the threat of being removed from a rulemaking proceeding for bias, even if they are highly partisan advocates for their cause. The case dramatically illustrates the extent to which courts now view rulemaking as a political process, in which value judgments and unprovable assumptions are more important than the kind of facts that can be found by a neutral, detached adjudicator.

C. EXECUTIVE OVERSIGHT

While courts have scaled back their attempts to supervise the rulemaking process in the years since *Vermont Yankee,* managerial activity within the executive branch has increased. At present the formal oversight function is exercised primarily by the

4. A further complication in the *National Advertisers* case was that Congress had directed the FTC to exercise its rulemaking authority through relatively formal procedures, resembling those used in adjudication; nevertheless, the proceeding clearly was designed to produce a rule, not an order, and thus the disqualification test for rulemakers was applicable.

Office of Information and Regulatory Affairs (OIRA), which engages in systematic scrutiny of proposed "significant" rules to determine whether they are cost-justified and consistent with administration policy. See pp. 64–67 supra.

To some observers, the extensive involvement of White House officials in rulemaking proceedings implicates the dangers of ex parte contacts in a particularly glaring fashion: private meetings between OIRA and officials at rulemaking agencies have been thought to subvert the essential procedural regularity and openness of the rulemaking process. However, in Sierra Club v. Costle, 657 F.2d 298 (D.C.Cir.1981) (discussed at pp. 336–37 supra), the court defended White House participation in rulemaking proceedings: "Our form of government simply could not function effectively or rationally if key executive policymakers were isolated from each other and from the Chief Executive. Single-mission agencies do not always have the answers to complex regulatory problems." The court thus declined to invalidate a rulemaking proceeding during which EPA officials had met with President Carter and his economic advisors but had not disclosed this meeting in the administrative record.[5] Nevertheless, the court suggested that disclosure of presidential contacts might be essential if the discussion brought important new factual information to the agency's attention. Accordingly, OIRA soon adopted a proce-

---

5. The court was also tolerant of pressures emanating from the legislative branch. See p. 50 supra.

dure for submitting such facts to the agency for inclusion in the administrative record.

The court's endorsement of executive supervision facilitated the growth of the Reagan oversight program. During the program's initial years, however, there were persistent reports that OIRA was pressuring agencies to weaken regulations in ways that were antithetical to the spirit of the statutes they were administering. In 1986, under threat of congressional intervention, OIRA adopted a set of procedural reforms, including a commitment that its formal written communications to agencies would be released to the public after a final rule was issued. Controls on "conduit communications" (in which OIRA passes along to an agency the views of interested outside parties) were also tightened. In his overhaul of the oversight program in 1993, President Clinton instituted further safeguards: OIRA is now required to maintain a public log disclosing the status of rules while they are under review; and an agency must identify, in the notice accompanying a published rule, any changes it made at the suggestion of OIRA. In the George W Bush administration, OIRA has gone even further, routinely posting its correspondence with agencies on its website. These reforms have served to improve the accountability of a reviewing office that, as a practical matter, usually operates independently of the President himself. However, informal contacts by the President's personal staff of policy advisors remain essentially unregulated by procedural checks in rulemaking, despite their increasing importance.

D. RULEMAKING BY NEGOTIATION

The image of rulemaking as a political process, which underlies decisions such as *Sierra Club* and *National Advertisers,* has given impetus to efforts by some agencies to use structured bargaining among competing interest groups as a means for developing certain rules. Initially, these experiments in consensus-seeking, generally called "regulatory negotiation" or "reg-neg," were pioneered by the Administrative Conference. Later, Congress codified the basic process in the Negotiated Rulemaking Act of 1990, 5 U.S.C.A. § 561 et seq. In a typical regulatory negotiation, concerned interest groups and the agency itself send representatives to bargaining sessions led by a mediator. Membership on the negotiating committee is to be balanced among the various interests that might be affected by the ultimate rule. The agreement that results from these sessions is then forwarded to the agency, which normally will publish it as a proposed rule and follow through with the standard APA rulemaking process. However, the agency is not obligated to accept the participants' compromise as a final rule, or even to propose it as a tentative rule. See USA Group Loan Services, Inc. v. Riley, 82 F.3d 708 (7th Cir.1996) (agency that repudiated reg-neg consensus agreement in its notice of proposed rulemaking was not guilty of "bad faith" negotiation).

At its best, regulatory negotiation can provide a superior format for encouraging cooperation rather than confrontation. If all affected interests, including the agency, participate in hammering out a consensual solution, the result is likely to be more acceptable to the participants than any policy that the agency or an external reviewer might seek to impose. Even the proponents of regulatory negotiation acknowledge, however, that in some situations the technique is not worth trying, such as where the number of interests needing representation is unmanageably high, or where agreement would be possible only if some participants compromised on a fundamental issue of principle. To date, the percentage of rulemaking proceedings handled through regulatory negotiation remains fairly low.

A built-in difficulty with the process is that the negotiating group's proposed rule may contain illogical compromises that were helpful in the search for consensus, but that the agency cannot easily justify as a rational exercise of its discretion under the governing statute. The Act attempts to counteract this tendency by providing that, on judicial review, a court should accord no greater deference towards a rule that is the product of negotiated rulemaking than it would display toward a rule developed through other rulemaking procedures. 5 U.S.C.A. § 570. In practice, however, most negotiated rules are never subjected to judicial review—precisely because they do embody a bargain that the participants are reluctant to disturb. The relatively low degree of external oversight to which negotiated rules are subjected puts a premium on ensuring that the negotiation is conducted with due attention to legality and the public interest when the participants forge their agreement in the first instance.

E. REQUIRED RULEMAKING

Agencies often choose to make policy in an individual adjudication rather than in a rulemaking proceeding, and for the most part the law respects this preference. The APA provides procedural models for both rulemaking and adjudication, but it does not direct an administrator to use one form of proceeding rather than the other. Nor do most substantive regulatory statutes limit an agency's choice of procedural vehicle; typically, they simply authorize the administrator both to issue rules and to adjudicate particular cases. As for judicial constraints, the general rule is well established: "the choice between proceeding by general rule or by individual, ad hoc litigation is one that lies primarily in the informed discretion of the administrative agency." SEC v. Chenery Corp., 332 U.S. 194, 203 (1947) *(Chenery II)*.

As *Chenery* recognizes, agencies often have legitimate reasons to make policy through adjudication. The agency may feel a need to consider the policy first in a concrete fact situation, building rules only incrementally in the fashion of common law courts. It may sense that the issues are too complex, or not ripe enough, for across-the-board treatment. Fundamental differences of perspective may prevent the members of a multi-member agency from uniting behind a common policy. Alternatively, the agency may not even have thought that a new policy was needed until the final stages of an adjudication, when the cost and delay of starting a new proceeding would be considerable. The agency may also have less attractive motives for shunning rulemaking: for example, it may calculate that it can avoid public or congressional criticism if its new policies are buried in fact-specific adjudications instead of being clearly articulated by rule. Usually, however, courts do not attempt to question the agency's motives or to second-guess its judgment as to how to develop policy.

Nevertheless, the *Chenery* principle has long troubled scholars and judges who have believed that rulemaking has sizable advantages in terms of both efficiency and fairness, see pp. 306–07 supra, and that some agencies rely too heavily on case-by-case adjudication to formulate policy. This critique has occasionally prompted courts to attempt to force agencies to make wider use of rulemaking in policy development. To date, however, exceptions to *Chenery* are rare and ill-defined.

A number of cases raising this issue have involved the National Labor Relations Board, which has been exceptionally reluctant to act through rules. In NLRB v. Wyman–Gordon Co., 394 U.S. 759 (1969), the Board ordered Wyman–Gordon to provide union organizers with a list of the names and addresses of employees eligible to vote in an election to select a collective bargaining representative. The Board's

directive was based on *Excelsior Underwear, Inc.,*
156 N.L.R.B. 1236 (1966), an earlier agency adjudication in which the Board had established the list
requirement, but had made it applicable only in
future cases. Wyman–Gordon claimed that the *Excelsior* requirement was equivalent to a "rule" and
was invalid because it had not been adopted in
accordance with the APA rulemaking procedures. In
the Supreme Court, the plurality opinion (for four
Justices) strongly criticized the NLRB's failure to
use rulemaking procedure to establish the *Excelsior*
list requirement. Nevertheless, the plurality upheld
the Board's action, because the agency had ordered
Wyman–Gordon to produce the list during a valid
adjudicative proceeding. Although the Board was
not entitled to treat the *Excelsior* decision as conclusively settling the propriety of the list requirement (as a rule would have done, see pp. 294–98
supra), it was free to rely on that decision as a
precedent while litigating against subsequent employers. That is just what it had done in Wyman–
Gordon's case. In effect, therefore, the Court held
that an agency *may* develop new policies through
adjudication, so long as each person to whom those
policies are later applied is given an individual right
to be heard on the question of whether the Board
should modify or abandon its case-law "rule."

The issue of choice between adjudication and
rulemaking returned to the Court in NLRB v. Bell
Aerospace Co., 416 U.S. 267 (1974). The agency
certified a bargaining unit of Bell's buyers, who
under previous Board policy would have been re-

garded as "managerial employees" who could not be given such rights. As in *Wyman–Gordon,* the company argued that a significant policy change of this nature had to be made in rulemaking rather than in an individual adjudication. Once again, the Supreme Court disagreed, reaffirming *Chenery* and stating that the Board's preference for adjudication in this case deserved "great weight." (The Court did indicate that a "different result" might have been required if the company had relied to its detriment on prior Board policy. However, this "different result" would probably not have been a demand for rulemaking. Generally, when courts discern unfair retroactivity in an agency order, their response is simply to hold that any attempt to apply the new policy to the respondent would be void as an abuse of discretion. See p. 107 supra.)

Notwithstanding this line of cases, the Court has on one occasion required an agency to engage in rulemaking. In Morton v. Ruiz, 415 U.S. 199 (1974), the Court reversed a decision of the Bureau of Indian Affairs denying benefits to Indians under a federal assistance program. The BIA had developed an internal policy of denying assistance to claimants who lived outside of the reservations, but it had never communicated this policy to the public. The Court held that, while this policy might be a reasonable response to limitations in the program's funding, it could not be implemented through ad hoc decisions; the BIA had to issue valid legislative rules, which would be published in the Federal Register, before it could cut off the claimants' eligibility in this fashion. A relatively systematic approach to dispensing public assistance payments was needed "so as to assure that [the agency's policy] is being applied consistently and so as to avoid both the reality and the appearance of arbitrary denial of benefits to potential beneficiaries."

Many commentators consider *Ruiz* irreconcilable with the *Chenery* line of cases. One explanation for these contrasting holdings is that Ruiz was relying on an interest that was not implicated in the other cases: an interest in obtaining fair consideration of his application for benefits that Congress intended to confer on persons such as himself. This, however, is only a partial explanation. The Court did not explain why Ruiz's case differed from that of many other statutory beneficiaries who might feel that an agency has not sufficiently spelled out the criteria by which it will dispense benefits.

While *Ruiz* is a unique case at the Supreme Court level, it was not without antecedents in administrative law. A handful of cases, decided under the due process clause, have held that an agency must make selections among applicants for scarce governmental benefits on the basis of "ascertainable standards." See Holmes v. New York City Housing Auth., 398 F.2d 262 (2d Cir.1968) (applications for public housing); Hornsby v. Allen, 326 F.2d 605 (5th Cir.1964) (applications for retail liquor licenses). Similarly, under a version of the nondelegation doctrine that now has apparently been abandoned, judicial refusals to strike down vague regulatory statutes were occasionally predicated on an expectation that the administering agency would develop standards to particularize the statute. See pp. 23–24 supra. To be sure, these cases can be read as having permitted the agencies to develop the requisite "standards" in adjudicative proceedings, obviating the need for regulations as such. The Court in *Ruiz* may have reasoned, however, that in a large nation-wide program like the BIA's, the only real protection for impecunious claimants like Ruiz lay in readily accessible rules that would ensure consistent behavior by the low-level bureaucrats who would effectively be the final decisionmakers in most instances.

In summary, agencies have almost complete freedom, in the absence of statutory restrictions, to choose between rules and orders as vehicles for policymaking. A few decisions have required rulemaking in order to ensure that applications for statutory benefits will be handled in a consistent and rational fashion. When *regulated* parties have raised the issue of mandatory rulemaking, however, the Supreme Court has been entirely unreceptive. (Regulated parties have occasionally prevailed in lower court cases, but these cases have not seriously attempted to distinguish *Bell Aerospace* and probably cannot be reconciled with it. See, e.g., Ford Motor Co. v. FTC, 673 F.2d 1008 (9th Cir.1981).) Of course, despite the absence of judicial compulsion, most agencies have, as mentioned earlier, expanded their rulemaking activity tremendously during the past two decades. Increasingly, therefore, agencies like the NLRB, which largely confine themselves to adjudicating, are aberrations in the federal administrative system. In fact, even the NLRB experimented during the 1980s with using rulemaking to streamline certain functions. The Supreme Court's unanimous confirmation of the Board's power to do so, American Hosp. Ass'n v. NLRB, 499 U.S. 606 (1991), may encourage further experimentation.

F. CONCLUSION: RULEMAKING IN TRANSITION

One of this chapter's principal themes has been the courts' view that federal agency rulemaking should remain relatively free of procedural complexity. Due to decisions such as *Florida East Coast*, *Vermont Yankee*, and *Sierra Club v. Costle*, agencies today can almost always develop rules without complying with the procedural expectations associated with trial-type hearings. Despite this trend in the case law, however, a number of prominent scholars have recently argued that notice and comment rulemaking is in fact becoming increasingly cumbersome and time-consuming. See, e.g., Thomas O. McGarity, *Some Thoughts on "Deossifying" the Rulemaking Process,* 41 Duke L.J. 1385 (1992). They attribute this development, which they sometimes call the "ossification" of the rulemaking process, to several factors. Both Congress and the White House now require agencies to conduct intensive analyses of the potential effects of significant proposed rules. Both branches have also become very active in reviewing the merits of individual proposed rules. See Chapter 2 supra. In addition, the judicial branch has made rulemaking more difficult by engaging in intrusive review of agency rules on appeal. The rigor of the courts' "hard look" puts pressure on agencies to write lengthy explanatory statements and build comprehensive records to support new regulations. See pp. 116–19 supra.

These scholars argue that, because of these external forces, agencies are becoming increasingly reluctant to commence rulemaking proceedings in the first place. "Ossification" can cause an agency to rely more frequently on interpretive rules and policy statements (which it can adopt without following APA procedures); or to develop new policies through case-by-case adjudication; or simply to downplay programs that could be pursued only through rulemaking, as one study found has occurred at the National Highway Traffic Safety Administration (see pp. 182–83 supra).

To be sure, there are also many observers who support the wide-ranging analyses that the legislative, executive, and judicial branches have induced agencies to prepare in significant rulemaking proceedings. They see these requirements as a necessary response to deficiencies in the thoroughness and wisdom of agency policymaking. The fundamental problem, then, is to determine how society can maintain adequate controls on the rulemaking process while not interfering unduly with agencies' ability to carry out their assigned missions. The lack of consensus among administrative lawyers on this issue should not be surprising. As the crucible of some of society's most important collective decisions, the administrative rulemaking process has quite naturally emerged as a focal point for major debates over the future of the regulatory state.

CHAPTER X

OBTAINING JUDICIAL REVIEW

A party seeking court reversal of an administrative decision may be met at the threshold with a series of technical defenses that could bar the court from reaching the merits of her claim. This complex and often overlapping set of doctrines is intended primarily to define the proper boundaries between courts and agencies—that is, to keep the courts from exceeding the limits of their institutional competence and intruding too deeply into the workings of the other branches of government. For example, administrators often make political or bargained decisions that do not readily lend themselves to judicial scrutiny. Parties sometimes seek judicial review of agency decisions in which they have no real stake. Or they seek review prematurely, creating a risk of early judicial intervention that could frustrate or delay the administrative process, and waste judicial resources. To deal with these kinds of problems, the courts have developed doctrines such as unreviewability, standing, and exhaustion of administrative remedies. Still, the trend of the past three decades has been toward breaking down these barriers and allowing liberal access to judicial review. The threshold defenses still have some bite, but review has become freely available to an extent that would have surprised lawyers of an earlier generation.

A. JURISDICTION: ROUTES TO REVIEW

The preliminary task in any attempt to obtain judicial review of an agency action in the federal system is to determine the proper court in which to seek relief. The APA contains a general guideline: If Congress has created a "special statutory review proceeding relevant to the subject matter," the party is expected to file her petition in the court specified in the statute; if no statutory review proceeding is available or adequate, the party may utilize "any applicable form of legal action" in a "court of competent jurisdiction." 5 U.S.C.A. § 703. These forms of proceeding are respectively known as "statutory review" and "nonstatutory review." In a given situation, it may be difficult to know which court to select. If a party mistakenly files in a court that lacks jurisdiction, however, the petition need not be dismissed: that court can transfer the case directly to a court that does have jurisdiction. 28 U.S.C.A. § 1631.

1. *Statutory Review.* Because they are individually enacted as part of the legislation prescribing the powers of an agency, special statutory review proceedings can take a variety of forms. Most commonly, however, they follow the pattern set by the Federal Trade Commission Act in 1914: after the agency's decision becomes final, an interested per-

son may file a petition for review in a federal court of appeals. The court reviews the decision on the basis of the record compiled by the administrator, and if the agency action is invalid, the reviewing court may vacate the decision or remand it for further proceedings. Under some administrative statutes, such as the Social Security Act, review occurs initially in a federal district court. The modern trend, however, is to allow petitioners to proceed directly to a court of appeals. Because even informal actions are now generally reviewed on an administrative record, the factfinding capabilities of a trial court are not needed; thus, immediate review in the court of appeals promotes judicial economy and has few offsetting disadvantages. See Florida Power & Light Co. v. Lorion, 470 U.S. 729 (1985).

Sometimes two or more parties file for review of a single agency decision in different courts of appeals. Until 1988, the first court to receive a petition would automatically acquire jurisdiction over the appeal. This rule occasionally induced rival challengers to engage in frantic "races to the courthouse," each hoping that the case would be heard by a court of appeals that it thought would favor its interests. Now, under a procedure enacted in 1988, a random selection method is used to determine which court will hear the case (subject to a change of venue motion). 28 U.S.C.A. § 2112(a).

2. *Nonstatutory Review.* When Congress has failed to create a special statutory procedure for judicial review, or when the procedure that does exist cannot furnish adequate relief, a party dissat-

isfied with an agency action must resort to "non-statutory review." This term is actually a misnomer, because judicial review is always based upon some statutory grant of subject matter jurisdiction. Thus, a party who wishes to invoke nonstatutory review will look to the general grants of original jurisdiction that apply to the federal courts. In most cases, plaintiffs simply proceed under the general federal question jurisdiction statute, 28 U.S.C.A. § 1331, which authorizes the federal district courts to entertain any case "arising under" the Constitution or laws of the United States. An action for injunctive or declaratory relief under § 1331 is generally the most straightforward route to obtaining nonstatutory review of an agency action.

An alternative basis for jurisdiction is the Mandamus and Venue Act, 28 U.S.C.A. § 1361, which permits the federal district courts to hear suits "in the nature of mandamus to compel an officer or employee of the United States or any agency thereof to perform a duty owed to the plaintiff." The Act is a direct outgrowth of the old common law system of writs (such as mandamus, certiorari, and prohibition), which served as the foundation for judicial review of administrative action before the modern system of civil procedure was developed. However, § 1361 applies only when the agency decision is "ministerial" or nondiscretionary, and thus its utility is fairly limited. In re Cheney, 406 F.3d 723 (D.C.Cir.2005). It should be noted that the APA itself cannot supply the jurisdictional basis for nonstatutory review; the Supreme Court has held that the APA merely tells the reviewing court what to do after it has obtained jurisdiction under some other statute. Califano v. Sanders, 430 U.S. 99 (1977).

Two other varieties of nonstatutory review should also be mentioned. First, instead of challenging an agency rule directly in court, a regulated party can simply choose not to comply with it, and then attack the validity of the rule in an enforcement action if the agency brings one. This strategy may be risky, however: if the rule survives, the challenger may suffer a stiff penalty for having violated it.[1] Second, all of the above forms of review provide relief only to litigants whose goal is to compel, enjoin, or set aside agency action. Those who seek to recover damages for harm inflicted by an administrative agency or official must rely on a separate set of remedies. See pp. 405–11 infra.

3. *Exceptions.* The right to judicial review under the APA applies to any "agency action." The Act defines that term very broadly, encompassing virtually every rule and adjudicative order. 5 U.S.C.A.

[1]. Another factor limiting the value of this strategy is that many modern regulatory statutes provide that a new rule may only be challenged within a short period after it is promulgated, such as sixty days. Courts have, however, carved out several exceptions to these restrictions. See National Mining Ass'n v. United States Dep't of Interior, 70 F.3d 1345 (D.C.Cir.1995); NLRB Union v. FLRA, 834 F.2d 191 (D.C.Cir.1987). Whether the proceeding is governed by the statutory review provision (and thus the time limit) or by nonstatutory review is sometimes unclear. Another option available to citizens who miss the deadline for challenging a rule is to petition the agency to rescind the rule, and then, if necessary, appeal from the agency's denial of the petition.

§ 551(13). Nevertheless, some types of executive activity fall outside the bounds of "agency action" and are therefore unreviewable under the Act. First, only a "circumscribed, discrete" decision or set of decisions can be treated as an agency action. Norton v. Southern Utah Wilderness Alliance, 542 U.S. 55 (2004). For example, in Lujan v. National Wildlife Fed'n, 497 U.S. 871 (1990), environmentalists sought judicial review to challenge maladministration of the Interior Department's program for withdrawing federal lands from public ownership. That program consisted of more than a thousand individual decisions, and the Supreme Court ruled that the plaintiff could not launch a "wholesale" attack on the entire program by characterizing it as an agency action (although a single regulation that applies program-wide *could* be a reviewable agency action). Second, the President is not an "agency" within the meaning of the APA and may not be sued under that Act (although common law remedies may be available on narrow issues, such as the constitutionality of the President's actions). Dalton v. Specter, 511 U.S. 462 (1994); Franklin v. Massachusetts, 505 U.S. 788 (1992). Third, the definition of "agency action" excludes various administrative acts that do not directly affect the rights and obligations of citizens, such as reports to Congress, Guerrero v. Clinton, 157 F.3d 1190 (9th Cir.1998), and educational publications. Flue–Cured Tobacco Coop. Stabilization Corp. v. U.S. EPA, 313 F.3d 852 (4th Cir.2002) (scientific study of health effects of second-tobacco smoke); Industrial Safety Equip.

Ass'n v. EPA, 837 F.2d 1115 (D.C.Cir.1988) (consumer guide comparing efficacy of various models of respirators).

B. UNREVIEWABLE ADMINISTRATIVE ACTIONS

In the contemporary administrative state, judicial review serves important social functions: it provides redress for persons who have been harmed by arbitrary or illegal government action, and it serves to keep the agencies faithful to the policy objectives and procedural safeguards established by the legislature. To promote these ends, the APA empowers the courts to review nearly all agency actions. At times, however, there are good reasons to exclude the courts from reviewing certain agency actions, or at least some of the findings underlying these actions. Two exceptions to the general availability of judicial review are codified in § 701 of the APA. Under this provision, judicial review is not available "to the extent that (1) statutes preclude judicial review; or (2) agency action is committed to agency discretion by law." 5 U.S.C.A. § 701. The first of these exceptions is primarily concerned with formal expressions of legislative intent, while the latter deals primarily with functional reasons why review would be difficult or harmful.

The words "to the extent" in § 701 are intended as a reminder that an action can be partially rather than totally unreviewable. In reaching any decision, an agency typically makes a series of determinations—some legal, some factual, and some discretionary. To say that an action is partially unreviewable is simply to say that the courts will examine some of these determinations and will not examine others. This qualification is important, because partial unreviewability is much more common than total unreviewability. Courts rarely pronounce an action "unreviewable" without adding that they would, nevertheless, entertain a challenge under limited circumstances—for example, if the action were alleged to be unconstitutional.

1. STATUTORY PRECLUSION OF REVIEW

Because Congress controls the jurisdiction of the federal courts, it is free to write into statutes particular exceptions to the general availability of judicial review—in other words, to "preclude" judicial review by statute. Courts are bound to follow these congressional directives so long as they are constitutional, but statutory preclusions run counter to a strong modern trend toward making judicial review freely available. In Abbott Laboratories v. Gardner, 387 U.S. 136 (1967), the Supreme Court formally acknowledged this presumption of reviewability. It held that judicial review of final agency action "will not be cut off unless there is persuasive reason to believe that [this] was the intention of Congress." Congressional intent to preclude review had to be demonstrated by "clear and convincing evidence."

The strength of the presumption of reviewability is reflected in the extraordinary feats of statutory construction that courts have performed in order to avoid concluding that particular statutes preclude judicial review. For example, in Johnson v. Robison, 415 U.S. 361 (1974), a statute provided that "the decisions of the Administrator on any question of law or fact under any law administered by the Veterans Administration providing benefits for veterans and their dependents or survivors shall be final and conclusive and no ... court ... shall have power or jurisdiction to review any such decision." Despite this extraordinarily clear expression of Congressional intent, the Supreme Court found a way to grant limited review. The claimant Robison was a conscientious objector who had performed alternative service, as required by the draft law. The VA concluded that he was ineligible for assistance under a statute that provided educational assistance to veterans who had "served on active duty." Robison asserted that this interpretation denied his constitutional rights to equal protection of the laws and free exercise of religion. The Court held that Robison escaped the statutory preclusion because he was not seeking review of an administrative decision *under* the statute, but rather was challenging the constitutionality of the statute itself.

The *Robison* opinion reflects a tendency of contemporary reviewing courts to seek a functional or institutional reason for prohibiting review, and to bar litigants only when there is a valid policy justification. The legislative history of the statutory preclusion for VA decisions suggested that it was designed to serve two policy goals: preventing burdens on the courts and the agency, and assuring national uniformity in the application of VA standards and policies. The Court reasoned that neither justification applied to constitutional claims like Robison's: the number of constitutional attacks was likely to be small, and the VA admittedly had no special competence in determining constitutional rights. Later, the Court extended *Robison* by permitting judicial review in situations in which a claimant contended that the VA had misinterpreted a statute other than its organic legislation. Traynor v. Turnage, 485 U.S. 535 (1988) (VA allegedly violated Rehabilitation Act by refusing to treat alcoholism as a disease). Finally, in 1988, Congress bowed to criticism of the broad VA preclusion statute, replacing it with a narrower one under which the VA's legal rulings (but not its factual or law-applying rulings) would be freely reviewable. 38 U.S.C.A. § 101.

At times, the Court has demonstrated that the presumption of reviewability can be overcome. In Block v. Community Nutrition Inst., 467 U.S. 340 (1984) *(CNI)*, the Court stated that the *Abbott Laboratories* "clear and convincing evidence" standard should not be applied in a "strict evidentiary sense"; rather, congressional intent to preclude review need only be "fairly discernible" in the statutory scheme. Indeed, in *CNI* itself, the Court was willing to find such intent despite the absence of any explicit preclusive language in the statute in controversy. A group of consumers challenged a marketing order in which the Secretary of Agriculture had established minimum prices that dairy farmers could charge to "handlers" (processors) of their milk products. As the Court noted, Congress, in the underlying statute, had designed a complex framework by which handlers could participate in the adoption of milk marketing orders at the administrative level, but it had not provided for consumer participation in those proceedings. Therefore, the Court reasoned, Congress must have meant to exclude consumers from the entire regulatory process, including the use of judicial review.

As in the veterans cases, the Court often tries to ensure that basic features of a program are subject to some judicial scrutiny, even if the agency's case-by-case judgments are not reviewable in detail. For example, in United States v. Erika, Inc., 456 U.S. 201 (1982), the Court construed a provision of the Medicare Act as impliedly forbidding federal courts from reviewing the amounts of reimbursements that the program paid to health care providers under Part B (optional coverage). The Court pointed to indications in the legislative history that Congress wanted to keep these "quite minor matters" out of federal court. In Bowen v. Michigan Academy of Family Physicians, 476 U.S. 667 (1986), however, in which a group of family physicians sought to contest regulations governing their Part B reimbursements, the Court construed the same provision in the Medicare Act more permissively and allowed the suit to proceed. The Court did not believe that the Act should be construed to bar statutory and constitutional challenges to the *method* by which reimbursement amounts would be determined.

On the other hand, the Court has been readier to find preclusion when the effect is basically to postpone judicial review rather than to foreclose it altogether. Thus, in Shalala v. Illinois Council on Long Term Care, Inc., 529 U.S. 1 (2000), an association of nursing homes brought suit to contest regulations that set forth the Secretary's procedures for imposing sanctions under the Medicare Act. The Court distinguished *Michigan Academy* and held that this challenge was barred by provisions in the Act that "channeled" these plaintiffs' claims through a special administrative process, with judicial review available thereafter. The Court deemed this "channeling" justified in light of the government's interest in maintaining the coherence of a complex program. Similarly, in Thunder Basin Coal Co. v. Reich, 510 U.S. 200 (1994), the Court held that a federal mine safety law impliedly precluded a coal company from suing in district court to prevent the Mine Safety and Health Administration from issuing a citation under the statute. Thus, a MSHA directive instructing the company to allow union representatives to participate in inspections of its mines could be contested only in an enforcement action initiated by MSHA. The Court found that the mine safety law provided a comprehensive scheme for administrative and judicial evaluation of employers' contentions, and that Congress had intended to make this scheme exclusive because of its concern about employer obstructionism. Although this holding meant that the company would have to tolerate inspections by the union representatives while the review proceedings were pending, or else risk monetary penalties, the Court was not persuaded that this choice would cause any intolerable hardship. As these cases illustrate, it is difficult to generalize about statutory preclusion, because every case ultimately turns on an examination of the meaning of a particular statute. While the presumption of reviewability is well entrenched, and reflects a prevalent judicial attitude, one cannot expect it to control the outcome of every case.

A major unresolved question in public law is whether, and how far, the Constitution *requires* that litigants be permitted to challenge agency actions in court. For example, commentators have often argued that, if courts are to fulfill their essential role of checking abuses by the political branches, they must at least be able to entertain arguments that a given administrative action is unconstitutional. Indeed, in one narrow setting the Court has held that due process requires some judicial review. United States v. Mendoza–Lopez, 481 U.S. 828 (1987) (when a criminal proceeding is based on a prior deportation, the alien must have had, or be given, a meaningful opportunity to challenge the validity of the deportation). However, the broader constitutional questions about Congress's power to preclude review are still unsettled—and are likely to remain so, due to the Court's persistent habit of adopting statutory interpretations (even strained ones, where necessary) that allow it to avoid addressing those questions. For example, even after holding that a personnel decision by the CIA was largely unreviewable, the Court construed the National Security Act to allow review of the constitutionality of this decision, in part because of the "serious constitutional question" that would otherwise arise. Webster v. Doe, 486 U.S. 592 (1988).

2. COMMITTED TO AGENCY DISCRETION

While statutory preclusion is concerned primarily with the legislature's intent to bar review, the exception for actions "committed to agency discretion" is more directly concerned with functional reasons for limiting or denying review. Courts are designed to make and review reasoned decisions—those which result from finding facts, drawing inferences from them, and applying legal principles to them. Agencies perform similar functions in both adjudication and rulemaking, but they also make other kinds of decisions as well—including political judgments or bargained decisions that the courts may not be competent to review. In addition, some areas of administration have a compelling need for speed, flexibility, or secrecy in decisionmaking that is inconsistent with the open and deliberate processes of judicial review. When the court finds that there is some compelling practical justification for avoiding review, it may conclude that the action is wholly or partly committed to the agency's unreviewable discretion. Of course, the fact that an agency has been granted *some* discretion by statute is not enough to trigger this exemption from judicial review. The phrase "committed to agency discretion" is a technical term, and the circumstances in which it is applicable are actually quite limited.

The Supreme Court's efforts to define the circumstances in which an agency action should be deemed "committed to agency discretion" have not been entirely satisfactory. In Citizens to Preserve Overton Park, Inc. v. Volpe, 401 U.S. 402 (1971), the Court stated with little discussion that this exemption from judicial review comes into play when there is "no law to apply" to the agency's decision. As the Court explained in Heckler v. Chaney, 470 U.S. 821 (1985), this test means that "review is not to be had if the statute is drawn so that a court would have no meaningful standard against which to judge the agency's exercise of discretion." The "no law to apply" test has often been quoted and followed in subsequent decisions, but it is somewhat misleading insofar as it suggests that a court will determine unreviewability by simply looking at the breadth of the statute under which the agency acted. In practice, although the openendedness of the statute is typically important to a finding that an action is "committed to agency discretion," courts look to a variety of other factors as well.

In fact, the Court has never used the "no law to apply" test as the sole basis for holding any administrative action unreviewable. When the Court held that a dismissed CIA employee could not challenge his termination in federal court (except on constitutional grounds), it relied not only on the breadth of the underlying statute, but also on the practical point that "employment with the CIA entails a high degree of trust that is perhaps unmatched in government service." Webster v. Doe, 486 U.S. 592 (1988). In a similar vein, the Court held in Lincoln v. Vigil, 508 U.S. 182 (1993), that an agency's allocation of funds from a lump-sum appropriation was unreviewable—not only because Congress had not tied the agency's hands, but also because of a tradition of leaving administrators free to balance competing spending priorities and to adapt to changing circumstances. And in ICC v. Brotherhood of Locomotive Eng'rs, 482 U.S. 270 (1987), the Court held that when a party argues that an agency's decision was erroneous when rendered and should be reconsidered, the agency's refusal to reconsider is unreviewable. The Court explained that review of such refusals has traditionally been unavailable and would be difficult to administer; it did not even mention the "no law to apply" test.

The Court's failure to treat the absence of "law to apply" as the sole test of unreviewability makes sense—not only because there are multiple justifications for unreviewability, as noted above, but also such a limitation would be illogical. When a court evaluates an agency action on the merits, it may look not only at whether the agency exceeded or misapplied statutory obligations, but also at other considerations, such as whether the agency acted inconsistently with past decisions, made factual errors, or failed to follow required procedures. Thus, an absence of statutory constraints would not necessarily deprive a reviewing court of judicially manageable standards, as the language of *Chaney* seemed to assume.

When read as a whole, the *Chaney* decision provides a good illustration of the Court's flexibility in applying the unreviewability doctrine. There, eight death row prisoners wrote to the Food and Drug Administration, contending that states' use of lethal drug injections in human executions violated the Food, Drug, and Cosmetic Act. They urged the FDA to bring suit to stop this practice, but the FDA refused. The Supreme Court declined to intervene, declaring broadly that an agency's refusal to initiate an enforcement proceeding is "presumptively unreviewable." Although this holding rested in part the absence of statutory standards and on an analogy to the tradition of prosecutorial discretion in the criminal justice system, the Court laid greater emphasis on some of the practical difficulties that judicial review of nonenforcement decisions can entail. Enforcing agencies usually do not have sufficient personnel or funds to pursue all possible violations of the laws they administer. As they allocate their investigative and litigating resources, they must make judgments about such factors as the seriousness of the offense, the nature and quality of proof available, the likelihood of obtaining a consent settlement or a favorable decision, the deterrent value of a prosecution, and the "opportunity cost" of other cases that will not be brought if resources are invested in this one. Courts have little competence to evaluate the rationality of discretionary choices such as these.

The *Chaney* opinion added, however, that when Congress lays down specific guidelines cabining an agency's enforcement discretion, a court can require the agency to respect its legislative mandate. In this regard, the Court cited with approval Dunlop v. Bachowski, 421 U.S. 560 (1975), in which it had upheld judicial review of the Secretary of Labor's refusal to challenge a union election under the Labor–Management Reporting and Disclosure Act. In *Dunlop* the Act itself had directed the Secretary to bring suit if he found probable cause to believe that a violation had occurred.

Although the courts have adhered to the core holding of *Chaney,* they have often striven not to extend it beyond its necessary limits. For example, when a plaintiff contends that an agency's nonenforcement decision resulted from a misunderstanding of the substantive law, rather than from an exercise of managerial judgment, the courts have usually been willing to reach these legal issues. See, e.g., Montana Air Chapter No. 29 v. FLRA, 898 F.2d 753 (9th Cir.1990). But see Crowley Caribbean Transp., Inc. v. Pena, 37 F.3d 671 (D.C.Cir.1994) (allowing review only if the agency's legal interpretation is expressed in a written policy, not just in an ad hoc enforcement decision). Similarly, courts have adhered to their pre-*Chaney* view that an agency's refusal to institute a rulemaking proceeding is subject to judicial review. Auer v. Robbins, 519 U.S. 452 (1997); see p. 125 supra.

In summary, the question of whether an administrative decision is committed to agency discretion depends largely on the presence or absence of "law to apply," but courts also consider functional matters. The relatively undeveloped nature of the law in this area is undoubtedly related to the courts' strong allegiance to the *Abbott Laboratories* presumption of reviewability. Mindful of the risks of unchecked administrative power, judges are usually not receptive to government counsel's pleas that particular agency decisions or findings should receive no judicial scrutiny whatever. Generally, therefore, courts rely on deferential scope-of-review principles, rather than applications of the doctrine of unreviewability, as the preferred tool for separating the administrative from the judicial spheres of responsibility.

C. STANDING

A person bringing a court challenge to an administrative decision must have standing to seek judicial review. The standing doctrine is a complex and frequently changing body of law, which has both a constitutional and a common law basis. The constitutional source of the standing doctrine is Article III, § 2 of the Constitution, which limits the federal judicial power to "cases" and "controversies." The American judicial process is an adversary system, which depends upon the litigants to gather and present the information needed for a sound decision. The "case or controversy" limitation, as embodied in the standing doctrine, seeks to assure sufficient opposition between the parties to make this system function properly. In addition, the law of standing is intended to help keep the judiciary within its proper orbit, so that the political branches of government will not be dominated by an "antimajoritarian" judiciary.

The difficulty, however, is that these considerations of institutional competence and legitimacy conflict with other strongly held values. The individual plaintiff's demand for redress from illegal government action can exert a powerful countervailing claim on the court's sense of justice. Moreover, judicial review serves as a method of assuring that bureaucratic actions are consistent with the Constitution and with mandates established by elected political actors. In light of these conflicting policy pulls, it is perhaps not surprising that the law of standing has had an erratic pattern of development.

1. EARLY CASE LAW

The early view was that a person seeking judicial scrutiny of agency action had to show that he had a legally protected interest—that is, one recognized by the Constitution, by statute or common law— that was adversely affected by the agency's decision. A personal or economic interest was not sufficient. E.g., Alabama Power Co. v. Ickes, 302 U.S. 464

(1938). Eventually, however, the "legally protected interest" test fell into disfavor. Critics claimed that it tended to confuse standing issues with merits issues, because the court would need to consider the merits of the plaintiff's assertions of administrative illegality in order to determine whether he had a sufficient legal interest to confer standing. Moreover, the test was excessively rigid, because it depended more upon ancient common law concepts than upon policy considerations such as the need for a judicial check on a growing federal bureaucracy. These defects led to a crumbling of the doctrinal barriers in the 1940s.

The first major breakthrough occurred in FCC v. Sanders Bros. Radio Station, 309 U.S. 470 (1940). The Court there held that the statutory language granting judicial review to "persons aggrieved" by an FCC license decision was broad enough to include competitors of a successful applicant, even though the substantive provisions of the Communications Act were intended to protect the public interest, not the economic interests of competitors such as the petitioner. The test of an "aggrieved person," in other words, was not limited to the assertion of a personal legal wrong. The Court reasoned that Congress "may have been of the opinion that one likely to be financially injured by the issuance of a license would be the only person having a sufficient interest to bring to the attention of the appellate court errors of law in the action of the Commission." *Sanders* gave rise to a series of cases in which private parties were granted standing under various statutory review provisions, on the assumption that Congress had viewed them as "private attorneys general" to enforce statutory requirements. See, e.g., Associated Indus. of New York v. Ickes, 134 F.2d 694, 704 (2d Cir.), vacated as moot, 320 U.S. 707 (1943). Once a claimant established that he was within the statutory language, he was free to challenge the legality of the agency action on all available grounds, even though some of them might not be relevant to his personal interest.

The adoption of the APA in 1946, providing in § 702 that a person "adversely affected or aggrieved by agency action within the meaning of a relevant statute" could obtain judicial review, eventually contributed to the liberalizing trend. Litigants began to argue that the Act did not merely codify the existing "legal interest" theory but rather expanded the availability of standing by allowing judicial review whenever the complainant could prove that he was adversely affected in fact. This theory met with mixed results in the lower courts. When, two and a half decades later, the Supreme Court finally addressed the meaning of § 702, it did not fully endorse the theory just mentioned, but it did propound a relatively permissive analytical framework. In Association of Data Processing Serv. Orgs. v. Camp, 397 U.S. 150 (1970), the Court reduced the law of standing to seek judicial review of administrative action to two questions: (1) whether the litigation involved a "case or controversy" under Article III of the Constitution, which the Court equated with asking "whether the plaintiff alleges that the challenged action has caused him injury in fact, economic or otherwise"; and (2) whether the plaintiff's interest was "arguably within the zone of interests to be protected or regulated by the statute or constitutional guarantee in question." Applying this two-pronged test, the Court found that sellers of data processing services could sue to prevent the Comptroller of the Currency from authorizing banks to compete with them, because (a) the Comptroller's ruling would cause them economic harm, and (b) federal banking legislation suggested, at least "arguably," that Congress desired to protect companies from having to compete with banks for nonbanking business. The *Data Processing* framework is still in use today, but it has undergone considerable evolution.

2. CONSTITUTIONAL STANDING

The initial, constitutional component of the *Data Processing* test has given rise to numerous bitter debates in the courts. The importance of this issue became clearly evident when the Sierra Club brought suit to block the development of a ski resort in a wilderness area. Sierra Club v. Morton, 405 U.S. 727 (1972). The Supreme Court conceded that threats to aesthetic, recreational, and environmental interests could constitute sufficient injury in fact to satisfy the standing requirement. Nevertheless, the Sierra Club's pleadings were inadequate, because they failed to allege that any Club members actually used the wilderness area that would be affected by the resort development; instead, the Club had merely relied on its status as a responsible environmentalist organization. This was not enough for standing. To satisfy the APA, the Court said, an organization had to demonstrate that the government was causing specific injury to it or its members.[2] A "mere 'interest in a problem'" would not entitle it to bring suit. *Sierra Club* soon gave rise to other cases refusing standing to litigants who could allege only an "abstract injury." E.g., Schlesinger v. Reservists Comm. to Stop the War, 418 U.S. 208 (1974) (plaintiff had no individualized stake in whether members of Congress retained membership in the Reserves).

In subsequent years, the Court has refined the constitutional test for standing into a multi-factor inquiry. The Court summed up the prevailing analysis in Allen v. Wright, 468 U.S. 737 (1984): "A plaintiff must allege personal injury fairly traceable to the defendant's allegedly unlawful conduct and

2. An association has standing to sue on behalf of its members when "(a) its members would otherwise have standing to sue in their own right; (b) the interests it seeks to protect are germane to the organization's purpose; and (c) neither the claim asserted nor the relief requested requires the participation of individual members in the lawsuit." Hunt v. Washington State Apple Advertising Comm'n, 432 U.S. 333 (1977). The second of these criteria is construed very leniently, National Lime Ass'n v. EPA, 233 F.3d 625 (D.C.Cir.2000), and the third comes into play only in suits for monetary relief, in which the amount of recovery might vary among individuals. See United Food & Commercial Workers Union Local 751 v. Brown Group, Inc., 517 U.S. 544 (1996). Usually, therefore, the only important question in litigation is whether the first criterion is met.

likely to be redressed by the requested relief." Generally, therefore, the standing inquiry is said to involve three variables: *injury, traceability*, and *redressability*. In practice, the latter two elements are closely related; they will be discussed together below. Because standing implicates subject-matter jurisdiction, a court must raise the issue on its own motion (if standing is doubtful), even where the parties do not dispute it. Moreover, the court must decide the standing issue first; it may not simply "assume" standing and proceed to the merits, even if the merits issue would be easier to resolve and would result in dismissal of the suit. Steel Co. v. Citizens for a Better Environment, 523 U.S. 83 (1998).

1.   *The Requisite Injury.* A challenger's failure to provide specific factual support for an asserted injury in fact, at least by the time the case reaches a summary judgment stage, makes the suit vulnerable to dismissal. For example, in Lujan v. National Wildlife Fed'n, 497 U.S. 871 (1990), an environmental organization alleged that the Bureau of Land Management's "land withdrawal program" was opening up too much public land to mining. The plaintiff had submitted affidavits in which two of its members asserted that they used lands for recreational and aesthetic purposes "in the vicinity" of the areas affected by the Bureau's actions. The Court held that this submission was too general. The areas named in the affidavits extended over millions of acres. Only small portions of these areas were affected by the Bureau's decisions, and the

affiants had not specifically asserted that they made use of those portions. See also DaimlerChrysler Corp. v. Cuno, ___ U.S. ___, 126 S.Ct. 1854 (2006) (taxpayers, as such, generally have no standing to object to specific government spending, because the impact of that spending on their tax liability is "minute and indeterminable").

Another illustrative case involved the requirement in the Endangered Species Act that a federal agency must consult with the Secretary of Interior before funding or carrying out activities that might jeopardize an endangered species. The Defenders of Wildlife brought suit to establish that this consultation requirement extends to projects that the federal government funds in foreign countries. Two members filed affidavits declaring that they had personally traveled to foreign sites in order to study certain endangered species that were threatened by development projects funded by the Agency for International Development. But the Court, in an opinion by Justice Scalia, found this insufficient for standing: the affiants had not mentioned any definite plans to return to the contested sites and thus had not established that they faced an actual or imminent injury. Lujan v. Defenders of Wildlife, 504 U.S. 555 (1992). Nor could plaintiffs establish standing by citing their generalized interest in having the Secretary "observe the procedures required by law." These holdings were particularly striking in light of the Act's provision stating that "any person" may bring suit to enforce the Act. The Court considered the "citizen suit" provision irrelevant in this case, because implementation of the laws is primarily the province of the executive branch, and Congress could not empower the courts to take over that function by intervening in the absence of a case or controversy under Article III of the Constitution.

A concurring opinion in *Defenders* suggested, however, that the result in that case might have been different if Congress had conferred on the plaintiffs a new legal interest, not just a right to sue. Subsequent cases have illustrated the utility of this escape route from the *Defenders* holding. In FEC v. Akins, 524 U.S. 11 (1998), a group of voters sued the Federal Election Commission for failing to require AIPAC, a pro-Israel lobbying organization, to file reports about its membership and finances, pursuant to the Federal Election Campaign Act. The Court found that the Act had conferred on plaintiffs (and everyone else) a right to obtain information from "political committees," a term that allegedly applied to AIPAC. A deprivation of that right was the kind of injury that would support standing. That the harm involved was "generalized," in the sense that numerous other voters could also have asserted it, did not matter, because this "informational injury" was concrete, not abstract. The Court has also found a statutory basis for standing in the "qui tam" provision of the False Claims Act, 31 U.S.C.A. § 3730. That provision enables a private individual to bring suit on behalf of the United States against a person who has defrauded the federal government. If the suit is successful, the government recovers for its losses, and the plaintiff or "relator" receives a share of the proceeds. In Vermont Agency of Natural Resources v. United States ex rel. Stevens, 529 U.S. 765 (2000), a citizen brought a qui tam suit against a Vermont environmental agency for overbilling the EPA in a federal grant program. The Court reasoned that the Act effectively made the relator an assignee of the United States's damage claim; therefore, he could treat the federal government's monetary loss as his own "injury" for standing purposes. (The relator lost his case anyway, however, because the Court also held that a state agency may not be a defendant in an FCA qui tam suit.)

2. *Causal Inquiries.* The traceability and redressability elements of the constitutional test for standing can be difficult to apply when the threat of harm to the plaintiff's interests is only remotely or indirectly attributable to agency action. This problem is especially likely to emerge when the government program uses subsidies, tax credits, or other such incentives to achieve a desired result, rather than providing for direct regulation or disbursements of benefits to claimants. At first, the Supreme Court seemed untroubled by causation issues of this kind. In United States v. Students Challenging Regulatory Agency Procedures, 412 U.S. 669 (1973) *(SCRAP)*, the plaintiffs were law students who wanted to contest the ICC's approval of a freight rate that they felt would discourage the use of recycled materials and thereby contribute to environmental pollution. To establish standing, they

alleged that the rate increase would lead to increased litter and depletion of minerals and other natural resources in forests or parks where they engaged in recreational activities. The Court thought this an "attenuated line of causation," but it did not bar the students from maintaining their action. Instead, it noted that the plaintiffs must be prepared to prove the allegations of harm in their complaint, and it remanded to the district court for further proceedings.

The liberality of *SCRAP,* however, proved shortlived. Later decisions of the Supreme Court have insisted that plaintiffs demonstrate that the government has caused them harm and that a favorable decision would likely redress that harm. For example, Simon v. Eastern Ky. Welfare Rights Org., 426 U.S. 26 (1976), involved tax exemptions for private hospitals providing medical care to indigents. When the IRS issued a revenue ruling reducing the amount of indigent care a hospital must provide in order to qualify for the exemption, a welfare organization and several indigent individuals sought judicial review. Despite allegations that the individual plaintiffs had been denied treatment as a result of the IRS ruling, the Court ordered the case dismissed for lack of standing. In the Court's view, it was purely speculative whether the plaintiffs would have been given any service in the absence of the ruling; nor was it clear that a favorable decision on the merits would be likely to redress the claimed injury, for the hospitals might continue to withhold care for indigents even without the tax incentive.

Similarly, in Allen v. Wright, 468 U.S. 737 (1984), parents of black children who attended public schools sued the IRS to force it to deny tax exempt status to racially discriminatory private schools. The parents (whose children had not applied for admission to the schools in question) claimed that the IRS's conduct caused these schools to flourish and thus impaired their children's right to attend an integrated school district. But the Court saw no reason to believe that elimination of the exemptions would make an appreciable difference in public school integration, and thus denied standing.

More recent cases have continued to explore these causal inquiries, but with mixed results. In *Defenders of Wildlife*, supra, four Justices adhered to the preceding cases' stringent approach to redressability. They argued that, even if the *Defenders* lawsuit led to a ruling that the Secretary of Interior must consult with other agencies about the possible impacts of their foreign projects upon endangered species, those other agencies (which were not parties to the lawsuit) might disagree with that ruling and decline to comply with it. Hence the suit was not "likely" to do the plaintiffs any good.[3] However, in another Endangered Species Act case, Bennett v. Spear, 520 U.S. 154 (1997), the Court held that

3. The Court noted in *Defenders*, however, that the redressability requirement is less stringent in cases involving procedural rights than elsewhere. A private party who contends that an agency committed a procedural error in reaching a decision does not have to show that rectification of the error would be likely to cause the agency to revise its action. Nevertheless, she does have to show that such a revised action would be likely to redress some harm to her concrete interests.

ranchers had standing to challenge a "biological opinion" rendered by the Fish and Wildlife Service. The biological opinion advised the Bureau of Reclamation to modify its plans for an irrigation project. The Court reasoned that this suit met the redressability test, because agencies usually do comply with these biological opinions, and the Bureau's failure to do so would expose its employees to legal jeopardy. See also Utah v. Evans, 536 U.S. 452 (2002) (Utah had standing to challenge a census calculation that disfavored it, because if the courts were to order the Secretary of Commerce to revise his calculation, the President and Congress would presumably accept the new figures).

Usually, the traceability element of the standing test (whether the agency's action caused or will cause the plaintiff's injury) and the redressability element (whether a judicial remedy would ameliorate that injury) are practically equivalent. They may diverge, however, where the defendant has discontinued the challenged conduct. In such a case, even if that conduct admittedly harmed the plaintiff in the past, a court decree would not necessarily make her better off in the future. Thus, in Steel Co. v. Citizens for a Better Environment, 523 U.S. 83 (1998), an environmental group brought suit against a manufacturer that had failed to file timely reports about its discharges of toxic chemicals, as required by law. However, the manufacturer had already brought its reports up to date, the plaintiff alleged no continuing or imminent violation, and any civil penalties that might be imposed on the manufacturer would be paid to the United States, not the plaintiff. In these circumstances, the Court saw no basis to predict that any of the relief sought would protect the plaintiff from future informational injuries. But the Court narrowly distinguished *Steel Co.* and reached a contrasting result in Friends of the Earth, Inc. v. Laidlaw Envtl. Services, 528 U.S. 167 (2000). There, local residents contended that a waste disposal company's discharges of mercury into a stream, exceeding the amounts allowed by its Clean Water Act permit, impaired their aesthetic and recreational enjoyment of the surrounding area. Although these violations were not currently ongoing, they had persisted even after the filing of the complaint and might well be resumed. These facts—coupled with evidence that Congress itself, in passing the Clean Water Act, had concluded that civil penalties would deter future violations—persuaded the Court to find that the likelihood that the suit would prevent future harms to plaintiffs was sufficient to meet Article III requirements.

The case law on Article III standing is often criticized as inconsistent and result-oriented. Probably, however, the Court's vacillation is partly a result of the very nature of its standing test, which requires judges to apply vague phrases such as "imminent injury" and "likelihood of redress" to always-unique fact situations. Given the inherently discretionary nature of these inquiries, frequent internal disagreements, as well as temptations to resolve doubts on the basis of one's ideological inclinations, may well be unavoidable.

3. ZONE OF INTERESTS

The "zone of interests" issue has proved to be the less contentious of the two prongs of the *Data Processing* test. The Court elaborated on the test in Clarke v. Securities Industry Ass'n, 479 U.S. 388 (1987). The facts closely resembled those of *Data Processing*: securities dealers challenged a ruling of the Comptroller allowing banks to offer discount brokerage services without conforming to federal restrictions on branch banking. The Court again found standing, noting that the zone of interests test is "not meant to be especially demanding" and prevents standing only when "the plaintiff's interests are so marginally related to or inconsistent with the purposes implicit in the statute that it cannot reasonably be assumed that Congress intended to permit the suit." Liberality also prevailed in National Credit Union Admin. v. First Nat'l Bank & Trust Co., 522 U.S. 479 (1998), in which banks sued to challenge an NCUA rule that allowed credit unions to serve employees of multiple companies. The Court found standing, even though the statute's limitations on credit union expansion were mainly designed to preserve the financial stability of credit unions, not to protect competitors.

To be sure, the zone test is not entirely toothless, as the Court showed in Air Courier Conf. v. American Postal Workers Union, 498 U.S. 517 (1991).

The Postal Service had issued a regulation partially waiving its statutory monopoly on mail service, so that private carriers would be free to engage in overnight delivery of letters to foreign postal systems. Concerned that this decision would adversely affect the employment opportunities of its members, two postal workers unions sued the agency, claiming that the regulation was unlawful. The Court held that the unions were not within the relevant zone of interests, because the statute establishing the postal monopoly "exists to ensure that postal services will be provided to the citizenry at-large, and not to secure employment for postal workers." Although Congress had also passed laws governing labor-management relations in the Postal Service, those laws had no significant relationship to the postal monopoly legislation and thus did not suffice for standing. *Air Courier* is, however, the only case in which the Court has ousted a challenger from court on the basis of the zone test. Only rarely does the test become a significant obstacle to judicial review of agency action.

Further diluting the force of the zone test are two additional principles. First, a litigant can satisfy the test by relying on the purpose of the specific provision underlying the suit, which may not be the same as the primary purpose of the overall regulatory scheme. The Court so held in Bennett v. Spear, 520 U.S. 154 (1997), in which ranchers and irrigation districts sued to overturn a biological opinion issued under the Endangered Species Act by the Fish and Wildlife Service. The opinion directed modifications in a water project in order to protect two species of fish. The plaintiffs claimed the FWS had not complied with a statutory directive to take into account the best available scientific data. This provision was largely intended to prevent overly zealous actions under the ESA and thus supported standing, even though the basic purpose of the Act is species protection. Second, as *Bennett* also held, the zone test is a prudential, nonconstitutional limitation on standing, and Congress can modify or dispense with it. Thus, because the ESA authorized "any person" to sue to redress certain violations, the zone test did not apply at all to those specific claims.

D. TIMING OF JUDICIAL REVIEW

Even when an agency's decision is reviewable and the plaintiff has standing to litigate, she may still be unable to get judicial review if she has brought the action at the wrong time. Finality, exhaustion, and ripeness are complementary doctrines that are designed to prevent unnecessary or untimely judicial interference in the administrative process. Theoretically, each of these three doctrines has a different focus and a different basis. The finality doctrine is primarily concerned with ensuring that the agency has reached a definitive, rather than preliminary or tentative, disposition of a particular case or issue. The exhaustion doctrine emphasizes the conduct of the party seeking review; in essence, it asks whether the appeal is an attempt to short-circuit the administrative process and whether the challenger has been reasonably diligent in pursuing relief through that process. And ripeness calls for a pragmatic judgment: it weighs the urgency of the challenger's need for guidance against the court's ability to resolve the dispute without waiting to see how the issues may develop over time. In practice, however, the three doctrines overlap each other and are not always carefully distinguished.

1.   FINALITY

Many statutory review provisions authorize a party to seek judicial review of any "final order" of an agency, and the APA states that "final agency action" is subject to judicial review. 5 U.S.C.A. § 704. For this reason, some cases, relying on an analogy to the general rule against interlocutory appeal in the federal courts, speak of timing problems as posing a question of whether the agency has taken "final" action. According to a prominent formula, two conditions are required for finality: the agency action "must mark the 'consummation' of the agency's decisionmaking process [and] not be of a merely tentative or interlocutory character"; and "the action must be one by which 'rights or obligations have been determined,' or from which 'legal consequences will flow.' " Bennett v. Spear, 520 U.S. 154 (1997) (a biological opinion rendered by the Fish and Wildlife Service "altered the legal regime" and was therefore final).

One implication of this formula is that an agency's decision to inquire further into a matter is not, standing alone, a final agency action. For example, when several oil companies charged in court that the FTC had issued a complaint for political purposes without determining that it had "reason to believe" that they had violated the antitrust laws, the Court held that the suit was premature because the FTC had not taken "final action." The agency's averment of "reason to believe," the Court said, was not a definitive agency position and imposed no burden on the companies other than the burden of litigating. FTC v. Standard Oil Co. of California, 449 U.S. 232 (1980). Realistically speaking, the Court's holding made the companies' claim unreviewable, because one could scarcely expect a reviewing court to vacate a final cease and desist order merely because the agency had lacked sufficient evidence of wrongdoing at the outset of the proceeding.

The finality doctrine also generally bars review of actions taken by a subordinate official whose decision will not directly affect the public. The Court used this argument in Franklin v. Massachusetts, 505 U.S. 788 (1992), to prevent APA review of the methodology that the Secretary of Commerce used in calculating the results of the 1990 census. The Secretary's decision was nonfinal because she merely sent a report to the President, who made the ultimate decisions regarding census figures. Similarly, a special commission's proposed list of military bases to be closed was held unreviewable under the APA, because the President was free to approve or disapprove the list. Dalton v. Specter, 511 U.S.

462 (1994). Ironically, the Court's holdings in *Franklin* and *Specter* meant that the challengers could not press their APA claims against anyone, because the President is not an "agency" for purposes of that Act. The only issues they could raise were constitutional claims arising outside of the APA.

Although these cases seem restrictive, other decisions reflect greater flexibility. Thus, in Whitman v. American Trucking Ass'ns, 531 U.S. 457 (2001), the EPA used the explanatory preamble accompanying its new ozone standards to set forth a strategy for implementing those standards. The Court held that the strategy itself was a final, reviewable action, because the agency had adopted it after an elaborate decisionmaking process and had said in later rulemakings that the strategy was not open to reconsideration.

The determination of whether an agency action is final can be difficult when the pronouncement in question is an informal statement such as an advice letter. In National Automatic Laundry & Cleaning Council v. Shultz, 443 F.2d 689 (D.C.Cir.1971), the court said that such a letter, if signed by the agency head, should be presumed to be final, although the agency head could overcome this presumption by filing an affidavit stating that the matter was still unresolved. However, no clear, durable lines have taken hold in this area. The courts are wary of interfering too readily with the ongoing process of policy development, but also of allowing agencies to coerce regulated persons informally without being held accountable for it. Compare Independent Equip. Dealers Ass'n v. EPA, 372 F.3d 420 (D.C.Cir. 2004) (no judicial review of a letter that restated position that agency had been following for some time), with Appalachian Power Co. v. EPA, 208 F.3d 1015 (D.C.Cir.2000) (guidance document was "final" because its insistent language made it effectively binding on companies).

2. EXHAUSTION

If review is sought while an agency proceeding is still under way, a court will usually dismiss the action because of the plaintiff's failure to exhaust administrative remedies. In a leading case, a company was served with an NLRB complaint alleging that it had engaged in unfair labor practices. The company went directly to court, taking the position that it was not operating in interstate commerce and hence that the NLRB had no jurisdiction. Despite the company's claim that it would suffer irreparable harm if it were forced to participate in an unnecessary evidentiary hearing, its effort to obtain immediate judicial review was turned aside. Myers v. Bethlehem Shipbuilding Corp., 303 U.S. 41 (1938). The principle of exhaustion has several purposes. It is designed to prevent regulated parties from delaying or obstructing the agency's ability to conduct an orderly proceeding. It also gives the court the benefit of the agency's factfinding capacity and expertise in analyzing the factual assertions that may underlie the plaintiff's complaint. Moreover, if a party has to postpone seeking judicial relief until the end of the proceeding, judicial involvement may not prove necessary at all—the agency might correct any initial errors at subsequent stages of the process, or the party might prevail on other grounds. Consequently, the exhaustion rule conserves judicial resources and reduces friction between the branches of government.

Although the exhaustion and finality doctrines basically overlap in a case like *Bethlehem*, exhaustion can reach further. Some of the policies just mentioned are also relevant when a private party goes to court in order to *induce* governmental action, rather than to prevent it. If the challenger has not pursued administrative remedies that might result in relief without the court's participation, the exhaustion doctrine may be applied in that context as well.

Courts do not always strictly enforce the requirement that the plaintiff exhaust administrative remedies before seeking judicial review. The courts' application of the doctrine is highly discretionary, although a few generalizations can be made. Immediate judicial review is usually permitted when a litigant establishes that the agency is clearly exceeding its jurisdiction. Leedom v. Kyne, 358 U.S. 184 (1958). Indeed, a few cases favor relaxing the exhaustion rule whenever the plaintiff's challenge is purely legal in nature, because the court may be able to resolve the dispute without any need for the agency's factfinding abilities. Since a desire for the agency's perspective is not the only justification for postponing review, however, most courts require exhaustion if the alleged statutory or constitutional violation is not obvious. See, e.g., Ticor Title Ins. Co. v. FTC, 814 F.2d 731 (D.C.Cir.1987) (opinion of Edwards, J.).

Another line of authority maintains that one is not required to exhaust administrative remedies that are "inadequate," such as where the agency lacks authority to grant the relief the plaintiff seeks, or where resort to administrative channels might cause undue delay. For example, in McCarthy v. Madigan, 503 U.S. 140 (1992), the Court held that a prisoner could file damage claims in court against penal officials without first invoking the prison's grievance mechanism, because the latter process did not authorize damage awards. See also Coit Indep. Joint Venture v. FSLIC, 489 U.S. 561 (1989) (creditors of failed bank could sue FSLIC as receiver in state court without first seeking administrative relief from the agency, because FSLIC had adverse interests and might delay resolution of the claim while the state's limitations statute ran out). On the whole, however, courts have striven to avoid recognizing exceptions to the exhaustion requirement that would swallow the rule. For example, the expense and disruption of defending oneself against administrative charges—a burden that every respondent could allege—is generally not a basis for interlocutory review.

Statutes sometimes impose exhaustion requirements that would not otherwise apply. For example, in Booth v. Churner, 532 U.S. 731 (2001), the Court abandoned the holding of *McCarthy v. Madigan,* supra, because Congress had passed intervening legislation that made clear that a prisoner must resort to the prison's grievance process before filing suit, even if his preferred remedy, damages, is not available through that process. Statutes that require exhaustion, irrespective of what courts might otherwise prefer, are often analyzed as preclusion provisions. See Shalala v. Illinois Council on Long Term Care, Inc., 529 U.S. 1 (2000), discussed at p. 364 supra. On the other hand, statutes can also narrow the scope of the exhaustion doctrine, by relieving a litigant from exhaustion requirements that might otherwise be imposed. See Patsy v. Board of Regents, 457 U.S. 496 (1982) (exhaustion is not a prerequisite to constitutional litigation against state officials under 42 U.S.C.A. § 1983). The APA itself plays this role in one specific procedural context: An agency action that is "otherwise final" is "final" for judicial review purposes regardless of whether the challenger has sought reconsideration or appealed to superior agency authority. 5 U.S.C.A. § 704. Although § 704 is written in terms of finality, the Court in Darby v. Cisneros, 509 U.S. 137 (1993), concluded that Congress must have meant to override exhaustion requirements in this situation as well. Thus, if a party has taken every available step at the agency level except for reconsideration or internal appeal, exhaustion and finality cease to be barriers to judicial review. (As § 704 also states, however, an agency may adopt regulations requiring an internal appeal; these rules must provide that the agency action will be inoperative while that appeal is pending.)

Courts use a variant of the exhaustion doctrine in deciding whether a party in civil or criminal proceedings should be barred from litigating an issue that could have been raised earlier in an administrative forum. In McKart v. United States, 395 U.S. 185 (1969), a draft registrant had failed to appeal his Selective Service reclassification from an exempt category to one that made him eligible for induction. He was prosecuted for draft evasion, and the government argued that the court should not entertain his claim to be exempt, because he had failed to exhaust his remedies within the Selective Service System. The Supreme Court, however, was reluctant to penalize a failure to exhaust when criminal sanctions were at issue, because the consequences of doing so could be severe: "The defendant is often stripped of his only defense; he must go to jail without having any judicial review of an assertedly invalid order." Moreover, the issues involved were straightforward questions of law that did not require the exercise of administrative expertise. Weighing these considerations, and the likelihood that few registrants would try to bypass the administrative process since they would risk criminal penalties by doing so, the Court held that the exhaustion doctrine did not bar the defendant from asserting the invalidity of his classification as a defense to the criminal prosecution. However, the Court distinguished *McKart* in McGee v. United States, 402 U.S. 479 (1971), another case involving prosecution of a draft resister who had bypassed remedies available from Selective Service authorities. McGee claimed to be a conscientious objector, a defense that turned on factual rather than legal issues. The Court invoked the exhaustion doctrine and held that he had lost his defense, because "[w]hen a claim to exemption depends ultimately on the careful gathering and analysis of relevant facts, the interest in full airing of the facts within the administrative system is prominent."

In addition to requiring a challenger to exhaust administrative *remedies*, courts usually insist on *issue exhaustion*. In other words, a court is usually not obliged to address issues that the challenger did not first present to the administrative decisionmaker. United States v. L.A. Tucker Truck Lines, Inc., 344 U.S. 33 (1952). This requirement is similar to a principle observed in civil litigation—that an appellate court need not consider arguments that were not preserved in the lower court. But see Sims v. Apfel, 530 U.S. 103 (2000) (issue exhaustion not required in Social Security disability proceedings, which are highly informal and thus not comparable to judicial proceedings). In practice, judges often apply the issue exhaustion requirement in a discretionary fashion. If a court is inclined to decide an issue, it may overlook the parties' failure to raise it below, especially if the issue is a purely legal argument that does not implicate the agency's factfinding competence or expertise. Conversely, when a court prefers not to confront an issue, a party's failure to have preserved the issue in earlier proceedings can provide an easy escape route.

3. RIPENESS

The ripeness doctrine typically comes into play when a party challenges a rule or other statement that an agency has made at a relatively early stage of the regulatory process, prior to actually seeking to enforce its policy against a given individual. The question becomes whether the court should allow the issue raised by the plaintiff to "ripen" until some later stage in the process. Practical considerations may weigh heavily in favor of postponement. The implications of an agency's legal or policy pronouncement often become clearer as it is implemented. Its scope may be ambiguous (perhaps because the agency intended to leave some points unsettled), and its consequences difficult to predict. Consequently, a court may feel that it could render a more reliable decision on the validity of the pronouncement if it were to await further developments. Or perhaps the anticipated collision between the plaintiff and the government would not occur at all, and the court could avoid an unnecessary confrontation with the executive branch. The ripeness doctrine attempts to give effect to these concerns, but also to reconcile them with the need of private parties for guidance as to their rights. The inquiry is similar to the kind of judgment a court would make in deciding whether to issue a declaratory judgment in civil litigation. To some degree, the ripeness defense serves to implement the policy behind Article III of the Constitution, which prohibits courts from issuing advisory opinions. Usually, however, the doctrine is analyzed as a nonconstitutional, prudential issue in administrative law cases.

The leading case of Abbott Laboratories v. Gardner, 387 U.S. 136 (1967), defined the primary factors that determine whether a claim is ripe for review: the court must "evaluate both the fitness of the issues for judicial decision and the hardship to the parties of withholding court consideration." In *Abbott Labs* itself, a ripeness defense was rejected. Drug manufacturers argued in that case that the FDA had exceeded its authority in issuing a rule that regulated the labeling that they placed on their products. The parties agreed that this dispute turned entirely on congressional intent. Therefore, further factual development by the agency was not needed, and the issue was appropriate for judicial resolution. Moreover, withholding review would have been burdensome for the companies, because they were threatened with fines, seizures, adverse publicity, and other penalties if they did not immediately change their labeling. As a result, the manufacturers were free to challenge the rule in court directly, instead of having to wait until the FDA commenced an enforcement proceeding against them.

In contrast, the rule at issue in a companion case, Toilet Goods Ass'n v. Gardner, 387 U.S. 158 (1967), was held unripe for review. It required companies using color additives in cosmetics to give FDA inspectors "free access" to their proprietary formulas.

If a manufacturer did not comply, the FDA could temporarily halt its certification services for that company. In this instance the Court believed that further development of the facts in the context of a specific enforcement proceeding might aid judicial review. Matters such as "an understanding of what types of enforcement problems are encountered by the FDA, the need for various sorts of supervision in order to effectuate the goals of the Act, and the safeguards devised to protect legitimate trade secrets" could all be more fully explored on the basis of an evidentiary record. At the same time, withholding immediate review would not injure the companies, because the rule did not force them to alter their primary conduct; their refusal to admit an inspector would "at most" lead only to a suspension of certification services, which could then be challenged in administrative and then judicial fora.

Today, judicial review of rules occurs at least as frequently in direct or "preenforcement" challenges as during enforcement actions. Indeed, the realities of modern administrative practice help to explain why such review is normally allowed pursuant to the *Abbott Labs* ripeness test. Now that agencies routinely build extensive records during rulemaking, a wide range of legal, policy, and even factual issues can be considered "fit" for review as soon as the rule is promulgated. Moreover, many of today's rules impose heavy compliance costs on regulated entities, and these entities have a strong interest in obtaining a court's view as to the rule's validity.

Nevertheless, courts do occasionally hold, upon applying the *Abbott Labs* test, that a rule is unripe for review. For example, in National Park Hospitality Ass'n v. Department of Interior, 538 U.S. 803 (2003), operators of concessions in national parks brought suit to overturn a National Park Service rule that asserted that their contracts with the Service were not subject to the remedial provisions of the Contract Disputes Act. The Court declined to address the validity of the rule in the abstract, noting that the applicability of that Act might depend on the characteristics of particular contracts. Moreover, the hardship to plaintiffs of postponing review would be minimal, because the challenged pronouncement did not affect their rights; it merely expressed the Service's litigation position, which the boards that actually administered the Act might not follow. Similarly, in Ohio Forestry Ass'n v. Sierra Club, 523 U.S. 726 (1998), environmentalists argued that a "forest plan" developed by the Forest Service would permit too much logging and clear-cutting in a forest in Ohio. The Court ordered the case dismissed, noting that the plan would have no impact until the Service implemented it in a decision pertaining to a specific site. The plaintiffs could pursue their legal challenge to the plan at that time, so postponement of litigation would cause them no hardship. On the other hand, such a postponement would allow the Service to adapt its plan to the circumstances of a particular site and would allow the court to conduct a more focused inquiry into the merits of logging at that site. Occasional holdings against ripeness, such as these, should not be particularly surprising, because the *Abbott Labs* test is designed to be highly discretionary.

E. PRIMARY JURISDICTION

Unlike the preceding topics examined in this chapter, the doctrine of primary jurisdiction is *not* a defense to judicial review of agency action. Indeed, it comes into play only in cases that fall within the original jurisdiction of the courts. However, it is often discussed in conjunction with exhaustion and ripeness because, like those doctrines, it is a tool by which courts seek to avoid interfering with an agency's ability to carry out its statutory functions in a coherent way. Briefly, primary jurisdiction questions arise when a court hearing a civil or criminal case encounters an issue that also falls within the distinctive competence of an administrative agency. If the court chooses to invoke the doctrine, it will suspend consideration of the disputed issue and direct the parties to take the matter to the agency for an initial determination. Thus, the primary jurisdiction doctrine is somewhat analogous to the federal courts' practice of abstaining from deciding an issue of state law so that state courts may address the issue.

There are two principal reasons for requiring a private litigant to resort to the administrative process before pursuing court litigation. First, a referral to the agency may preserve needed uniformity in a regulatory program. Thus, in Texas & Pac. R.R. v.

Abilene Cotton Oil Co., 204 U.S. 426 (1907), a shipper sued the railroad in state court, alleging that the railroad's rates, which had been approved by the Interstate Commerce Commission, were unreasonably high. The Court held that this question was within the primary jurisdiction of the ICC, because a major objective of the Interstate Commerce Act had been to achieve national uniformity of rates, and this goal would be frustrated if numerous courts across the country could enforce ad hoc judgments as to whether individual rates were excessive. Second, the litigation may involve issues that go beyond the conventional experience of judges, and on which the expertise of the agency could be helpful. In United States v. Western Pacific R.R., 352 U.S. 59 (1956), a railroad shipped napalm in steel casings for the Army, charging its established rate for "incendiary bombs." The Army claimed that the (lower) rate for "gasoline in steel drums" applied, and the railroad sued for payment in the Court of Claims. On appeal, the Supreme Court again referred the question to the ICC: since that agency had approved the tariffs in which the two rates appeared, it was in the best position to know whether the purposes underlying the high rate for "incendiary bombs" were implicated in this situation.

On the other hand, if an issue raised in the court action falls outside the ambit of the agency's special expertise or unique authority, the claim will not be barred by the primary jurisdiction doctrine. An airline that had the bad luck or bad judgment to "bump" Ralph Nader from a flight on which he held a confirmed reservation learned this lesson in Nader v. Allegheny Airlines, Inc., 426 U.S. 290 (1976). Nader brought a damage action for fraudulent misrepresentation, claiming that the airline deceptively failed to disclose that it might "overbook" its flights and deny boarding to passengers with confirmed reservations. One of the airline's defenses was that the question fell within the primary jurisdiction of the Civil Aeronautics Board, because that agency had power to issue cease and desist orders against regulated carriers that had engaged in "unfair or deceptive practices." The Supreme Court disagreed. The CAB's statutory power to abate deceptive practices was not synonymous with common law fraud and misrepresentation, and the Board had no power to immunize carriers from this kind of liability. More significantly, the issue was not one on which a decision "could be facilitated by an informed evaluation of the economics or technology of the regulated industry"; rather, the common law fraud standards "are within the conventional competence of the courts, and the judgment of a technically expert body is not likely to be helpful in the application of these standards to the facts of this case."

As these cases suggest, the basic justification for the doctrine of primary jurisdiction is to coordinate the work of agencies and courts. Their activities are most likely to come into conflict where the agency's regulation is pervasive, and where uniform interpretations are necessary to assure effective regulation. Therefore, the doctrine has most often been applied in cases concerning intensively regulated industries—where agencies control entry, price, and nature and quality of service. In recent decades, of course, policies of deregulation have greatly reduced the number of industries that fall into this category (indeed, the ICC and CAB no longer exist), and so primary jurisdiction is less frequently invoked than in the past. In the end, however, invocation of the doctrine is highly discretionary and seems to depend on whether the court actually feels out of its depth as it confronts the issues raised by the parties.

In any event, the doctrine does not transfer *exclusive* jurisdiction from court to agency; it only allocates jurisdictional priority. Once the agency renders its decision, recourse to the courts—through the normal mechanisms for judicial review of agency action—is still available. In Far East Conf. v. United States, 342 U.S. 570 (1952), an association of steamship companies gave preferential rates to shippers who dealt exclusively with association members. The Justice Department challenged this dual-rate scheme under the antitrust laws, but the Court held that the matter fell within the Federal Maritime Board's primary jurisdiction. Subsequently, the FMB ruled that the dual-rate system was valid, but the Supreme Court reversed this ruling on direct appeal. FMB v. Isbrandtsen Co., 356 U.S. 481 (1958). Thus, the Court got the benefit of the agency's views, but also refused to overlook the possibility that the agency had been "captured" by the industry that it was created to regulate. This best-of-both-worlds outcome is somewhat unusual, however: in most cases, allowing the agency the first opportunity to decide an issue (or case) probably means giving it the dispositive voice as well.

F. DAMAGE ACTIONS AGAINST THE GOVERNMENT

Persons who are harmed by administrative action often seek to recover damages from the government to compensate them for their injuries. Such efforts always require a statutory basis, for otherwise they might founder on the ancient doctrine of sovereign immunity, i.e., the principle that the government may not be sued without its consent. (In the typical judicial review proceeding to compel or set aside an agency action, sovereign immunity is not an issue, because the APA waives this defense. 5 U.S.C.A. § 702. But the APA waiver does not extend to claims for "money damages,"[4] and thus a litigant who hopes to recover damages from the United States must find a statutory waiver elsewhere.) For example, in the Tucker Act, 28 U.S.C.A. § 1491, the United States has consented to be sued for damages in the U.S. Claims Court for a breach of contract or a "taking" of property without just compensation. For tort claims, the proper avenue for redress is the Federal Tort Claims Act.

4. Claims for equitable monetary relief, such as reimbursement of specific sums, are not considered claims for "money damages" and thus can be pursued through the normal APA review mechanisms. Bowen v. Massachusetts, 487 U.S. 879 (1988).

The FTCA generally renders the government liable in tort for any "negligent or wrongful act or omission ... in the same manner and to the same extent as a private individual under like circumstances." 28 U.S.C.A. §§ 1346(b), 2674. However, the Act also lists a number of exceptions that effectively preserve much of the sovereign immunity doctrine. One of these exceptions denies tort liability for a wide variety of intentional torts, including defamation, misrepresentation, deceit, and interference with contract rights. Id. § 2680(h). Originally the same provision also excluded liability for assault, battery, false arrest, and malicious prosecution; since 1974, however, these latter torts have been actionable if committed by law enforcement officers. Id.

The most sweeping of the FTCA exceptions bars suit if the responsible officials were exercising a "discretionary function," regardless of whether they abused their discretion. Id. § 2680(a). In United States v. S.A. Empresa de Viacao Aerea Rio Grandense (Varig Airlines), 467 U.S. 797 (1984), the Court explained that Congress had intended the discretionary function exception "to prevent judicial 'second-guessing' of legislative and administrative decisions grounded in ... policy through the medium of an action in tort." Thus § 2680(a) should be read "to encompass the discretionary acts of the Government acting in its role as a regulator of the conduct of private individuals." Later, however, the Court limited *Varig Airlines* by holding that the exception applies only to "the permissible exercise of policy judgment." Berkovitz v. United States, 486 U.S. 531 (1988). This formula had two important implications. First, the exception cannot apply to government conduct that violates a "statute, regulation, or policy [that] specifically prescribes a course of action for an employee to follow." In such a case, "there is no discretion in the [officer's] conduct for the discretionary function exception to protect." Second, the exception protects only judgments based on public policy considerations, not every exercise of judgment by a government employee.

The Court elaborated on the teachings of *Berkovitz* in United States v. Gaubert, 499 U.S. 315 (1991). The plaintiff was the chairman and largest stockholder of a financially troubled savings and loan association. The Federal Home Loan Bank Board had assumed supervisory control over the institution, and Gaubert's suit alleged that the Board's management decisions had been negligent. The Court reaffirmed the *Berkovitz* reasoning, but added that, when an agency's regulations allow a government employee to exercise discretion, there is a strong presumption that the employee's actions were grounded in policy and thus not actionable. Since the Board's enabling statute afforded it wide discretion in deciding how to supervise thrift institutions, and the Board's day-to-day exercise of this power was evidently grounded in the policies of the statute, the Court ordered Gaubert's complaint dismissed. That the Board's alleged mismanagement had occurred in routine decisions reached at the "operational level" of the savings and loan's business was not an obstacle to immunity.

G. DAMAGE ACTIONS AGAINST OFFICERS

When a litigant seeks to recover damages from the pocket of a government official, sovereign immunity is not an obstacle, but a related doctrine, official immunity, may be. The longstanding rule has been that a federal employee is absolutely immune from common-law tort liability for any act performed "within the outer perimeter of [his] line of duty." Barr v. Matteo, 360 U.S. 564 (1959). The rationale for this strict rule is that officials should feel free to make decisions according to their concept of the public interest, without the threat that they might have to bear monetary loss if a member of the public is injured in the process. In 1988 the case law started to move away from the absolute rule of *Barr,* see Westfall v. Erwin, 484 U.S. 292 (1988), but Congress quickly acted to restore it in substance. The so-called Westfall Act provides that, in any tort suit brought against a federal employee for actions he took within the scope of his employment, the United States will be substituted as the defendant and the plaintiff's rights will be determined in accordance with the FTCA. 28 U.S.C.A. § 2679(d). Tort recovery from the employee is specifically foreclosed, id. § 2679(b), even if the claim against the United States is worthless because of an FTCA exemption. United States v. Smith, 499 U.S. 160 (1991). However, the substitution occurs only if the Attorney General certifies that the employee was acting within the scope of his employment, and this certification is judicially reviewable. Gutierrez de Martinez v. Lamagno, 515 U.S. 417 (1995).

When the basis for a damage claim is not the common law of tort but an officer's violation of the Constitution, the Westfall Act does not apply, and the parties' rights are determined by an entirely separate body of case law. This line of authority stems from Bivens v. Six Unknown Named Agents of the Federal Bureau of Narcotics, 403 U.S. 388 (1971), where the Court held that an individual could bring a suit under the Fourth Amendment to recover for injuries resulting from the actions of federal narcotics agents during an unlawful search of his apartment. The Court has extended the *Bivens* holding to violations of constitutional provisions generally, but it has also held that in some specific contexts the remedy is not available. These include situations in which Congress has already set up an elaborate remedial system, see Schweiker v. Chilicky, 487 U.S. 412 (1988) (Social Security disability claims); Bush v. Lucas, 462 U.S. 367 (1983) (grievances by federal civil servants), or where there are other "special factors counseling hesitation," such as in the military context. United States v. Stanley, 483 U.S. 669 (1987).

In a *Bivens* action, official immunity is again a factor, but usually in a modified form. In Butz v. Economou, 438 U.S. 478 (1978), the Court held that federal officers should have the same immunity defenses that the Court had been applying for some years in "constitutional tort" actions against state officials under the Civil Rights Act of 1871, 42 U.S.C.A. § 1983. Balancing the injustice of denying redress to an injured plaintiff against the injustice of imposing liability on an official who had exercised his discretion in good faith, and taking account of the risk that liability would make administrators overly cautious in reaching important decisions, the Court stated that the scope of official immunity depended upon the kind of function the official was performing. Executive officers exercising discretion were accorded only a "qualified" immunity: an official would be protected from liability only if he had a good faith belief that his conduct was lawful, and the belief was reasonable. In thus breaking from the strict principle of immunity represented by *Barr,* the Court did not seem to be motivated by any strong sense that an additional check on federal officers was needed, but rather by a belief that it would be incongruous to hold federal officers to a more lenient standard than state officers.

However, the Court went on to recognize that state judges and prosecutors have been accorded absolute immunity in § 1983 litigation. This led the Court to hold that their counterparts exercising judicial functions in the federal bureaucracy—such as ALJs and staff attorneys acting in a prosecutorial capacity—should also enjoy absolute immunity, even in constitutional tort cases. The Court felt that this complete immunity was necessary to assure that "judges, advocates, and witnesses can perform their respective functions without harassment or intimidation." At the same time, absolute immunity for officers exercising judicial functions would not be likely to cause many unredressed injuries, because the safeguards built into the formal adjudicatory process would provide substantial protection against possible constitutional violations.

A few years after *Economou,* the Court revised the standard for qualified immunity in *Bivens* actions. The test became whether the defendant "violate[d] clearly established statutory or constitutional rights of which a reasonable person would have known." Harlow v. Fitzgerald, 457 U.S. 800 (1982). The prior "good faith" standard, with its emphasis on motives, had led to burdensome discovery and had been difficult for courts to apply except by holding a trial; the *Harlow* test is purely objective and turns primarily on legal issues, so that groundless cases can often be terminated through summary judgment. Partly because of the stringency of the *Harlow* test, successful constitutional tort actions against federal officers have been extremely sparse, and probably will remain so. One can argue, however, that the real significance of the *Bivens* cause of action does not lie in its practical role as part of a compensation system, but in its symbolic reminder that executive decisionmaking must always remain subordinate to the dictates of the Constitution.

APPENDIX I

SELECTED CONSTITUTIONAL AND STATUTORY PROVISIONS

UNITED STATES CONSTITUTION

Article I

Section 1. All legislative Powers herein granted shall be vested in a Congress of the United States, which shall consist of a Senate and House of Representatives.

Section 7. [1] All Bills for raising Revenue shall originate in the House of Representatives; but the Senate may propose or concur with Amendments as on other Bills.

[2] Every Bill which shall have passed the House of Representatives and the Senate, shall, before it become a Law, be presented to the President of the United States; If he approve he shall sign it, but if not he shall return it, with his Objections to that House in which it shall have originated, who shall enter the Objections at large on their Journal, and proceed to reconsider it. If after such Reconsideration two thirds of that House shall agree to pass the Bill, it shall be sent, together with the Objections, to the other House, by which it shall likewise be reconsidered, and if approved by

two thirds of that House, it shall become a Law. But in all such Cases the Votes of both Houses shall be determined by yeas and Nays, and the Names of the Persons voting for and against the Bill shall be entered on the Journal of each House respectively. If any Bill shall not be returned by the President within ten Days (Sundays excepted) after it shall have been presented to him, the Same shall be a Law, in like Manner as if he had signed it, unless the Congress by their Adjournment prevent its Return, in which Case it shall not be a Law.

[3]   Every Order, Resolution, or Vote to Which the Concurrence of the Senate and House of Representatives may be necessary (except on a question of Adjournment) shall be presented to the President of the United States; and before the Same shall take Effect, shall be approved by him, or being disapproved by him, shall be repassed by two thirds of the Senate and House of Representatives, according to the Rules and Limitations prescribed in the Case of a Bill.

Section 8, The Congress shall have Power ...

[18]   To make all Laws which shall be necessary and proper for carrying into Execution the foregoing Powers, and all other Powers vested by this Constitution in the Government of the United States, or in any Department or Officer thereof.

Article II

Section 1. [1] The executive Power shall be vested in a President of the United States of America....

Section 2. [1] The President shall be Commander in Chief of the Army and Navy of the United States; . . . he may require the Opinion, in writing, of the principal Officer in each of the executive Departments, upon any Subject relating to the Duties of their respective Offices. . . .

[2]   He shall have Power, by and with the Advice and Consent of the Senate, to make Treaties, provided two thirds of the Senators present concur; and he shall nominate, and by and with the Advice and Consent of the Senate, shall appoint Ambassadors, other public Ministers and Consuls, Judges of the supreme Court, and all other Officers of the United States, whose Appointments are not herein otherwise provided for, and which shall be established by Law; but the Congress may by Law vest the Appointment of such inferior Officers, as they think proper, in the President alone, in the Courts of Law, or in the Heads of Departments. . . .

Section 3. He shall from time to time give to the Congress Information of the State of the Union, and recommend to their Consideration such Measures as he shall judge necessary and expedient; . . . he shall take Care that the Laws be faithfully executed, and shall Commission all the Officers of the United States.

Section 4. The President, Vice President and all civil Officers of the United States, shall be removed from Office on Impeachment for, and Conviction of, Treason, Bribery, or other high Crimes and Misdemeanors.

Article III

Section 1. The judicial Power of the United States, shall be vested in one supreme Court, and in such inferior Courts as the Congress may from time to time ordain and establish. . . .

Section 2. [1] The judicial Power shall extend to all Cases, in Law and Equity, arising under this Constitution, the Laws of the United States, and Treaties made, or which shall be made, under their Authority;—to all Cases affecting Ambassadors, other public Ministers and Consuls;—to all Cases of admiralty and maritime Jurisdiction;—to Controversies to which the United States shall be a Party;—to Controversies between two or more States;—between a State and Citizens of another State;—between Citizens of different States;—between Citizens of the same State claiming Lands under the Grants of different States, and between a State, or the Citizens thereof, and foreign States, Citizens or Subjects.

Amendment I [1791]

Congress shall make no law respecting an establishment of religion, or prohibiting the free exercise thereof; or abridging the freedom of speech, or of the press; or the right of the people peaceably to assemble, and to petition the Government for a redress of grievances.

Amendment IV [1791]

The right of the people to be secure in their persons, houses, papers, and effects, against unreasonable searches and seizures, shall not be violated, and no Warrants shall issue, but upon probable cause, supported by Oath or affirmation, and particularly describing the place to be searched, and the persons or things to be seized.

Amendment V [1791]

No person shall be held to answer for a capital, or otherwise infamous crime, unless on a presentment or indictment of a Grand Jury, except in cases arising in the land or naval forces, or in the Militia, when in actual service in time of War or public danger; nor shall any person be subject for the same offence to be twice put in jeopardy of life or limb; nor shall be compelled in any criminal case to be a witness against himself, nor be deprived of life, liberty, or property, without due process of law; nor shall private property be taken for public use, without just compensation.

Amendment VII [1791]

In Suits at common law, where the value in controversy shall exceed twenty dollars, the right of trial by jury shall be preserved, and no fact tried by a jury, shall be otherwise re-examined in any Court of the United States, than according to the rules of the common law.

Amendment XIV [1868]

Section 1. All persons born or naturalized in the United States, and subject to the jurisdiction thereof, are citizens of the United States and of the State wherein they reside. No State shall make or enforce any law which shall abridge the privileges or immunities of citizens of the United States; nor shall any State deprive any person of life, liberty, or property, without due process of law; nor deny to any person within its jurisdiction the equal protection of the laws.

ADMINISTRATIVE PROCEDURE ACT

UNITED STATES CODE, TITLE 5

CHAPTER 5—ADMINISTRATIVE PROCEDURE

§ 551.   Definitions

For the purpose of this subchapter—

(1) "agency" means each authority of the Government of the United States, whether or not it is within or subject to review by another agency, but does not include—

(A) the Congress;

(B) the courts of the United States;

(C) the governments of the territories or possessions of the United States;

(D) the government of the District of Columbia;

or except as to the requirements of section 552 of this title—

(E) agencies composed of representatives of the parties or of representatives of organizations of the parties to the disputes determined by them;

(F) courts martial and military commissions;

(G) military authority exercised in the field in time of war or in occupied territory; or

(H) functions conferred by sections 1738, 1739, 1743, and 1744 of title 12; chapter 2 of title 41; subchapter II of chapter 471 of title 49; or sections 1884, 1891–1902, and former section 1641(b)(2), of title 50, appendix;

(2) "person" includes an individual, partnership, corporation, association, or public or private organization other than an agency;

(3) "party" includes a person or agency named or admitted as a party, or properly seeking and entitled as of right to be admitted as a party, in an agency proceeding, and a person or agency admitted by an agency as a party for limited purposes;

(4) "rule" means the whole or a part of an agency statement of general or particular applicability and future effect designed to implement, interpret, or prescribe law or policy or describing the organization, procedure, or practice requirements of an agency and includes the approval or prescription for the future of rates, wages, corporate or financial structures or reorganizations thereof, prices, facilities, appliances, services or allowances therefor or of valuations, costs, or accounting, or practices bearing on any of the foregoing;

(5) "rule making" means agency process for formulating, amending, or repealing a rule;

(6) "order" means the whole or a part of a final disposition, whether affirmative, negative, injunc-

tive, or declaratory in form, of an agency in a matter other than rule making but including licensing;

(7) "adjudication" means agency process for the formulation of an order;

(8) "license" includes the whole or a part of an agency permit, certificate, approval, registration, charter, membership, statutory exemption or other form of permission;

(9) "licensing" includes agency process respecting the grant, renewal, denial, revocation, suspension, annulment, withdrawal, limitation, amendment, modification, or conditioning of a license;

(10) "sanction" includes the whole or a part of an agency—

(A) prohibition, requirement, limitation, or other condition affecting the freedom of a person;

(B) withholding of relief;

(C) imposition of penalty or fine;

(D) destruction, taking, seizure, or withholding of property;

(E) assessment of damages, reimbursement, restitution, compensation, costs, charges, or fees;

(F) requirement, revocation, or suspension of a license; or

(G) taking other compulsory or restrictive action;

(11) "relief" includes the whole or a part of an agency—

(A) grant of money, assistance, license, authority, exemption, exception, privilege, or remedy;

(B) recognition of a claim, right, immunity, privilege, exemption, or exception; or

(C) taking of other action on the application or petition of, and beneficial to, a person;

(12) "agency proceeding" means an agency process as defined by paragraphs (5), (7), and (9) of this section;

(13) "agency action" includes the whole or a part of an agency rule, order, license, sanction, relief, or the equivalent or denial thereof, or failure to act; and

(14) "ex parte communication" means an oral or written communication not on the public record with respect to which reasonable prior notice to all parties is not given, but it shall not include requests for status reports on any matter or proceeding covered by this subchapter.

§ 552. Public information; agency rules, opinions, orders, records, and proceedings [Freedom of Information Act—excerpts only]

(a) Each agency shall make available to the public information as follows:

(1) Each agency shall separately state and currently publish in the Federal Register for the guidance of the public—

(A) descriptions of its central and field organization and the established places at which, the employees (and in the case of a uniformed service, the members) from whom, and the methods whereby, the public may obtain information, make submittals or requests, or obtain decisions;

(B) statements of the general course and method by which its functions are channeled and determined, including the nature and requirements of all formal and informal procedures available;

(C) rules of procedure, descriptions of forms available or the places at which forms may be obtained, and instructions as to the scope and contents of all papers, reports, or examinations;

(D) substantive rules of general applicability adopted as authorized by law, and statements of general policy or interpretations of general applicability formulated and adopted by the agency; and

(E) each amendment, revision, or repeal of the foregoing

Except to the extent that a person has actual and timely notice of the terms thereof, a person may not in any manner be required to resort to, or be adversely affected by, a matter required to be published in the Federal Register and not so published. . . .

(2) Each agency, in accordance with published rules, shall make available for public inspection and copying—

(A) final opinions, including concurring and dissenting opinions, as well as orders, made in the adjudication of cases;

(B) those statements of policy and interpretations which have been adopted by the agency and are not published in the Federal Register;

(C) administrative staff manuals and instructions to staff that affect a member of the public;

(D) copies of all records, regardless of form or format, which have been released to any person under paragraph (3) and which, because of the nature of their subject matter, the agency determines have become or are likely to become the subject of subsequent requests for substantially the same records; and

(E) a general index of the records referred to under subparagraph (D);

unless the materials are promptly published and copies offered for sale. For records created on or after November 1, 1996, within one year after such date, each agency shall make such records available, including by computer telecommunications or, if computer telecommunications means have not been established by the agency, by other electronic means. . . . A final order, opinion, statement of policy, interpretation, or staff manual or instruction that affects a member of the public may be relied on, used, or cited as precedent by an agency against a party other than an agency only if—

(i) it has been indexed and either made available or published as provided by this paragraph; or

(ii) the party has actual and timely notice of the terms thereof.

(3)(A) Except with respect to the records made available under paragraphs (1) and (2) of this subsection, ... each agency, upon any request for records which (i) reasonably describes such records and (ii) is made in accordance with published rules stating the time, place, fees (if any), and procedures to be followed, shall make the records promptly available to any person.

(B) In making any record available to a person under this paragraph, an agency shall provide the record in any form or format requested by the person if the record is readily reproducible by the agency in that form or format. Each agency shall make reasonable efforts to maintain its records in forms or formats that are reproducible for purposes of this section. . . .

(4)(A)(i) In order to carry out the provisions of this section, each agency shall promulgate regulations, pursuant to notice and receipt of public comment, specifying the schedule of fees applicable to the processing of requests under this section ...

(B) On complaint, the district court of the United States in the district in which the complainant resides, or has his principal place of business, or in which the agency records are situated, or in the District of Columbia, has jurisdiction to enjoin the agency from withholding agency records and to order the production of any agency records improperly withheld from the complainant. In such a case the court shall determine the matter de novo, and may examine the contents of such agency records in camera to determine whether such records or any part thereof shall be withheld under any of the exemptions set forth in subsection (b) of this section, and the burden is on the agency to sustain its action. . . .

(E) The court may assess against the United States reasonable attorney fees and other litigation costs reasonably incurred in any case under this section in which the complainant has substantially prevailed. . . .

(b) This section does not apply to matters that are—

(1)(A) specifically authorized under criteria established by an Executive order to be kept secret in the interest of national defense or foreign policy and (B) are in fact properly classified pursuant to such Executive order;

(2) related solely to the internal personnel rules and practices of an agency;

(3) specifically exempted from disclosure by statute (other than section 552b of this title), provided that such statute (A) requires that the matters be withheld from the public in such a manner as to leave no discretion on the issue, or (B) establishes particular criteria for withholding

or refers to particular types of matters to be withheld;

(4) trade secrets and commercial or financial information obtained from a person and privileged or confidential;

(5) inter-agency or intra-agency memorandums or letters which would not be available by law to a party other than an agency in litigation with the agency;

(6) personnel and medical files and similar files the disclosure of which would constitute a clearly unwarranted invasion of personal privacy;

(7) records or information compiled for law enforcement purposes, but only to the extent that the production of such law enforcement records or information (A) could reasonably be expected to interfere with enforcement proceedings, (B) would deprive a person of a right to a fair trial or an impartial adjudication, (C) could reasonably be expected to constitute an unwarranted invasion of personal privacy, (D) could reasonably be expected to disclose the identity of a confidential source, including a State, local or foreign agency or authority or any private institution which furnished information on a confidential basis, and, in the case of a record or information compiled by criminal law enforcement authority in the course of a criminal investigation or by an agency conducting a lawful national security intelligence investigation, information furnished by a confidential source, (E) would disclose techniques and proce-

dures for law enforcement investigations or prosecutions, or would disclose guidelines for law enforcement investigations or prosecutions if such disclosure could reasonably be expected to risk circumvention of the law, or (F) could reasonably be expected to endanger the life or physical safety of any individual;

(8) contained in or related to examination, operating, or condition reports prepared by, on behalf of, or for the use of an agency responsible for the regulation or supervision of financial institutions; or

(9) geological and geophysical information and data, including maps, concerning wells.

Any reasonably segregable portion of a record shall be provided to any person requesting such record after deletion of the portions which are exempt under this subsection. The amount of information deleted shall be indicated on the released portion of the record, unless including that indication would harm an interest protected by the exemption in this subsection under which the deletion is made. If technically feasible, the amount of the information deleted shall be indicated at the place in the record where such deletion is made. . . .

(d) This section does not authorize withholding of information or limit the availability of records to the public, except as specifically stated in this section. This section is not authority to withhold information from Congress. . . .

§ 552a. Records maintained on individuals

[This section, known as the Privacy Act, is omitted.]

§ 552b. Open meetings

[This section, known as the Government in the Sunshine Act, is omitted.]

§ 553. Rule making

(a) This section applies, according to the provisions thereof, except to the extent that there is involved—

(1) a military or foreign affairs function of the United States; or

(2) a matter relating to agency management or personnel or to public property, loans, grants, benefits, or contracts.

(b) General notice of proposed rule making shall be published in the Federal Register, unless persons subject thereto are named and either personally served or otherwise have actual notice thereof in accordance with law. The notice shall include—

(1) a statement of the time, place, and nature of public rule making proceedings;

(2) reference to the legal authority under which the rule is proposed; and

(3) either the terms or substance of the proposed rule or a description of the subjects and issues involved.

Except when notice or hearing is required by statute, this subsection does not apply—

(A) to interpretative rules, general statements of policy, or rules of agency organization, procedure, or practice; or

(B) when the agency for good cause finds (and incorporates the finding and a brief statement of reasons therefor in the rules issued) that notice and public procedure thereon are impracticable, unnecessary, or contrary to the public interest.

(c) After notice required by this section, the agency shall give interested persons an opportunity to participate in the rule making through submission of written data, views, or arguments with or without opportunity for oral presentation. After consideration of the relevant matter presented, the agency shall incorporate in the rules adopted a concise general statement of their basis and purpose. When rules are required by statute to be made on the record after opportunity for an agency hearing, sections 556 and 557 of this title apply instead of this subsection.

(d) The required publication or service of a substantive rule shall be made not less than 30 days before its effective date, except—

(1) a substantive rule which grants or recognizes an exemption or relieves a restriction;

(2) interpretative rules and statements of policy; or

(3) as otherwise provided by the agency for good cause found and published with the rule.

(e) Each agency shall give an interested person the right to petition for the issuance, amendment, or repeal of a rule.

§ 554. Adjudications

(a) This section applies, according to the provisions thereof, in every case of adjudication required by statute to be determined on the record after opportunity for an agency hearing, except to the extent that there is involved—

(1) a matter subject to a subsequent trial of the law and the facts de novo in a court;

(2) the selection or tenure of an employee, except a[n] administrative law judge appointed under section 3105 of this title;

(3) proceedings in which decisions rest solely on inspections, tests, or elections;

(4) the conduct of military or foreign affairs functions;

(5) cases in which an agency is acting as an agent for a court; or

(6) the certification of worker representatives.

(b) Persons entitled to notice of an agency hearing shall be timely informed of—

(1) the time, place, and nature of the hearing;

(2) the legal authority and jurisdiction under which the hearing is to be held; and

(3) the matters of fact and law asserted.

When private persons are the moving parties, other parties to the proceeding shall give prompt notice of issues controverted in fact or law; and in other instances agencies may by rule require responsive pleading. In fixing the time and place for hearings, due regard shall be had for the convenience and necessity of the parties or their representatives.

(c) The agency shall give all interested parties opportunity for—

(1) the submission and consideration of facts, arguments, offers of settlement, or proposals of adjustment when time, the nature of the proceeding, and the public interest permit; and

(2) to the extent that the parties are unable so to determine a controversy by consent, hearing and decision on notice and in accordance with sections 556 and 557 of this title.

(d) The employee who presides at the reception of evidence pursuant to section 556 of this title shall make the recommended decision or initial decision required by section 557 of this title, unless he becomes unavailable to the agency. Except to the extent required for the disposition of ex parte matters as authorized by law, such an employee may not—

(1) consult a person or party on a fact in issue, unless on notice and opportunity for all parties to participate; or

(2) be responsible to or subject to the supervision or direction of an employee or agent engaged in the performance of investigative or prosecuting functions for an agency.

An employee or agent engaged in the performance of investigative or prosecuting functions for an agency in a case may not, in that or a factually related case, participate or advise in the decision, recommended decision, or agency review pursuant to section 557 of this title, except as witness or counsel in public proceedings. This subsection does not apply—

(A) in determining applications for initial licenses;

(B) to proceedings involving the validity or application of rates, facilities, or practices of public utilities or carriers; or

(C) to the agency or a member or members of the body comprising the agency.

(e) The agency, with like effect as in the case of other orders, and in its sound discretion, may issue a declaratory order to terminate a controversy or remove uncertainty.

§ 555. Ancillary matters

(a) This section applies, according to the provisions thereof, except as otherwise provided by this subchapter.

(b) A person compelled to appear in person before an agency or representative thereof is entitled to be accompanied, represented, and advised by counsel or, if permitted by the agency, by other qualified representative. A party is entitled to appear in person or by or with counsel or other duly qualified representative in an agency proceeding. So far as the orderly conduct of public business permits, an interested person may appear before an agency or its responsible employees for the presentation, adjustment, or determination of an issue, request, or controversy in a proceeding, whether interlocutory, summary, or otherwise, or in connection with an agency function. With due regard for the convenience and necessity of the parties or their representatives and within a reasonable time, each agency shall proceed to conclude a matter presented to it. This subsection does not grant or deny a person who is not a lawyer the right to appear for or represent others before an agency or in an agency proceeding.

(c) Process, requirement of a report, inspection, or other investigative act or demand may not be issued, made, or enforced except as authorized by law. A person compelled to submit data or evidence is entitled to retain or, on payment of lawfully prescribed costs, procure a copy or transcript thereof, except that in a non-public investigatory proceeding the witness may for good cause be limited to inspection of the official transcript of his testimony.

(d) Agency subpenas authorized by law shall be issued to a party on request and, when required by rules of procedure, on a statement or showing of general relevance and reasonable scope of the evidence sought. On contest, the court shall sustain the subpena or similar process or demand to the extent that it is found to be in accordance with law. In a proceeding for enforcement, the court shall issue an order requiring the appearance of the witness or the production of the evidence or data within a reasonable time under penalty of punishment for contempt in case of contumacious failure to comply.

(e) Prompt notice shall be given of the denial in whole or in part of a written application, petition, or other request of an interested person made in connection with any agency proceeding. Except in affirming a prior denial or when the denial is self-explanatory, the notice shall be accompanied by a brief statement of the grounds for denial.

§ 556. Hearings; presiding employees; powers and duties; burden of proof; evidence; record as basis of decision

(a) This section applies, according to the provisions thereof, to hearings required by section 553 or 554 of this title to be conducted in accordance with this section.

(b) There shall preside at the taking of evidence—

(1) the agency;

(2) one or more members of the body which comprises the agency; or

(3) one or more administrative law judges appointed under section 3105 of this title.

This subchapter does not supersede the conduct of specified classes of proceedings, in whole or in part, by or before boards or other employees specially provided for by or designated under statute. The functions of presiding employees and of employees participating in decisions in accordance with section 557 of this title shall be conducted in an impartial manner. A presiding or participating employee may at any time disqualify himself. On the filing in good faith of a timely and sufficient affidavit of personal bias or other disqualification of a presiding or participating employee, the agency shall determine the matter as a part of the record and decision in the case.

(c) Subject to published rules of the agency and within its powers, employees presiding at hearings may—

(1) administer oaths and affirmations;

(2) issue subpenas authorized by law;

(3) rule on offers of proof and receive relevant evidence;

(4) take depositions or have depositions taken when the ends of justice would be served;

(5) regulate the course of the hearing;

(6) hold conferences for the settlement or simplification of the issues by consent of the parties or by the use of alternative means of dispute

resolution as provided in subchapter IV of this chapter;

(7) inform the parties as to the availability of one or more alternative means of dispute resolution, and encourage use of such methods;

(8) require the attendance at any conference held pursuant to paragraph (6) of at least one representative of each party who has authority to negotiate concerning resolution of issues in controversy;

(9) dispose of procedural requests or similar matters;

(10) make or recommend decisions in accordance with section 557 of this title; and

(11) take other action authorized by agency rule consistent with this subchapter.

(d) Except as otherwise provided by statute, the proponent of a rule or order has the burden of proof. Any oral or documentary evidence may be received, but the agency as a matter of policy shall provide for the exclusion of irrelevant, immaterial, or unduly repetitious evidence. A sanction may not be imposed or rule or order issued except on consideration of the whole record or those parts thereof cited by a party and supported by and in accordance with the reliable, probative, and substantial evidence. The agency may, to the extent consistent with the interests of justice and the policy of the underlying statutes administered by the agency, consider a violation of section 557(d) of this title sufficient grounds for a decision adverse to a party who has knowingly committed such violation or knowingly caused such violation to occur. A party is entitled to present his case or defense by oral or documentary evidence, to submit rebuttal evidence, and to conduct such cross-examination as may be required for a full and true disclosure of the facts. In rule making or determining claims for money or benefits or applications for initial licenses an agency may, when a party will not be prejudiced thereby, adopt procedures for the submission of all or part of the evidence in written form.

(e) The transcript of testimony and exhibits, together with all papers and requests filed in the proceeding, constitutes the exclusive record for decision in accordance with section 557 of this title and, on payment of lawfully prescribed costs, shall be made available to the parties. When an agency decision rests on official notice of a material fact not appearing in the evidence in the record, a party is entitled, on timely request, to an opportunity to show the contrary.

§ 557. Initial decisions; conclusiveness; review by agency; submissions by parties; contents of decisions; record

(a) This section applies, according to the provisions thereof, when a hearing is required to be conducted in accordance with section 556 of this title.

(b) When the agency did not preside at the reception of the evidence, the presiding employee or, in cases not subject to section 554(d) of this title, an employee qualified to preside at hearings pursuant to section 556 of this title, shall initially decide the case unless the agency requires, either in specific cases or by general rule, the entire record to be certified to it for decision. When the presiding employee makes an initial decision, that decision then becomes the decision of the agency without further proceedings unless there is an appeal to, or review on motion of, the agency within time provided by rule. On appeal from or review of the initial decision, the agency has all the powers which it would have in making the initial decision except as it may limit the issues on notice or by rule. When the agency makes the decision without having presided at the reception of the evidence, the presiding employee or an employee qualified to preside at hearings pursuant to section 556 of this title shall first recommend a decision, except that in rule making or determining applications for initial licenses—

(1) instead thereof the agency may issue a tentative decision or one of its responsible employees may recommend a decision; or

(2) this procedure may be omitted in a case in which the agency finds on the record that due and timely execution of its functions imperatively and unavoidably so requires.

(c) Before a recommended, initial, or tentative decision, or a decision on agency review of the decision of subordinate employees, the parties are entitled to a reasonable opportunity to submit for the consideration of the employees participating in the decisions—

(1) proposed findings and conclusions; or

(2) exceptions to the decisions or recommended decisions of subordinate employees or to tentative agency decisions; and

(3) supporting reasons for the exceptions or proposed findings or conclusions.

The record shall show the ruling on each finding, conclusion, or exception presented. All decisions, including initial, recommended, and tentative decisions, are a part of the record and shall include a statement of—

(A) findings and conclusions, and the reasons or basis therefor, on all the material issues of fact, law, or discretion presented on the record; and

(B) the appropriate rule, order, sanction, relief, or denial thereof.

(d)(1) In any agency proceeding which is subject to subsection (a) of this section, except to the extent required for the disposition of ex parte matters as authorized by law—

(A) no interested person outside the agency shall make or knowingly cause to be made to any member of the body comprising the agency, administrative law judge, or other employee who is or may reasonably be expected to be involved in the decisional process of the proceeding, an ex parte communication relevant to the merits of the proceeding;

(B) no member of the body comprising the agency, administrative law judge, or other employee who is or may reasonably be expected to be involved in the decisional process of the proceeding, shall make or knowingly cause to be made to any interested person outside the agency an ex parte communication relevant to the merits of the proceeding;

(C) a member of the body comprising the agency, administrative law judge, or other employee who is or may reasonably be expected to be involved in the decisional process of such proceeding who receives, or who makes or knowingly causes to be made, a communication prohibited by this subsection shall place on the public record of the proceeding:

(i) all such written communications;

(ii) memoranda stating the substance of all such oral communications; and

(iii) all written responses, and memoranda stating the substance of all oral responses, to the materials described in clauses (i) and (ii) of this subparagraph;

(D) upon receipt of a communication knowingly made or knowingly caused to be made by a party in violation of this subsection, the agency, administrative law judge, or other employee presiding at the hearing may, to the extent consistent with the interests of justice and the policy of the underlying statutes, require the party to show cause why his claim or interest in the proceeding should not be dismissed, denied, disregarded, or otherwise adversely affected on account of such violation; and

(E) the prohibitions of this subsection shall apply beginning at such time as the agency may designate, but in no case shall they begin to apply later than the time at which a proceeding is noticed for hearing unless the person responsible for the communication has knowledge that it will be noticed, in which case the prohibitions shall apply beginning at the time of his acquisition of such knowledge.

(2) This subsection does not constitute authority to withhold information from Congress.

§ 558. Imposition of sanctions; determination of applications for licenses; suspension, revocation, and expiration of licenses

(a) This section applies, according to the provisions thereof, to the exercise of a power or authority.

(b) A sanction may not be imposed or a substantive rule or order issued except within jurisdiction delegated to the agency and as authorized by law.

(c) When application is made for a license required by law, the agency, with due regard for the rights and privileges of all the interested parties or adversely affected persons and within a reasonable time, shall set and complete proceedings required to be conducted in accordance with sections 556 and 557 of this title or other proceedings required by law and shall make its decision. Except in cases of willfulness or those in which public health, interest, or safety requires otherwise, the withdrawal, suspension, revocation, or annulment of a license is lawful only if, before the institution of agency proceedings therefor, the licensee has been given—

(1) notice by the agency in writing of the facts or conduct which may warrant the action; and

(2) opportunity to demonstrate or achieve compliance with all lawful requirements.

When the licensee has made timely and sufficient application for a renewal or a new license in accordance with agency rules, a license with reference to an activity of a continuing nature does not expire until the application has been finally determined by the agency.

§ 559.   Effect on other laws; effect of subsequent statute

This [Act does] not limit or repeal additional requirements imposed by statute or otherwise recognized by law. Except as otherwise required by law, requirements or privileges relating to evidence or procedure apply equally to agencies and persons. Each agency is granted the authority necessary to comply with the requirements of this subchapter through the issuance of rules or otherwise. Subsequent statute may not be held to supersede or modify this [Act], except to the extent that it does so expressly.

Subchapter III—Negotiated Rulemaking Procedure

[This subchapter, known as the Negotiated Rulemaking Act, is omitted.]

Subchapter IV—Alternative Means of Dispute Resolution in the Administrative Process

[This subchapter, known as the Administrative Dispute Resolution Act, is omitted.]

CHAPTER 6—THE ANALYSIS OF REGULATORY FUNCTIONS

[This chapter, known as the Regulatory Flexibility Act, is omitted.]

CHAPTER 7—JUDICIAL REVIEW

§ 701. Application; definitions

(a) This chapter applies, according to the provisions thereof, except to the extent that—

(1) statutes preclude judicial review; or

(2) agency action is committed to agency discretion by law.

(b) For the purpose of this chapter—

(1) "agency" means each authority of the Government of the United States, whether or not it is within or subject to review by another agency, but does not include—

(A) the Congress;

(B) the courts of the United States;

(C) the governments of the territories or possessions of the United States;

(D) the government of the District of Columbia;

(E) agencies composed of representatives of the parties or of representatives of organizations of the parties to the disputes determined by them;

(F) courts martial and military commissions;

(G) military authority exercised in the field in time of war or in occupied territory; or

(H) functions conferred by sections 1738, 1739, 1743, and 1744 of title 12; chapter 2 of title 41; subchapter II of chapter 471 of title 49; or sections 1884, 1891–1902, and former section 1641(b)(2), of title 50, appendix; and

(2) "person", "rule", "order", "license", "sanction", "relief", and "agency action" have the meanings given them by section 551 of this title.

§ 702. Right of review

A person suffering legal wrong because of agency action, or adversely affected or aggrieved by agency action within the meaning of a relevant statute, is entitled to judicial review thereof. An action in a court of the United States seeking relief other than money damages and stating a claim that an agency or an officer or employee thereof acted or failed to act in an official capacity or under color of legal authority shall not be dismissed nor relief therein be denied on the ground that it is against the United States or that the United States is an indispensable party. The United States may be named as a defendant in any such action, and a judgment or decree may be entered against the United States: *Provided,* That any mandatory or injunctive decree shall specify the Federal officer or officers (by name or by title), and their successors in office, personally responsible for compliance. Nothing herein (1) affects other limitations on judicial review or the power or duty of the court to dismiss any action or deny relief on any other appropriate legal or equitable ground; or (2) confers authority to grant relief if any other statute that grants consent to suit expressly or impliedly forbids the relief which is sought.

§ 703. Form and venue of proceeding

The form of proceeding for judicial review is the special statutory review proceeding relevant to the subject matter in a court specified by statute or, in the absence or inadequacy thereof, any applicable form of legal action, including actions for declaratory judgments or writs of prohibitory or mandatory injunction or habeas corpus, in a court of competent jurisdiction. If no special statutory review proceeding is applicable, the action for judicial review may be brought against the United States, the agency by its official title, or the appropriate officer. Except to the extent that prior, adequate, and exclusive opportunity for judicial review is provided by law, agency action is subject to judicial review in civil or criminal proceedings for judicial enforcement.

§ 704. Actions reviewable

Agency action made reviewable by statute and final agency action for which there is no adequate remedy in a court are subject to judicial review. A preliminary, procedural, or intermediate agency action or ruling not directly reviewable is subject to review on the review of the final agency action. Except as otherwise expressly required by statute, agency action otherwise final is final for the purposes of this section whether or not there has been presented or determined an application for a declaratory order, for any form of reconsideration, or, unless the agency otherwise requires by rule and provides that the action meanwhile is inoperative, for an appeal to superior agency authority.

§ 705. Relief pending review

When an agency finds that justice so requires, it may postpone the effective date of action taken by it, pending judicial review. On such conditions as may be required and to the extent necessary to prevent irreparable injury, the reviewing court, including the court to which a case may be taken on appeal from or on application for certiorari or other writ to a reviewing court, may issue all necessary and appropriate process to postpone the effective date of an agency action or to preserve status or rights pending conclusion of the review proceedings.

§ 706. Scope of review

To the extent necessary to decision and when presented, the reviewing court shall decide all relevant questions of law, interpret constitutional and statutory provisions, and determine the meaning or applicability of the terms of an agency action. The reviewing court shall—

(1) compel agency action unlawfully withheld or unreasonably delayed; and

(2) hold unlawful and set aside agency action, findings, and conclusions found to be—

(A) arbitrary, capricious, an abuse of discretion, or otherwise not in accordance with law;

(B) contrary to constitutional right, power, privilege, or immunity;

(C) in excess of statutory jurisdiction, authority, or limitations, or short of statutory right;

(D) without observance of procedure required by law;

(E) unsupported by substantial evidence in a case subject to sections 556 and 557 of this title or otherwise reviewed on the record of an agency hearing provided by statute; or

(F) unwarranted by the facts to the extent that the facts are subject to trial de novo by the reviewing court.

In making the foregoing determinations, the court shall review the whole record or those parts of it cited by a party, and due account shall be taken of the rule of prejudicial error.

CHAPTER 8—CONGRESSIONAL REVIEW OF AGENCY RULEMAKING

[This chapter, known as the Congressional Review Act, is omitted.]

[ADMINISTRATIVE LAW JUDGES]

§ 3105. Appointment of administrative law judges

Each agency shall appoint as many administrative law judges as are necessary for proceedings required to be conducted in accordance with sections 556 and 557 of this title. Administrative law judges shall be assigned to cases in rotation so far as practicable, and may not perform duties inconsistent with their duties and responsibilities as administrative law judges.

§ 7521. Actions against administrative law judges

(a) An action may be taken against an administrative law judge appointed under section 3105 of this title by the agency in which the administrative law judge is employed only for good cause established and determined by the Merit Systems Protection Board on the record after opportunity for hearing before the Board.... [Actions covered include removal, suspension, and reduction in grade or pay.]

§ 5372. Administrative law judges

... There shall be 3 levels of basic pay for administrative law judges [as specified in detail in this section].

§ 3344. Details; administrative law judges

An agency as defined by section 551 of this title which occasionally or temporarily is insufficiently staffed with administrative law judges appointed under section 3105 of this title may use administrative law judges selected by the Office of Personnel Management from and with the consent of other agencies.

§ 1305. Administrative law judges

For the purpose of [the administrative law judge employment provisions of this Act], the Office of Personnel Management [and] the Merit Systems Protection Board may investigate, require reports by agencies, issue reports, including an annual report to Congress, prescribe regulations, appoint advisory committees as necessary, recommend legislation, subpena witnesses and records, and pay witness fees as established for the courts of the United States.

APPENDIX II

THE FEDERAL ALPHABET SOUP: A GUIDE TO COMMON ABBREVIATIONS AND ACRONYMS

A common source of confusion is the tendency of courts, commentators and administrators themselves to refer to agencies by their initials. This Appendix provides a translation of some of these acronyms into their English equivalents. General information about the functions and organization of each federal agency can be found in the current edition of the Government Manual.

ACUS	Administrative Conference of the United States (terminated; some functions transferred to DOJ)
AEC	Atomic Energy Commission (superseded; functions now divided between NRC and DOE)
BATF	Bureau of Alcohol, Tobacco, Firearms and Explosives
BIA	Board of Immigration Appeals or Bureau of Indian Affairs
CAB	Civil Aeronautics Board (some functions terminated, others transferred to DOT)

CBO	Congressional Budget Office
CFTC	Commodity Futures Trading Commission
CIA	Central Intelligence Agency
CMS	Centers for Medicare and Medicaid Services (previously HCFA)
CPSC	Consumer Product Safety Commission
CSC	Civil Service Commission (superseded; functions transferred to OPM, MSPB)
DOC	Department of Commerce
DHS	Department of Homeland Security
DOD	Department of Defense
DOE	Department of Energy
DOI	Department of the Interior
DOJ	Department of Justice
DOL	Department of Labor
DOT	Department of Transportation
DVA	Department of Veterans Affairs (formerly VA)
DEA	Drug Enforcement Administration

EEOC	Equal Employment Opportunity Commission
EPA	Environmental Protection Agency
FAA	Federal Aviation Administration
FBI	Federal Bureau of Investigation
FCC	Federal Communications Commission
FDA	Food and Drug Administration
FDIC	Federal Deposit Insurance Corporation
FEC	Federal Election Commission
FEMA	Federal Emergency Management Agency
FERC	Federal Energy Regulatory Commission (formerly FPC)
FHA	Federal Housing Administration
FHWA	Federal Highway Administration
FLRA	Federal Labor Relations Authority
FMB	Federal Maritime Board
FmHA	Farmers Home Administration
FMSHRC	Federal Mine Safety and Health Review Commission
FPC	Federal Power Commission (superseded by FERC)

FRB   Federal Reserve Board

FTC   Federal Trade Commission

FSLIC   Federal Savings and Loan Insurance
            Corporation (terminated; functions
            transferred to FDIC)

FHLBB   Federal Home Loan Bank Board (super-
            seded by OTS)

FWS   Fish and Wildlife Service

GAO   Government Accountability Office (for-
            merly General Accounting Office)

GSA   General Services Administration

HCFA   Health Care Financing Administration
            (now CMS)

HEW   Department of Health, Education, and
            Welfare (superseded; functions divided
            between HHS and Department of Edu-
            cation)

HHS   Department of Health and Human Ser-
            vices (formerly HEW)

HUD   Department of Housing and Urban De-
            velopment

ICC   Interstate Commerce Commission
            (some functions terminated, others
            transferred to DOT)

INS   Immigration and Naturalization Service (terminated; functions transferred to DHS)

IRS   Internal Revenue Service

ITC   International Trade Commission

MSHA   Mine Safety and Health Administration

MSPB   Merit Systems Protection Board (formerly part of CSC)

NASA   National Aeronautics and Space Administration

NCUA   National Credit Union Administration

NHTSA   National Highway Traffic Safety Administration

NIRA   National Industrial Recovery Administration (terminated)

NLRB   National Labor Relations Board

NMB   National Mediation Board

NOAA   National Oceanic and Atmospheric Administration

NRC   Nuclear Regulatory Commission

NSA   National Security Agency

NSC   National Security Council

NTSB   National Transportation Safety Board

OCC	Office of Comptroller of Currency
OIRA	Office of Information and Regulatory Affairs (part of OMB)
OMB	Office of Management and Budget
OPA	Office of Price Administration (terminated after World War II)
OPM	Office of Personnel Management (formerly part of CSC)
OSHA	Occupational Safety and Health Administration
OSHRC	Occupational Safety and Health Review Commission
OTA	Office of Technology Assessment (terminated)
OTS	Office of Thrift Supervision
PBGC	Pension Benefit Guaranty Corporation
PTO	Patent and Trademark Office
SBA	Small Business Administration
SEC	Securities Exchange Commission
SSA	Social Security Administration
TVA	Tennessee Valley Authority
USDA	Department of Agriculture

VA   Veterans' Administration (superseded
            by DVA)

*

INDEX

References are to Pages

457

BIAS AND PREJUDGMENT—Cont'd
Adjudicative proceedings, affected by, 286–91
APA provision governing, 286
Due process requirements, 237–40, 290
Financial interests causing, 238–39, 290–91
Legal or policy positions causing, 287–89
Prior exposure to evidence causing, 240, 290, 291
Procedure for ruling on claims of, 286
Rule of necessity, 288–89
Rulemaking proceedings affected by, 338–39
Speeches indicating, 289–80, 338–39

BURDEN OF PROOF
See Formal Adjudications, Evidence, Burden of proof

CASE OR CONTROVERSY REQUIREMENT
See Access to Judicial Review, Case or controversy requirement

CHEVRON DOCTRINE
See Scope of Judicial Review, Legal issues

CHOICE OF ADJUDICATION OR RULEMAKING
Advantages of rulemaking, 306–07
Authority to issue legislative rules, 308–09
Discretion in, 344–50
Foreclosure of adjudication through rulemaking, 294–98
Reasons for failure to use rulemaking, 307, 344–45
Reasons for increased use of rulemaking, 307–09
Required rulemaking, 344–50
Statutes affecting, 308, 344

COLLATERAL ESTOPPEL
See Scope of Judicial Review, Collateral estoppel

COMBINATION OF FUNCTIONS
See Separation of Functions

COMMERCIAL DATA
See Confidentiality of Records, Proprietary information

COMMITTED TO DISCRETION
See Access to Judicial Review, Committed to agency discretion

COMPULSORY PROCESS
See Investigations

CONFIDENTIALITY OF RECORDS
See also, Information Disclosure; Publicity

PROCEDURAL DUE PROCESS—Cont'd

PROPOSED FINDINGS AND CONCLUSIONS

†